Surveying
Small Craft

By the same author

Sea Saint
Log of the *Maken*
Building the *St Mary*
Ian Nicolson's Guide to Boat Buying
Dinghy Cruising
Outboard Boats and Engines
Designer's Notebook
Small Steel Craft
Marinise Your Boat
Boat Data Book
Cold Moulded Boatbuilding
Build Your Own Boat
Yacht Designer's Sketchbook

Ian Nicolson, FRINA CEng

Surveying Small Craft

Fault-finding in Boats

Second Edition

Drawings by the author

**SHERIDAN
HOUSE**

Published in the United States of America 1984 by
Sheridan House Inc., 145 Palisade St, Dobbs Ferry,
New York 10522

Published in Great Britain 1974 by
Adlard Coles Ltd, Granada Publishing Ltd, 8 Grafton St, London W1X 3LA
Reprinted with amendments 1978
Second edition 1983

Library of Congress Cataloging in Publication Data
Nicolson, Ian, 1928–
        Surveying small craft.
        Includes index.
        1. Boats and boating–Inspection. I. Title.
VM321.N53   1984   623.8'202   83–13554
ISBN 0–911378–47–2

Printed in the United States of America

To Martin and
Kathy Barnes

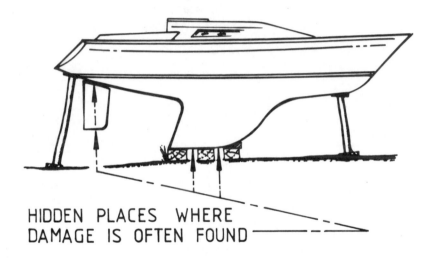

HIDDEN PLACES WHERE
DAMAGE IS OFTEN FOUND

A surveyor has to lie on his back and look upwards at some of the inaccessible areas under the hull and rudder. Why is it that there are always such large puddles under boats, just where the surveyor has to lie? He also looks down on the top edge of a fibreglass rudder for cracks at the join line.

Contents

Illustrations

Photographs

Drawings

General Considerations

The Surveyor's Lot

A surveyor has to be both a scientist and an artist. Basically his work is technical detection. He has to notice past troubles and impending ones; from small clues he has to deduce what has gone wrong and what may fail. Good eyesight is his chief asset, more important than ultrasonic testers or probes or drills or laboratory tests. It is most often his eyesight that gives the first clue, finds the followup and interprets the result of scientific testing.

Some of the best surveyors spend long minutes sitting and staring at one part of a boat, or leaning back in the cockpit mulling over how subtle signs of trouble fit together to form a basic pattern. Anyone can deduce that a 10 m (32 ft) boat with two electric bilge pumps suffers from leaking. But it takes experience to tell whether a fresh coat of paint is hiding a multitude of troubles or is there because the owner looks after his boat well and repaints as often as necessary. Once a surveyor has established whether a boat is truly well maintained or not, much of his job is simplified.

This part of the detection is complex because, in practice, boats tend to have successive owners, some who look after their charge and others who neglect her. Experience and study are needed to discern the signs of neglect which occurred years previously, if the current owner takes a lot of trouble with his maintenance.

This Book is for Amateur Surveyors

With practice, with experience and by reading it is possible for anybody to become a judge of a boat's condition. Anyone intending to buy a boat usually looks at a selection and decides that two or three seem to suit the requirements. It can be an expensive business to have several boats fully surveyed when only one is to be bought. An amateur can make a good preliminary survey of the boats under consideration and decide which is the soundest, before calling in a professional surveyor.

Plenty of *new* boats have myriad faults, so an owner who is a good amateur surveyor can save himself time and money by forestalling troubles. A firm which exhibits at a boat show presumably offers a boat specially and carefully prepared. But any experienced surveyor, amateur or professional, can detect all sorts of faults, some of them downright serious, on boats in any show.

This Book is for Owners

It takes years to learn how to do a *deep* survey. But this is a guide for an owner who wants to maintain his boat better and forestall accidents, as well as reduce maintenance. There are books about fitting out and laying up; this work aims at reducing the work of looking after a boat on the principle that prevention is better than cure.

This Book is for Professional Surveyors

The only way to become a good surveyor is to blot up a tremendous amount of knowledge about every type of craft.

Surveying should have become easier over the last few years because boats are now built, for the most part, in production runs of identical craft. Once a surveyor has examined two or three of a class, in theory he can predict much of the trouble he is likely to find on any other boat of the same make. In practice things are rather different. For a start, many builders introduce modifications; sometimes annual changes are made to a class. Not all these alterations are *improvements* for if a builder is making an inadequate profit he may reduce scantlings or substitute inferior materials and workmanship to cut production costs. This book is a contribution to the knowledge which a professional surveyor needs.

A good surveyor concentrates intensely throughout the job and as a result he does not like anyone to be present during the examination. Above all, the owner or buyer are usually unpopular if they linger near the craft while the surveyor is at work. Few people can bear to see someone prying and prodding a boat in which they have an interest. So professional surveyors need the tact, and sometimes the bluntness, to get rid of spectators, particularly those who are biased one way or another. Surveyors also have to be thick-skinned, because so often they bring bad tidings. Everyone tends to assume that unless a boat appears to be falling to pieces she is in good order, whereas all boats have defects and the majority have a lot of inbuilt trouble, either imminent or potential.

Professional surveyors appreciate that the only successful way to carry out their job is to be ruthless. They all know horror stories about boats which have been lost due to unsoundness. For instance, there was the case of the cruiser which was wrecked in Wemyss Bay against the sea wall. The crew were drowned and their bodies, encased in lifejackets, were recovered the next day. The flesh of the hands of each victim was completely torn away right down to the bone where these drowning men had tried to scale the vertical sea wall . . . if only they had had a surveyor's warning they never would have gone to sea in that particular boat.

Time Afloat—the essential ingredient

Surveyors need a deep knowledge of small craft construction. They must know all about mast making, keel casting, the manufacture of fastenings and cushions, the ins and outs of engines and electrical equipment, insurance and salvage, glass cloth lay-up and lamination, corrosion and erosion, and many more technicalities. But above all they need experience afloat. Boats get into trouble on the water and that is where surveyors have to start learning their job. Anyone who has been through a big gale in a small boat is unlikely to make a slovenly surveyor.

The Money Side

When a vessel is being sold it is usual for the *buyer* to retain the services of the surveyor and to pay him. The surveyor writes out a report which he hands or posts *only* to the buyer. He takes some trouble to keep the report confidential since it may have a considerable effect on the value of the ship.

Sometimes the buyer who has commissioned the survey does not go ahead with the sale and a second buyer comes along. The surveyor will not sell a copy of the report without getting permission from the person who originally commissioned the survey, and the cost will be well under the normal full price.

The cost of a survey varies according to a good many circumstances, but the normal basis of the charge is on the size of the craft. The UK Yacht Designers, Brokers and Surveyors Association's standard fee scale is widely used and officially approved. It is: Yacht's overall length × Beam divided by a constant. This constant decreases every few years to deal with inflation and in 1983 was 1.6. This formula gives the price in pounds sterling.

Surveyors charge not only for their work but also their travelling and other outgoing expenses such as overnight accommodation in hotels. By tradition surveyors travel first class on trains and charge for their meals during the day of the survey.

A man buying a boat may have two or even four different craft in mind, each possibly of the same class, or generally similar. He may be having some trouble making up his mind which one to purchase and the decision may largely depend on the condition of the various boats. When this situation occurs it often pays to retain the surveyor 'by the day' and have him go from boat to boat, giving each one a general examination. He then carries out a full survey on the craft which seems to be in the best condition. This works out cheaper than having full or even partial surveys on each of the boats under review. A survey generally costs about a week's wages for a blue collar worker per surveyor-day, plus expenses.

Because travelling is so expensive, surveying very small boats like dinghies and miniature cruisers seems to be very expensive when compared with the purchase price of the boat. One way to minimise costs is to club together with another buyer in the same area so that the surveyor can do two boats in the same day. Again the surveyor would be retained by the day. Another technique is to commission the survey, stating that the work is to be carried out when the surveyor happens to be in the area where the boat is. This saves travelling expenses and most surveyors, who are busy men for the most part, are pleased to save unprofitable travelling time.

In practice, commissioning a survey is akin to buying insurance. The money spent confers peace of mind first and foremost. Secondly it protects the value of the investment, and often—very often—saves a great deal of money. It has to be remembered that quite a small accident afloat can result in a hefty bill. If half this is spent on a survey just to avoid one minor accident, then the profit might reasonably be measured at 100 per cent.

The vast majority of people selling small craft honestly do not know the defects which their boats have. As a result virtually every survey throws up a dozen, and maybe forty, defects. In general the seller will concede at least part of the cost of putting these defects right, and this reduction in the selling price virtually always more than pays for the cost of the survey.

Here is an approximate guide to the relation between the cost of a professional survey and the size of the boat. For a boat 24 ft (7·5 metres) overall, the cost is roughly equivalent to the weekly wage of a blue collar worker. The cost is doubled for a boat 40 ft (12 metres) overall, trebled for a boat 55 ft (16·5 metres) overall, and so on, pro rata.

Travel and other expenses are extra.

Professional Surveyors

Leading surveyors in Europe are generally members of the Yacht Brokers, Designers and Surveyors Association (YBDSA). A good way for a buyer or owner to get the services of a reliable surveyor is to write to this Association's office at 'Wheel House', 15 Station Road, Liphook, Hants GU30 7DW, England. Members of the Association are based in Britain and the Channel Isles, Eire, Holland, France and Malta. They are in demand for survey work on small craft all over the world because of their reputation and integrity. The frequency and speed of jet travel means that British surveyors are to be found at work in the Caribbean, in Greece, in Gibraltar, all round the coasts of Scandinavia—in fact wherever small craft are to be found.

All YBDSA surveyors have at least five years' experience before they are accepted for Associated Membership. They have to serve another five years in this capacity before becoming full members. In practice, the majority of surveyors on the YBDSA list have quite twenty years' experience at their job. Many have served apprenticeships or had similar training, and historically they are probably as efficient as any generation because their experience has spanned the changeover years from wood and steel craft to fibreglass. Quite a few have tackled aluminium and concrete boats. There has never been a time when the range of materials was so wide, and certainly surveyors can never have been so busy, so that the total amount of experience each professional surveyor has packed in during the last few years will in general be more than that of his predecessors.

In addition the YBDSA insists that its members have professional indemnity insurance. In practice insurance companies will not take on an inexperienced surveyor, so anyone commissioning a survey from a YBDSA member has this additional safeguard.

The other main surveying institution is Lloyds, whose address is 71 Fenchurch Street, London EC3M 4BS. Lloyds also have world coverage and they provide an additional service to ensure that small craft are kept up to a good standard. In the last chapter of my book *Small Steel Craft* there are details of Lloyds' services, and the various misconceptions about boats built to Lloyds' standards. (This book is published by Adlard Coles Ltd in UK and International Marine in USA.)

A YBDSA surveyor cannot by the rules of his association accept a share in the commission which arises when a vessel is sold, except in special circumstances and only when everyone concerned agrees that payment of a commission is due. The YBDSA lays down a standard scale of charges, and this is followed to a very large extent by those competent surveyors not in the Association.

There are longshoremen, retired seamen and others who set up as fringe surveyors. Their characteristics are a tendency to undercut the normal scale of charges, and to produce skimpy reports which are suspiciously unsigned. A man who takes four hours to survey a 60 ft craft and charges a third of the normal price is swindling the owner in two ways. Firstly, he is only partly doing the job, and secondly, he is overcharging for the number of hours put into the job.

Limitations of Survey

The only fully effective way of examining a boat is to slice up every single component into thin slivers so that each can be examined meticulously. This would give a very good idea of the condition of the craft prior to her being reduced to a pile of granulated waste! The surveyor has to steer a course between on one hand doing damage in order to discover the condition of the structure and on the other being so cautious that no proper research is carried out.

To make matters worse there are areas which cannot be seen at all and so they can scarcely be surveyed. Even regions which can be viewed are sometimes out of reach even of a long-handled spike or hammer. Again, there are large areas which can only be seen on one side. For instance, decks which are sheathed over are more likely to have trouble on top than underneath, yet the top is normally wholly inaccessible.

In this connection there are certain well-established procedures which some surveyors use, having first got the owner's permission to carry out the semi-destructive work needed to get a better view. For instance some surveyors take borings and examine the chips which are bored out. This can be done with both fibreglass and wood, and is particularly favoured where the scantlings of the boat are very heavy so that the drilled out hole causes no significant weakening of the structure. A typical instance is in the beam ends of a fishing boat built to the typical massive rough standards, such as are much favoured by fishermen. In the same way, where a deck has been skinned over with one of the plasticised cloths like Trakmark, if the sheathing is already showing fairly advanced signs of wear and tear then it seems reasonable to get the owner's permission to lift the edge of this and view the deck beneath. Since repairs are going to be needed in any case, the surveyor is merely helping the shipwright to do the preliminary dismantling work.

But where the topsides are perfect, perhaps beautiful new fibreglass or a perfect enamel job, what is the surveyor to do? I know of one Lloyds surveyor who uses a very sharp-pointed pricker, which he applies at very close intervals, the argument here being that the hole made is so tiny that it is not noticed. This seems to be a fallacy since repeated piercing of the watertight skin lets in moisture, and in any case shows up in spite of the small size of pricker. Incidentally this type of pricker requires special skill in its use since it is liable to penetrate very easily into soft timber and give the impression that the wood is defective whereas it is perfectly sound. As a general rule surveyors steer clear of enamelled topsides when using a pricker, but they do hammer test and listen for the dead sound of rotten wood. A much more limiting situation is the absence of staging or a reasonably portable ladder round a boat which stands high above the ground. When this situation is presented to the surveyor the best he can do is to work round the deck, reaching down as far as possible, and working up from the ground as far as he can reach.

It is usual for a surveyor to indicate the parts of the ship which have not been surveyed, but the inference always is that items not detailed are either sound or are out of reach. If a surveyor is to give a detailed list of everything not inspected the report becomes extremely long with a high percentage of useless information.

However, there is yet another dilemma. Where is the line to be drawn between normal refitting work and repairs? It is not enough to say that refitting work is something which is done every year: this would be most misleading and for the most part untrue. As a broad guideline, I believe that the fitting-out items which are done every year need not be mentioned, but any defect in the vessel or her equipment which might be missed during fitting out should be included in the report. For example, it seems unnecessary to mention that a boat requires antifouling, but it is only good sense to draw attention to a bent rigging screw. There are plenty of riggers who will ignore a mild bend in the stem of a rigging screw in the mistaken belief that it survived last year and therefore might well do another season.

Equipment, or the absence of it, raises frequent problems. Is the surveyor to draw attention to the absence of berth leeboards? On the whole I would have thought not, unless the vessel is intended for offshore cruising and the buyer has specifically asked for the fullest possible information on such equipment. But virtually no cruising yacht should put to sea with only one anchor, and if the surveyor finds that there is no second anchor it would seem good policy to mention this.

The surveyor's job is probably most difficult when he is looking at a new or virtually new craft. Here both buyer and seller will have a reverent attitude towards the pristine finish. Both parties will be extremely wroth if the surveyor leaves a trail of damage, however tiny the test marks may be. There cannot be any complete answer to this situation; no solution which will entirely satisfy the requirements of a ruthless inspection without leaving the least sign. A great deal can be done with electronic and similar non-destructive testing but the equipment is not widely available and tests can be misleading.

No boat designed and fabricated by human hand will be absolutely perfect, and one of the curses of production line technique is that a mistake made in the first prototype is not always spotted, and is then repeated in every craft built to the same design. So a fault found in one of a class may be expected in many, if not all of her sister ships. If the fault is not visible it can only be mentioned as a possibility, a difficult task to do without being inaccurate or unfair to one person or another.

Assessing Ability

Just occasionally a surveyor is asked to comment on the probable performance or the general ability of a craft. Some surveyors even do this regularly without being asked, though the practice seems to have a number of acute dangers. These arise because different people have different conceptions of what is 'seaworthy' or 'fast' or 'good looking' and so on. A second source of potential trouble is that boats are subject to a very large number of outside influences, so that an apparently good boat may fail to achieve a reasonable speed or may not trim level when underway even though there is ample external evidence that the craft should behave as predicted.

To take a simple example, plenty of potential buyers will ask the surveyor whether a yacht is likely to carry weather helm. The surveyor may honestly think that a certain craft is going to be light on the helm and his opinion may be backed by the knowledge that she comes from the board of a well-known designer, all of whose products are celebrated for their docile behaviour. But it may just happen that the boat in question was one of his earliest designs, completed before he achieved his true level of artistic and scientific skill. Just to make the situation more confusing, some design offices grow so big that relatively junior draughtsmen are responsible for the lines of some of the secondary boats which come from that particular office. If the maestro himself happens to be away on holiday or ill when the hull form is settled, a boat with his name on the design may not be well-mannered.

For such reasons a surveyor with a lot of experience generally hedges any comments about ability with a large number of defensive clauses.

If assessing qualities like weather helm and seakindliness is risky, predicting speed is outrageously dangerous. Since any vessel can lose 10 per cent of her speed through a distorted or bad propeller, it is not even safe to say that because one craft does 10 knots then her sistership should do the same speed. I have come across a pair of apparently identical propellers, one of which was 12 per cent off the specification in pitch, and the other 23 per cent in error. Further examination showed that neither propeller even had the *diameter* called for on the plans!

As a large number of small craft actually displace more than the designed weight, often owing to the addition of extra gear and unconsidered trifles like hidden pockets of bilgewater, predicting speed is difficult and risky. Another problem is that a very large number of small craft engines never reach their designed peak r.p.m., so the theoretical horsepower is not available. All in all, the surveyor who makes comments about probable speeds, even after an exhaustive examination of a ship, is risking his reputation and his bank balance.

Surveyors are occasionally asked to sign certificates of seaworthiness. I cannot see how anyone can give an unqualified certificate, simply because there is no such thing as a 'totally seaworthy' vessel. The Royal National Life-boat Institution spends thousands of pounds building a relatively small number of craft to stand up to bad weather. The very best workmanship and material, the finest equipment and the best available seamen are assembled to produce what should be totally seaworthy boats. But there are widows all around the coasts to prove that even the RNLI craft do not always come home. Governments and companies, corporations and navies all strive to build completely seaworthy ships which are utterly reliable, yet losses continue. If all these ships, big and small, backed by the best, the most, the wealthiest, fail to be 100 per cent safe, then the average craft which small craft surveyors inspect can seldom be deemed more than moderately seaworthy.

At least half the truth is that the word 'seaworthy' can only be coupled with a combination of ship plus crew. The best ship is very dependent on its crew, and the best crew is no more than human. If a surveyor is asked to sign any document resembling a certificate of seaworthiness he should lay down limitations and defensive clauses, since the boat which is given a clear bill of health, in writing, is so often the one that gets into trouble. By the same token it is quite extraordinary how old, decrepit boats which are found to be in poor if not downright unsound condition make extraordinary passages across dangerous oceans, just to confound the surveyor's opinion. It all boils down to the fact that seaworthiness is a quality which is never found in a perfect form, and is in any case only attributable to the team of ship-plus-crew and never to the ship alone.

Preparing Craft for Surveying

All sorts of advantages accrue if the surveyor can visit the boat a few days before doing the survey. He can see just how grubby the bilge is, how much internal ballast there is, and even mark the fastenings he wants withdrawn. The necessary instructions can then be given to the yard, or the owner or buyer. If the preparations are left to the surveyor to do he will waste a lot of time which should have been spent on his true job. Just as important, the sharp edge will have been taken off his concentration. Surveying is gruelling hard work on many occasions, and it is wholly unsatisfactory if the survey is preceded by an hour's strenuous exercise, humping ballast up through narrow companionways and over the side.

In addition, in some yards the management do not allow certain work to be done by anybody except yard employees. Elsewhere there are trade union restrictions which mean that only certain men, employed by the yard, are allowed to do jobs like removing fastenings or lifting out ballast.

Ideally, the ship should be exactly upright and on a level keel, if for no other reason than for sighting along sheer and keel for fairness. In practice very few ships are exactly level or upright. Also relatively few owners are interested in extra expenditure to achieve this desirable state. Just occasionally, however, a boat is found to be positively unstable because she is tilted too much, so extra chocking after lifting her more upright is essential.

Before going on board the surveyor has to check the bilge chocks and other supports, and in this connection it is important to remember that a glossy fibreglass shell does not allow props and wedges to grip easily. This means that any support should be well under the turn of bilge, and should be angled as near as possible normal to the shell to prevent a wedging action forcing props away. One reason for employing only a professional surveyor is that his professional indemnity insurance policy should cover the cost of repairing damage if his movement on board a boat causes her to tip over. In this connection it is important to remember that a boat which tips over in a yard may well be close to others and start a chain reaction, knocking over all adjacent vessels!

Before a surveyor arrives, not only should the main hatch be unbolted but also the fore hatch and any semi-portable hatches, to give access wherever possible. At the same time manhole covers, traps doors and other portable or semi-portable panels should be removed.

All loose gear should be taken off the yacht with the exception of the fire extinguishers. It is just as important to remove warps and fenders from the aft lazarette as it is to take out the cushions. All anchor chains should be removed from the chain locker, skylight covers and winch covers should be taken off; in short, every part of the boat and every component should be made easily viewable.

Ideally all floorboards and all lining and ceiling should be taken out. In practice this could prove a long, expensive job and it is quite usual to lift only the centre floorboards. Quite often only alternative pieces of lining, or possibly every third piece, are taken out. A lot depends here on the age of the vessel and her intended use. Just occasionally the surveyor may find that he can just detect trouble behind a piece of lining which has not been removed, in which case he will call for a ship-wright to take down the ceiling which is blocking his view. The rule here must be: when in doubt, take everything out.

Internal ballast should be removed, though in practice it is quite usual for 30 per cent to be lifted. It may very well be necessary to make a plan of how the ballast is stowed so that it can be refitted correctly.

When a ship is laid up it should have the bung removed from the lowest part of the bilge so that all water drains away automatically. If this has not been done it may be necessary to pump the bilge, and if this is done in the presence of the surveyor it gives him a good opportunity to assess the effectiveness of the bilge pumping arrangements. A very dirty bilge should be cleaned out to give the surveyor every chance to see the structure low down.

It is not universal practice to remove keel bolts and skin fittings before the surveyor arrives, partly because some surveyors defer this work until everything else is done. They work on the principle that if the vessel has serious defects the buyer will not wish to incur the expense of taking out fastenings unnecessarily. The trouble with this approach is that some keel bolts are difficult to remove, so that two shipwrights may still be struggling at the job after the surveyor has finished his work.

Nominally every ship hauled up, particularly if she is in a shed, should have all fuel tanks empty. It is a requirement of insurance companies that boats laid up ashore have no bottled gas nor any fuel aboard. In practice this rule is honoured in the breach! Certainly a partly filled tank is more likely to show any leaks in the fuel system than one that is completely empty. However, tanks for fuel or water which are not empty cannot always have inspection plates taken off. Even if the manholes are on top, liquid in a tank prevents full inspection.

For the fullest possible survey all tanks should be lifted right out of the hull prior to inspection, partly to allow the structure behind the tanks to be viewed. Occasionally the engine is taken out to be inspected fully, and to look at the caverns normally hidden by the machinery. Dismantling gives opportunities to work on the engine and the tanks, as well as the exposed parts of the ship. Painting should also be carried out, after intensive cleaning.

Partial Surveys

A job half done seldom satisfies anyone. Partial surveys are almost always unsatisfactory though there are a number of special circumstances which make them necessary. For instance, an owner who is uncertain which of two boats to buy may commission partial surveys on both until either one or other is found to have a serious defect, or until it is clear that one boat is better than the other. This is rather a special case because in the end the boat finally bought is given a *full* survey.

A more common case is a survey for insurance purposes, when the vessel is afloat. The majority of insurance companies accept a survey carried out on a boat in the water without asking for the craft to be hauled up, or even beached and inspected at low tide. They appear to work on the premise that if nothing serious is shown up inside the boat, and there is nothing too important on deck and round the topsides, the assumption can be made that the craft is in reasonable order. In practice, insurance underwriters, once they have got used to a particular surveyor's style, can assess the standard of risk when they are reading the survey report. Underwriters know from experience that the vast majority of small craft are very far from perfect. They appreciate that batches of certain types are deficient in particular departments. For instance, inshore fishing boats are notoriously badly equipped with ground tackle.

Partial surveys tend to be valueless unless they cover about 65 per cent of the important parts of the ship and at least 40 per cent of the lesser factors. A survey of this extent will almost always indicate to a technically qualified person the general state of the craft. For quite a number of purposes such as insurance, or the purchase of a craft like a contractor's launch, such a partial report is sometimes adequate.

It must be emphasised that no survey is 100 per cent complete. It would only be possible to give an utterly comprehensive report by dismantling every part of the craft and cutting out multiple sections at quite close intervals. This would amount to total destructive testing, and though it would give a great deal of information it would eliminate the craft as a useful entity!

Those professional organisations and associations which guard surveyors' interests are against partial surveys, though they recognise the facts of life: they realise that some partial surveys have to be done but recommend that a full list be made of the items not inspected. Since one reason for not carrying out a full survey may be shortage of time, a comprehensive list of all parts not examined may take up almost as much time as completing a full survey!

One reason why surveys afloat are not satisfactory is the difficulty of working around the outside of the hull. An ordinary dinghy is most unsatisfactory as a platform since it is too mobile and lacks stability. It also tends to bump the topsides continuously. A rubber dinghy is in some respects better, normally having more stability and no tendency to damage pristine paintwork. The trouble here is that even in an enclosed harbour waves will splash up between the main hull and the dinghy so that the surveyor soon finds himself saturated, a condition he is probably used to. What he cannot tolerate is spray all over his notebook.

A painter's raft is a handy vehicle for working round a hull, but only useful in very sheltered waters because it lacks freeboard. Whatever tender is used to examine the outside of a hull, it is almost always essential to have an assistant to move the platform every few minutes, and also to attend any fenders.

Examining a boat afloat is doubly bad in a strong tide or severe weather, so arrangements should be made for the craft to be moved away from exposed moorings. It is general practice for the surveyor to have somebody else move the boat, partly to avoid being responsible for damage or other trouble, and partly because he is often pressed for time.

When surveying a vessel with masts standing it is seldom satisfactory to go aloft without assistance. Even a young, tough surveyor cannot be expected to cling precariously to a spar, dozens of feet above the deck, and make dispassionate notes after prolonged careful scrutiny.

It is probably fair to say that a partial survey properly carried out gives a reasonable *indication* of the quality, level of maintenance and safety standards of a ship.

The Basis of Surveying

A survey is carried out by carefully examining every part of the ship concerned. The surveyor crawls and climbs all over the hull and superstructure. He burrows and peers into all the dark inaccessible corners, he sometimes goes up the masts if they are standing, he goes under, over, round and through wherever he can reach. Where he cannot go himself he sends in a torch beam and looks wherever possible.

He is looking for future, present and past troubles. If he sees poor ground tackle he knows that the craft is likely to drag ashore the first time she is caught in an exposed anchorage by an onshore gale. Prevention is far better than cure, and this is one of the most important ways that the surveyor earns his fee. Troubles which are already present tend to be easier to detect, but they are certainly not all obvious. For instance, real rot is less common than inadequate fastenings. It takes experience to notice that a pair of knees are doing little more than support their own weight owing to a paucity of through-bolts.

Past troubles have to be scrutinised to make sure that repairs have been adequately carried out. It is not enough to double over a fractured frame if the strength of the doubler is no more than the strength of the frame which has already *proved* inadequate. At the same time the cause of the fracture should be discovered, if only to lead the surveyor to other troubles arising from the same accident.

The surveyor has to use his experience and imagination the whole time. Anybody can detect galloping rot—the smell alone is usually ample evidence. But a hatch which is so designed that it can chop off a man's fingers is not such an obvious defect, yet it can be every bit as dangerous as a corroded lifeline or a worn tiller link. In the same way, most enginerooms on small craft are badly lit. But that is no excuse for letting another boat go to sea in this dangerous condition.

A surveyor's duty is to his clients; it is to save life, limb and property. He also has a duty to the insurance underwriter who covers the craft, and to the owners and crew of other ships. All this means that he has to be fearless in making his report, and this means he is likely to make enemies.

One of the hardest parts of the job is to be dispassionate when making a report and yet imaginative when predicting practical troubles.

Sources of Error

New Boats

It is a fallacy that new boats do not need survying. This never was true, and now that boats are more and more often built in factories, with an increasing tendency to follow light engineering practice rather than traditional boatbuilding, new boats often need a very full survey. This is partly because they get little or no inspection on completion in some factories. Added to this, boats now get sent considerable distances from the place where they were built to the launching point. These journeys generate all kinds of faults, from external scratches to loosened bulkheads.

In some years something like 5 per cent of the surveys I do are on boats which are new or nearly new. The defect rate used to be high; sometimes there were faults which required several hundred pounds worth of labour and material to put them right. To be sure, this was during the early years of fibreglass boats, when some manufacturers had not grasped the implications of the new material. There were not only construction problems but also excessive price cutting to increase sales. This resulted in weak mast supports, shoddy engine installations, piping and wiring installed without any clips or securing arrangements, rudders and steering gear with no factor of safety, and so on.

It has to be remembered that a boat is more complex than a car since it has more departments. After all, relatively few cars have cooking and toilet facilities in them. Since a boat has so many facets, it follows that the chances of defects are more numerous. No one needs reminding just how many faults a new car has, and a new boat is likely to be at least as bad.

It is well known that most boats are better in their second year of production, when teething troubles have been worked out. This applies to all types of vessel and to the majority of builders.

The Value of a Survey Report

It is a mistake to think that a survey remains up to date for many months. An hour after it has been completed the boat may run aground, perhaps in quite a mild way. This type of accident can introduce a variety of hidden defects from fractured engine beds to uprooted toilets.

This brings out another point. Certain defects remain completely hidden unless radical dismantling takes place. In the majority of small craft there are hidden corners, such as at the extreme bow and down inside hollow keels, which cannot be seen and tested. There are places like those under tanks and engines which may be just visible at a distance, and other localities which cannot be seen but can be reached. It is probably fairly accurate to say that a normal condition survey can only cover 80 per cent of the surface area of any vessel. This figure is wildly approximate and depends a great deal on the type and size of craft. One result of this inaccessibility is that estimates for repair work which are made on the basis of a survey report should include a factor for defects which come to light when dismantling and repairs commence.

State No Opinion During a Survey

It is wrong to make any full judgment on a ship until the very end of the survey. Unobtrusive lockers are likely to be missed till the surveyor is making his final check through. If a surveyor misses this half-hidden space it is possible that maintenance staff will have done the same. It is not unusual to find the major part of a ship entirely sound with just two or three pockets of trouble, but these defective areas may not be discovered until the very end of the inspection. What seemed to be developing into an encouraging report suddenly becomes a disappointing one only ten minutes before the surveyor finally climbs out of his overalls.

It is also unwise to come to a comprehensive opinion about a vessel until after the report has been typed out and read through. Those pages of cryptic jottings in the surveyor's notebook may seem to be nothing more than a few hundred pounds worth of defects. Maturer reflection can throw up new aspects to the situation: the boat may have to be moved before repairs can be started; the marine engineer may consider the propeller shaft wear so excessive that serious engine misalignment is probable; another expert called in by the surveyor, such as a sailmaker, may multiply the woes the surveyor has already listed, and so on.

Surveyors get asked about craft they are working on, and it is tempting to reply, even if only to get rid of the distractions. This temptation has to be resisted. If the questioner has commissioned the survey it is unfair to give him an unformed opinion. Added to this, the surveyor is likely to be tired, or hungry, or sweaty, or grubby—probably all four. He is in no condition to give a useful answer. If the questioner has *not* commissioned the survey, he is not entitled to any answer. He is asking for confidential information which someone else is about to pay for. He should be sent packing.

Misleading Specifications

It is not unusual to start a survey primed with information which is wrong. Through roguery or ignorance, owners and brokers tell surveyors that a ship is built of iron, when she turns out to be of steel. The former material has quite astonishing lasting powers; for instance there are well-documented stories of wooden boats which have totally rotted away, leaving behind the iron fastenings in usable condition. Of course there is a great difference between good and poor iron; the best rusts away slowly, the worst has no more lasting ability than steel.

In practice, it is unlikely that a craft built after 1912 will be found to have iron plating or frames. If the age of the ship can be accurately determined, a convenient cross-check is thus available as to her true specification. Lloyds Registers are a convenient source of reference, and the larger public libraries have copies dating back to the early years of the century. Some craft listed in these tomes have a note against the entry stating the construction material. However, the entries are often sent in by owners, and are not to be trusted implicitly.

The safe way to confirm the material of construction is to take samples for analysis. When doing a steel or iron ship, the drillings may be used for analysis, or a small piece can be cut out from an area where there is corrosion and repairs are inevitably going to be needed. There are almost always places where the structure is relatively unimportant or easily renewed; these are good areas for taking samples. A small section should be cut out so that renewal will involve down-hand welding so far as possible.

The situation is complicated by the difficulty, almost impossibility, of getting iron for repairs. A vessel built originally of iron of the best quality may suffer damage or local corrosion, and have to be repaired with steel. The steel is likely to rust at its usual rate and need renewing in due course, while the rest of the ship soldiers on in fine condition. So before accusing anyone of sharp practice, it is a good idea to make sure that a ship reputedly of iron is indeed mainly of that material, with perhaps a few patches of inferior material.

A comparable situation exists with wooden craft. Many times I have found patches of rot in superb craft. Careful probing and a lot of thoughtful beavering has thrown up the fact that the basic hull is still in good condition, but low- or middle-quality repairs have become defective. One corollary is that the surveyor should where possible recommend repairs to be carried out with a better-quality material than in the main structure. This applies to all construction materials.

Yachts are sometimes built with teak bottom planking and a lighter timber on the topsides. The object is to have the advantages of teak over the immersed areas, with its valuable resistance to worm and relatively low water absorption. The lighter timber is used high up to improve stability and make it easier to obtain a fine finish. A boat having this construction may be described as 'teak planked'. If she also has teak decks and teak coamings she is quite likely to be listed as 'all teak', which is patently untrue because the beams, shelves, carlines, probably the keel and stem, the knees, lining, berth battens and so on are not teak. I have seen lots of boats listed as 'all teak' and have yet to find this claim more than 85 per cent true.

Occasionally teak planking is used only for the lower four or five planks. The idea is to have this best of woods in way of the metal floors because this is where electrolytic action is so common. Teak minimises this trouble, whereas mahogany seems to be very prone to it. A hull with only the bottom planks of teak may be described as having a 'teak bottom'. This in itself would be misleading, but there is a more serious aspect. Because the bottom of the boat is swept up at each end and the planks run relatively horizontally, it is common to find that towards the bow and stern the floor fastenings come in the higher, less noble timber. Naturally there are only a few of these fastenings outside the teak-planked region, but they are very likely to be the ones which give trouble. So even when the surveyor is told that the bottom planking is of teak, he should treat the information with suspicion and study the wood round the upper fastenings of the floors towards the ends of the waterline. If in doubt, patches of wood should be scraped clean.

For wood scraping I like to use an old file with the end heated and bent over, then ground and sharpened. This is not just my Scottish reluctance to throw away old files: the tool has weight and inertia, so that it is easy to sweep along a thick skin of paint and whip it off. Sharpening is easy once the knack has been practised, no one steals or borrows this type of scraper, and it stands up to the hurly-burly of years of use. It does not lose its edge quickly even when it lies with other tools in the bottom of the survey bag.

In practice, surveyors do not scrape away large areas of paint themselves They seldom have the time. When there is doubt about the bottom condition of a wood boat it is a good plan to get the purchaser's and owner's permission to have the whole of the underbody burnt off. This is the only way to get a *view* of the condition of the wood: sighting is every bit as important as spike testing.

If the owner protests that the bottom has recently been burnt off, there is cause for suspicion. Why should he worry about burning off again? He is not paying for it, and he is presumably confident that the hull is sound, so he should have no worries about adverse effects of burning off two years running. In practice the bad side-effects of burning off are few, and seldom matter.

What is Flimsy?

Most professional surveyors of any standing can look at a boat, or any part of it, and give a useful opinion as to its strength. Years spent in close proximity with ships implants a scale of soundness which automatically evaluates everything. When I go aboard anything from a racing machine to a dumb barge I glance up and round, at the beams, frames, floors, the edge mouldings, the way the fittings are secured. It means that I appear extremely rude, and owners wonder why I'm apparently distracted, vague, and not properly involved in the conversation. They misjudge me: I'm vastly interested in everything they have to say, for there is no quicker way to learn about a boat than to listen to her owner. But it is impossible to keep the eyes from straying.

Over the years surveyors learn to assess the worth of different scantlings. They know that below a certain thickness each item becomes progressively less able to stand up to the rough and tumble of life afloat. They know that if a scantling is just a little too weak there will be signs of movement, traces of leaking, paint cracks, giveaway signs. The further below the safety limit a part is, the more blatant these signs become, on anything except a very new vessel.

A weak component throws an unfair load on the adjacent structure. A rudder that is too thin bends and causes upper and lower bearings to wear. I remember surveying a fabulous ocean racer which had a rudder which was thick enough by any normal standards, or it would have been if there had been the usual number and spacing of rudder straps. But to cut down every interruption to water flow the designer had omitted all straps. Inevitably the rudder bent in the middle when the helm was put over when the yacht was travelling fast. The wear at the bottom bearing was very serious, and unusual in appearance. The owner complained that the rate of wear was disconcerting, even though the best bearing material was used. This is a reminder that the best designers sometimes err, or hand over some of their detail design work to lesser men and boys.

An experienced surveyor relies on his years of experience, and usually knows instinctively what will stand up to a force 10 gale. In time he will probably cast a measuring eye over the pearly gates, to see if they will stand up to their job. For other mortals there are Lloyds' scantlings rules, which cover many types of ships. They are printed in special books, for fibreglass, wood, aluminium, composite and steel construction.

One trouble about these rules is that they are designed for particular classes of vessel. However, the rules can be adapted with intelligence. The yacht rules may be 'beefed up' for fishing boats, special attention being paid to the frames forward and in way of any trawl-handling gear. Naturally a fishing boat needs massive side rubbers, extra thick decks where heavy fishing gear is handled and so on. Some fishing boat scantlings are listed by the Government body which oversees the commercial fishing industry, and their publications are a useful source of information. In Britain, the name of this body varies almost as often as the government changes and is at present the 'Sea Fisheries Industry Authority'.

Lighter craft, used for racing or inland waters, can have more delicate scantlings. Many racing craft are too lightly built, especially in classes which are highly competitive. A surveyor finding delicate scantlings in a racing boat should remember two principles: the sea does not mitigate its force for the convenience of racing boats; and in order to win it is first necessary to finish—which no one does in a flimsy shell.

Damage
Surveys

Right at the start, when carrying out a damage survey, it is important to discover the real cause of the trouble. A factor which seems the obvious culprit is sometimes a secondary reason for the damage, so that a little intensive detective work is needed. To take a common example, fractured or bent stanchions are seen every week. The stanchion sockets should be examined, because the vertical type, when fitting onto a well-rounded deck, tilts the stanchion outboard so that it is virtually bound to get damaged in the course of time. Simply putting back new stanchions will not truly cure the trouble. The sockets either have to be replaced with an angled pattern or have wedges put in beneath the base flanges. Alternatively, if there already are pads under the base flanges they should be tapered so that the stanchions stand vertical.

It is almost always essential to put back more strength than the craft originally had, when carrying out a repair. After all, if damage is there the structure has not proved adequate for the stresses which it has suffered. Certain high performance craft have to be kept as light as possible, however, and this may conflict with the principle of putting back ample extra strength.

When adding this additional stiffening it is important to taper away the new scantlings. If this is not done there will be new hard spots, and therefore new weak regions. This principle needs detailing even to good yards, and it is an aspect of materials properties not appreciated by all boatbuilders. It applies regardless of what material is being used and is particularly important in craft with light or flexible scantlings.

Another important precept is that existing structure should be disturbed as little as possible. Good boatyards appreciate this and often fit doublers rather than cut out a scantling and scarph in a new piece. To be sure, scarphing virtually always looks neater, whereas a doubler normally lowers the value of a boat by indicating that a repair has been carried out. Doubling up is nearly always quicker and cheaper, which means that the vessel is back in service sooner.

Even when the surveyor is retained by an insurance company, he has a duty to the owner of the craft. Where the boat is needed back afloat as quickly as possible the owner's interests may be served best by fitting a doubler, even when this is not the most elegant type of repair. On older boats it is very often downright bad practice to take out frames or knees or bulkheads which have been in place a long time, just to make a repair. Far better to put in a new scantling close by, through-fastened to the existing structure. On occasions where there is damage on the port side, it may be better to fit a new piece on both port *and* starboard in order to match up the appearance, rather than take out a damaged part and put in a new one on the damaged side only. This applies to elegant cockpit coamings which are fitted in a complicated way. Rooting out or patching only one coaming so often causes an uneven appearance.

It is clearly a case of selecting 'horses for courses'. The repair has to be commensurate with the type of craft and its usage. A contractor's launch is usually wanted back in service in a hurry; there are seldom reserve boats available and no one is going to mind about a fancy finish. In contrast, a new yacht should be put back to a new standard. This can mean stripping out all movable and semi-portable equipment from a moderately severely damaged GRP hull and transferring everything to a new hull. It is not unusual for the insurance company to sell the badly damaged hull to an enthusiastic amateur shipwright so that the cost of repairs can be partly offset by the sale. The buyer of the fractured hull must be somebody who does not mind spending a lot of time and trouble dealing with the damage. He ends up with a hull which is likely to show extensive patching on the inside. This type of patched hull may look perfect from the outside but it will fetch a lower market price when sold, which is why the original owner can reasonably reject an extensively repaired hull, always provided the boat was relatively new when the damage occurred. From the insurance underwriter's point of view it may be cheaper to transfer the equipment to a new shell.

This is a field where there is no unanimity among insurance companies, owners or boatyards. The surveyor stands in the middle and tries to achieve an equitable settlement. He has to remember that his aim is to look after the person or company who retains his services, and has to put up with the fact that he is virtually bound to upset one party or another, often seriously.

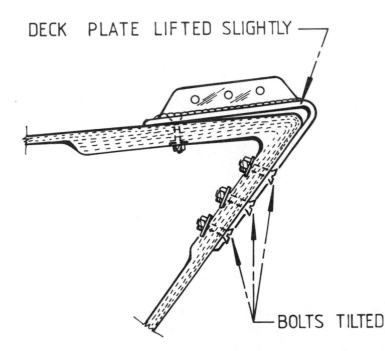

A glance over the bow may show that the bolts holding the stem-head fitting are tilted slightly. Then peer closely at the flat plate on the deck, and see if it has pulled up just slightly. This means there will be leaks through the deck, and in time the whole fitting may come adrift. Check the back-stay chain plate for tilted bolts too.

Examining
the Hull

Tools

Tools for Wood Surveying

Spikes

The common bradawl with a wood handle seldom lasts long in the hands of a professional surveyor. The metal spike breaks off close to the handle, or comes out of the wood. The moral of this is to take two or three on a survey if the better type of bradawl (which has a plastic handle) cannot be found. This improved type is made by Wm. Marples of Dronfield, Sheffield, and comes in a range of sizes. I prefer the large version with the yellow handle for most jobs. For fine work a medium size with a red handle, or a fine one with a blue handle are useful. These bradawls are in the Trigrip range; their handles have three deep dimples round the circumference which helps the grip in cold wet weather, but makes for blisters if the hand has become softened. They are nothing like so handy as the circular-sectioned handles of the common wood bradawl when it comes to tapping, and as so much surveying involves tapping and spiking alternately, the Marples tools are not everyone's choice. I have tried carrying two all the time, but this can be dangerous. If a cork is not kept on the spike which is not in use, there is a good chance of being impaled on the unguarded point while climbing into some cramped hole. A bradawl spike goes through overalls and clothes easily. This is one reason why I do not use the Marples Type 1838, which has a very fine sharp point. I know at least one Lloyds surveyor who favours this model, but I find it misleading. I prefer the flat blade used with the grain of the wood. It is more sensitive and telling.

In practice, after a dozen surveys most people will decide just how sharp they like their bradawl to be, and grind it accordingly.

For working up behind beam shelves or into counters or chain lockers, in fact anywhere out of reach, a long thin electrician's screwdriver is useful. The point has to be ground off, but not so sharp that it bends easily when accidentally pushed against a metal fastening.

Of the various other tools sometimes used, a knife is likely to make too much damage and its 'feel' varies too much according to whether it is along or across the grain. Also the handle is seldom comfortable for a long day's surveying. The same applies to a small electrician's screwdriver.

Hammers
Hammer handles may be drilled and fitted with a wrist loop. For general work a 700 g (1½ lb) long-handled hammer or even a 350 g (¾ lb) version are useful. The pein-headed type are generally used. A telephone or pin hammer with a head weight of about 110 g (4 oz) is needed for light work. It has a handle about 330 mm (13 in.) long, which makes it easy to use. Some surveyors use a 1·8 kg (4 lb) hammer on rough craft such as fishing boats, though I personally do not favour this particular tool for this job.

Tools for Steel Surveys

Hammers
A long-handled 1·8 kg (4 lb) hammer is good for a wide variety of work. For lightly plated craft a 700 g (1½ lb) hammer, again with a long shank, is useful.

For measuring thickness of plating and frames an internal vernier caliper gauge is needed. The ordinary caliper gauge is no use because it cannot be used to measure the thickness of plate round a very small hole. It is seldom adequate to test plate thickness at an open edge, such as the inner edge of a frame flange. The normal procedure is to drill a hole in a typical vulnerable place and measure the plate thickness at the hole. A vernier caliper gauge capable of working through a 6 mm ($\frac{1}{4}$ in.) hole is needed. This standard type is not always easy to obtain, but some ordinary vernier caliper gauges can be ground away for use inside small holes.

Drills
Generally speaking, a shipwright will be called in to drill the holes for the surveyor. This is necessary to save time, to accord with trade union requirements, and so on. However, in some yards and locations where surveys have to be carried out the surveyor himself will have to do the drilling. For such situations one of the electric drills which carries its own charge and does not need mains supply is useful, though of course these drills have a limited electrical capacity. It is also possible to buy electric drills which work off a car battery. However, these too are relatively impotent compared with a proper electric drill plugged into the mains.

Portable Lights

Wandering leads
Far and away the best type of lighting for a surveyor is a wandering lead. Even the best torch can only be described as a moderately adequate substitute for mains electric lighting. As a good view of every nook and cranny in a ship is the first essential of surveying, lighting should take priority. Every effort should be made to get mains electricity into a boat during a survey even if this means laying on long leads, or setting up a portable generator.

A well-protected wandering lead is needed, with a wire cage right round the bulb. Even with this it is likely that the bulb will be shattered, so a couple of spares are needed in the surveyor's equipment. My own preference is for 60-watt bulbs with *clear* glass. When the light fails it is easy to see if the trouble is at the bulb and no time is wasted sorting through the various primitive connections found in small yards.

There must be a shade on the wandering lead so that all the light is directed on the job and none comes back into the surveyor's face, blinding him. Some wandering leads have clamps or alligator type spring-loaded clips so that they can grip bulkhead edges, beams or any other protruding structure. This is certainly an advantage, though care has to be taken that the clamp does not bite into furniture and cause damage. If the clamp is too sharp it is softened by gluing cloth over the teeth.

It is possible to buy neon lamps with wandering leads, but they are not easy to find. One of their advantages is that they are particularly rugged: I have seen a demonstration of one which included frequent attempts to break the light by treading on it.

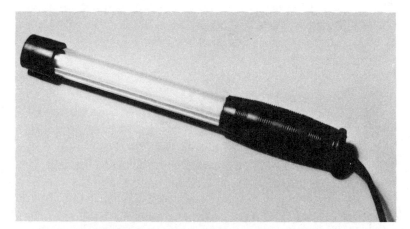

A shatter-proof portable neon light makes a good surveyor's torch. It needs an ample length of cable, so that it can be lowered into deep bilges and tanks.

Some small craft have their own wandering leads but these are often not powerful enough. The combination of low voltage and low amperage combined with loss of voltage along the wire results in pretty poor illumination. On the other hand, the small-size wandering leads used in aircraft hangers are probably the best of the lot. They are designed for low voltage (for safety) but have a high current, and have a shade which directs the light in a beam which is just about right, not too narrow and intense and yet not over-diffused. They have a clamp on the back and are nevertheless light, compact and easily worked into small apertures.

Torches
A surveyor needs at least two torches, simply because his equipment leads a very rough life. For instance, when working in engine compartments it is inevitable that there is a lot of grease about and torches get dropped when they become slippery. Even the rubber type cannot stand unlimited dropping from great heights. Some torches have rings at the top so that safety straps can be added, but it can be difficult to write without removing the safety strap and taking it off and on becomes too tedious.

Only the very best torch should be used, since the brightest beam is essential. I use a type of torch made for railways, by Bardic of Southampton, England. It carries a long-life battery, is semi-waterproof, with a wide base and a good handle. It is not too heavy, which is convenient during a long day's work, and inside the case is a spare bulb. The reflector is protected by a rubber rim and the light does not shine back at all. The same firm make a neon-type light which has advantages such as long battery life, but would need the addition of a shade to prevent the light from blinding the surveyor.

For working in deep bilges and similar inaccessible holes I have made up for myself a special torch. A 12-volt unbreakable neon light made by GP International Electronics Ltd of Pickwick Road, Corsham, Wiltshire, England, is wired to a waterproof battery. The cable is about 4 m (12 ft) long, strongly bonded into the handle on the light, so that it can be used to lower the light into dark places. As the handle is rubber and there is a rubber ferrule at the opposite end of the tube, the light is well cushioned. Also the tube is protected by a plastic transparent casing, so that to date it has withstood the rough and tumble of surveying. This light can be used off a car battery, but it may be advisable to park the car on a slope, because few vehicles have starting handles nowadays!

Another alternative is a miner's type of lamp which may be clipped onto a hat. Power is from a rechargeable Nife battery. It is also possible to buy portable Nife batteries with integral lights which certainly give a good beam. However, they are rather heavy and expensive.

The traditional type of torch with a cylindrical body is seldom powerful enough. If this type is used then a model with a clean well-made reflector should be bought and batteries must be changed frequently. The bulb should be the most powerful which will fit.

Spike Handling

It is essential to tell the difference between wood which is deteriorating and wood which by its nature has always been relatively soft. The surveyor has to develop a 'feel', and he can only do this with one hand until he is fully experienced. When using a spike to test wood structures a right-handed person should only use his right hand. Because the job is tiring, it is necessary to stop every so often to give the hand a rest. This is an occasion to write up notes, which in any case should be made fairly continuously. In theory it is a good idea to only write notes every half hour, on the principle that time is wasted cleaning the hands, getting the notebook out of its waterproof case when it is raining, finding somewhere to sit or stand out of the wind and so on. But in practice it is very easy to forget some small detail, so notes have to be put down more or less continuously.

A beginner is advised to get hold of a piece of spruce, a piece of mahogany, a piece of teak and so on, each in good condition and each planed all over. These are used as test pieces, so that if there is some doubt as to whether the spike has discovered wood in the first stages of rot or merely a rather soft grade of one of the pines, it is easy to try spiking the test pieces with the same amount of force to see what the situation truly is.

The boat should be spiked all over, but not with the same intensity at every point. It is a mark of bad surveying if the boat is left in a lacerated condition. In general the surveyor concentrates on the underwater part of the hull when on the *outside*, and on the inside he spikes mostly in lockers and in dark corners where the spike mark is unobjectionable.

It is essential to work to a pattern in order to avoid missing areas. Go from bow to stern, concentrating first on one side and then on the other. Work from the keel up to the sheer in a continuous line of jabs. Expect to find trouble wherever there are edges: at the deck edge, at the keel edge, round bolt heads, at butts and at seacocks are likely places for softening. Each rectangular piece of wood has six sides and as many of these as possible should be tried.

Above all, intelligence has to be used. A forty-year-old fishing boat is virtually bound to be riddled with troubles and as rough as a mountain road. Testing her with unabashed energy is not going to reduce her quality and it is essential to find out just how far she has gone downhill. In contrast, a two-year-old racing boat built to the finest specification and maintained with total disregard to expense should be handled very gently. Widespread tapping with the handle of the spike will show if any of the wood is waterlogged or rotten: it will give a dull sound in contrast to the ringing of sound wood. Even where the planking is locally stiffened by a bulkhead, there will still be a degree of 'ring' as compared with the flat, unresonant 'bump' when the handle hits real rot. Beginners may be lucky or clever enough to get hold of a piece of planking which includes a length of rot. This should be carefully painted over to give the effect of smart topsides. The handle of the spike can then be tapped first on the sound area and then on the defective region to acclimatise the ear to the different sound responses. There is no reason why this sample should not be carried around during the early surveys, as a guide.

Marking Trouble

It is common for surveyors to mark defects with chalk. My preference is for some different medium, because chalk wipes off easily and washes away in the mildest rain. It is not always easy to get coloured chalk, but white is unsatisfactory because so many craft are white outside or inside. White chalk shows up badly on many pale colours and all chalk tends to be illegible on rough surfaces. Only on varnish or wood to be varnished is chalk satisfactory because it is easy to eradicate.

Various felt-tipped pens are convenient for indicating troubles. There are some which are slightly indelible, and others which remain visible even when washed by torrential rain. My preference is for the kind which is not totally indelible, because indelible marks are hard to blot out by painting. A selection of three colours is handy to designate different levels of seriousness, or various types of trouble. More than three colours tends to become confusing.

Regardless of marking, it is considered good practice to detail accurately in a survey report the troubles found. This is to help anyone reading the survey when not actually aboard, and also to ensure that the trouble is easily and quickly located. It is infuriating for a busy yard foreman to be told that a forward floor needs repairs, if it takes him half an hour to haul up rows of floorboards to examine every single floor in the forward part of the vessel. When a defective scantling is inaccessible, down in a cramped double bottom for instance, it is particularly important to help the men who have to interpret the survey. On the outside of the hull defects can be given co-ordinates. A thin plate might be described as '1 m below the LWL and 2·5 m aft the forward scuttle (portlight)'. (Side openings with glass in them are known variously as portlights, scuttles, portholes, sidelights and so on.)

This brings up a recurring trouble when writing out survey reports: parts of a vessel have different names in different regions, even within nominally the same language. The most notorious example of this is the scantling which runs fore and aft up near the deck edge. This is called the shelf, beam shelf, beam ledge, deck stringer, top stringer, beam stringer and so on and on. It would not be so bad if these different names were found clearly in defined regions, but in one county the same thing may be called by different names in different yards.

My own method of getting over this problem is to recommend a consultation after the survey report has been read, to ensure that it has been understood fully.

Fairness

It is occasionally argued that the fairness of a hull is no concern of a surveyor. This attitude ignores two principles: the first is that the surveyor must protect the buyer's financial interests; and secondly, any unfairness may be the result of an accident, or weakening structure. Fairness is clearly an imperfection and therefore should be mentioned in a report. It may, in certain cases, be left to the reader of the report to assess the significance of the unfairness. For instance, a half inch hollow spread over a metre (3 ft) on a steel fishing boat scarcely calls for a raised eyebrow. However, it may be an indication of poor plating technique or locked-up welding stresses, or it may be the result of a collision which has perhaps caused other damage. It should therefore be noted. The same degree of unfairness on a racing yacht, even one 25 m (80 ft) long, is a great deal more serious. Even if it is not the result of an accident, it cannot be left to offend both the sweet flow of the water and the eye of anyone who appreciates yacht standards.

It is virtually impossible to have fixed criteria when it comes to acceptable fairness. By precision engineering standards no boat is fully fair or symmetrical. Suffice to say that when concerned with craft like yachts, directors' launches and other prestige craft, the eye should not be able to detect any unfairness or unevenness in a moderate light from the distance of two or three times the boat's length. In practice, a really skilled craftsman can almost always detect subtle discrepancies in a good light on the most carefully made boat, provided he stands close enough.

Whatever the craft, she should have smooth sweeping lines fore and aft, though athwartships she may be angular, with unexpected hollows and bumps. Some of the latter are to get round restricting rules for racing, tonnage limitations, etc.

To assess fairness it is important to stand well back and take a diagonal view first from one bow and then the other, and afterwards from the quarter on the port and then the starboard side. Ideally these views should also be taken from below the waterline and from well above. In practice craft ashore or afloat are usually set around with obstructions like other boats, buildings and so on. The surveyor just has to take as many views as he can.

It is easy to be misled by bad paint lines which distort the waterline, and sometimes even the sheer. In addition hard shadows may give a false picture. Occasionally the port and starboard sheers may seem different, and a quick check may be made by taking a straightedge and laying it across the gunwales every few feet from bow to stern. A carpenter's level laid on the straightedge shows whether the sheer on the two sides is closely similar.

Generally the bottom of the run of any boat, whether sail or power driven, should be a smooth, almost straight, line sweeping gradually up over the last third of the vessel. A notable exception to this is the breed of Sparkman & Stevens racing and cruising auxiliary yachts produced during the period between 1946 and 1960. Quite a number of these boats had a slight reverse hook towards the aft waterline end. In the same way some shallow draft power boats sweep up in a straight rising line towards the propeller with a peak somewhere near the screw; the line then reverses and comes gradually down towards the aft end, so that when a propeller blade swings up to the top of its circle it is near or even above the waterline. It is important to realise that *these* hog-back shapes in a ship's bottom are intentional, because in some instances this same curious appearance is produced by structural weakness. Long, lightly built motor cruisers which are not carefully laid up ashore with ample blocks under the keel develop hogged backbones with all sorts of subsequent troubles such as binding propeller shafts and worn stern bearings. In an extreme case I even discovered that a propeller shaft was rubbing against a bulkhead.

Fibreglass boats, particularly those with thin shells and a low standard of construction, may have quite noticeable mild undulations in the topsides. Some builders aim to get a glossy finish and do not worry about these subtle hills and valleys. Often the discrepancies can only be discovered by laying a batten along the topsides and noting the way the hull does not touch the batten continuously throughout its length.

Just occasionally a GRP shell is pulled out of a mould too soon, with odd results. A thin keel may not hang exactly vertically below the vessel's canoe body. If the eye detects signs of this type of fault it is a good idea to cut a wood or cardboard template to fit on one side and then check it against the other side. If one side of the hull is in bright sunlight and the other in dark shadow the eye may be misled, in which case the template is a useful check. Also, if the vessel is not chocked vertically upright it is difficult, particularly for the inexperienced eye, to discern whether there is indeed a lack of symmetry.

However, when offering the template up it is important to remember that tolerance must be allowed. For instance on a 10 m (30 ft) cruiser the difference of 6 mm ($\frac{1}{4}$ in.) in the tuck is not significant and scarcely calls for comment. On a racing boat a difference of more than 1·5 mm ($\frac{1}{16}$ in.) can matter, particularly when it comes to measuring a boat to ensure that she complies with class rules or ratings.

When viewing the sheer it is important to look for humps in way of the mast of a sailing vessel. If she is built of fibreglass it is possible that the deck may be lifting slightly. On a wooden boat, built throughout with bent frames, after a few seasons' hard racing mild hogging in way of the mast is quite common. In old boats the trouble may be repeated aft where the runners come down to the deck.

Where a number of boats are built from one mould, or one set of patterns, certain defects are repeated inevitably. This trouble is not confined to GRP boats. A whole generation of carvel Folkboats produced in Eastern Europe have a noticeable lack of symmetry at the garboards. It must be admitted that some of these boats have had good racing results in spite of this defect.

An experienced surveyor naturally builds up a casebook of class defects, and if he surveys a boat which does not have one of the 'standard' troubles, he should pursue the matter. It may be that he is surveying the wrong vessel! Or the boat may be masquerading under the wrong title, or she may have been altered without the knowledge of the builders, or perhaps without adequate skill.

The lands on a clinker boat, or simulated clinker craft, should taper evenly towards each end. It is not unusual to find that the two sides of a traditional clinker boat are different, because two teams of shipwrights, one on each side, have worked in opposition rather than with full co-operation.

Deck camber unfairness is hard to detect by eye unless it is very serious. It can be quickly checked by laying a straightedge across the ship. The vertical distances at 30 cm, 60 cm, 90 cm, etc., from the centre should be the same port and starboard. A light held beyond the straightedge should show similar shapes of gaps port and starboard, but with a boat over twenty years old some leniency must be allowed. A camber which has collapsed is usually easy to see. It is usually given away by a beam failure or two, and the deck tends to be flexy.

When it comes to rudders, fishing boats appear to get away with murder. They have in some cases rudders which do not appear to be vertical when viewed from astern, even to the most inexperienced eye. The results under way are seldom noticeable. However, a racing yacht must have a rudder made and fitted with a good deal of precision. Any boat loses a little value if any part of her is visibly unsymmetrical or inaccurately assembled.

Any troubles found should be traced back as far as possible, to discover their cause. A boat with no drain-hole may have been laid up all one winter with tons of rainwater in the bilge. A boat with long overhangs may have had props put under them which sank into the ground, allowing the bow and stern to droop. This happened, for instance, with a number of 30 Square Metres which were laid up in muddy boatyards.

Ballast
Keel

If a surveyor comments unfavourably on the amount of ballast in a given boat he will probably displease the seller and also the selling broker. Both will claim that the surveyor's job is to assess the condition of the structure and avoid disparaging remarks about the basic design. However, a sailing boat's ability to stand up to bad weather and fight away from a lee shore is dependent on her stability. If she does not have adequate stability, which usually means ample weight low enough down, she cannot stand up to the blast. She will merely lurch to leeward at every breaking wave. It boils down to the undeniable fact that ballast ratio and safety are linked. However, a boat with a reliable engine of adequate power may get away with a very poor ballast ratio since the engine can compensate for the lack of windward ability under sail.

The problem is further complicated by the difficulty of assessing the total weight of ballast, particularly when the iron or lead is entirely enclosed and hidden inside a fibreglass shell or a steel fin keel. In practice, surveyors tend not to comment on ballast ratios unless they are specifically asked to do so, or unless there are very clear indications that the ballast has been cut down. If there are signs that a boat has less ballast than her sister ships, they may well comment. There was a very popular, much advertised miniature cruiser, a hard chine boat which started off life built in plywood and then production changed over to GRP. The Mark II version had more ballast than the Mark I though the design was otherwise unchanged. Mark III had even more ballast, which confirmed what every intelligent surveyor knew, namely that the first two versions were under ballasted. Though the published descriptions and the advertisements claimed that this class was suitable for offshore work, in practice these boats should never have been used except in sheltered waters. The surveyor's dilemma is to make this clear, because owing to luck and thoroughly good seamanship quite a number of these tiny boats have made deep-sea passages. This does not alter the fact that they should not go where there is risk of being caught by an onshore breeze in excess of force 7.

The surveyor's dilemma is sharpened further because he cannot simply recommend additional ballast to be put on the keel. Extra stiffening is needed to support the greater weight, usually in the form of floors but also possibly in frames and even occasionally extra stringers.

A commercial boat or cruising yacht is generally acceptable with a relatively rough keel. If the lead is dented or the iron rusty and pitted, the owner is not likely to worry unduly. For race winning the keel has to be as smooth as the rest of the hull and this means that dents and scratches on the keel need cleaning up and filling. An iron keel must be scoured to remove rust and the pitting filled. It has to have a proper build-up of paint, first to prevent rust and then to fill in undulations, and finally to give a proper antifouling coverage which includes a barrier paint between the rust preventive and the actual antifouling. Where an iron keel has protruding sharp edges no paint can be expected to adhere well. These sharp edges should be ground or filed to at least a small radius of curvature to prevent rust starting and to ensure that the antifouling works properly.

A deep gouge on the bottom of a lead keel suggests that the boat has been driven aground hard, and the surveyor will know he must look for the other signs of trouble which this kind of accident produces, such as broken frames. If the grounding has been very severe the whole ballast keel may be fractionally moved relative to the rest of the hull. The problem here is that some externally fitted ballast keels are built so that they do not exactly align with the shell. It is quite common even on well-built boats to find stopping on the keel or on the hull to fill a gap and avoid the crude appearance of an ill-fitting ballast keel. The surveyor has to decide whether the keel was originally fitted badly or whether it has been strained sideways. If the forward starboard side of the keel stands out from the shell, and the aft port side also protrudes, the indications are that the keel has been bashed over to starboard as it hit the ground. The keel bolt heads should be checked to see if they show subtle indications that they have been twisted the same way. If the forward end of the keel has been knocked to starboard, the indications are that the forward keel bolts will have forced their washer plates into the keel top on the port side. After a very bad grounding there are sometimes cracks under the keel bolt washer plates, which give a good idea of the severity of the accident.

A ballast keel which is sealed inside a fibreglass hull must be entirely protected from any contact with water. The majority of these keels are iron, or a mixture of iron and concrete if the boat is cheaply built. If water gets at this iron rusting follows. Because rust takes up more space than the iron which forms it, the top sealing is forced upwards. This means that more and more water can seep down so that the rusting gets progressively worse. Just as important, the ballast may be no longer held securely into the shell so that if the vessel gets knocked down in very severe conditions the ballast may come tumbling out and rampage about inside the hull. This is why it is so important to examine the area below the floorboards for any signs of cracks or minute openings in the fibreglass which bonds the keel in.

The use of concrete is popular in cheap boats because it is an inexpensive material. It is also relatively light so it is not an efficient ballast. Concrete is seldom 100 per cent efficient at sealing in ballast so that after a few years, sometimes after only a few months, water tends to work its way down between the concrete and the shell. If this water is fresh, or only slightly salt, trouble is likely during the winter because freezing water takes up more space than liquid water and so the separation between shell and ballast becomes worse.

Where a steel hull has internal ballast sealed off with cement the steel shell tends to get a line of pitting along the top of the sealing. Very few bilge pumps will suck out every last drop of water, and there is always a small puddle on top of the cement. Because this washes to and fro it is well aereated, and so it forms the ideal rusting agent. As a result a steel shell is attacked quickly in this area. Part of the cure is to ensure that there is a sump, so that the last drop of water in the bilge drops into this. This makes it easier to get out the maximum amount of water and also ensures that there are no shallow puddles left sloshing about on top of the cement and in contact with the steel. The sump itself should, of course, be a cavity entirely surrounded by cement.

A great many craft, particularly power-driven vessels, built on traditional lines have keel bands. These take a great deal of punishment, being scratched every time the vessel is slipped or grounded. As a result the metal rusts quickly, and fastenings have their heads torn sideways, chafed and generally treated in the roughest way. A keel band is not easy to repair because the ship has to be supported clear of the band with keel blocks removed, to get the metal strip out. This raises a number of complications and involves awkward hard work. It tends to be difficult and expensive and generally unpopular so that not surprisingly keel bands are neglected. They can tolerate a certain amount of neglect but eventually the joins and particularly the forward end may pull away, which can be dangerous. Because the fastenings are often corroded and bent they can be difficult to withdraw. On commercial craft the most sensible repair procedure is very often the addition of a new set of fastenings intermediate between the existing ones, with an extra pair of fastenings at the forward end.

Cement and Pitch in the Bilges

Beneath the sole may be found either cement or pitch, sometimes deep, sometimes quite shallow. The purpose of this material may be to cover ballast, to keep out water, or to fill pockets so that bilgewater flows aft easily to a pump sump without leaving puddles. If the material is put in for this last purpose it is usually obvious, because only the pockets will be filled and the top of the keel (or what serves as the keel) will be visible between the infill. Whatever the purpose of the filling material, there should be no cracks, or powdering, on top or around the edge, and no loose pieces.

For the most part cement or pitch over internal ballast tends to be an indication of inexpensive building; it has a suggestion of cheapness, but not necessarily shoddiness.

Sometimes filling material is put in when the craft is new. Ideally there is a certificate made out by the builder, dated and signed, stating that the cement or pitch was put in for a set purpose which should be listed and noting that the work was done when the vessel was brand-new and had never been put afloat. In practice these certificates are seldom with the craft after ten years and it is almost always very difficult for the surveyor to find out when and why the infill was put in.

Cement itself is not particularly heavy and is often used to cover internal ballast in the form of iron bars or punchings. Some fibreglass and ferrocement boats have this form of inside ballast. The edge of the cement should be carefully examined for chipping or cracking because this may indicate that the fibreglass is moving relative to the cement.

Signs of red rust at the edge of the cement, or in cracks across the cement, are serious because they indicate that water is getting down to the iron. The rust is likely to force the cement apart, widening the cracks.

Cement should be smooth and clean on top, free from chipping and powdering. It should adhere well to the entire

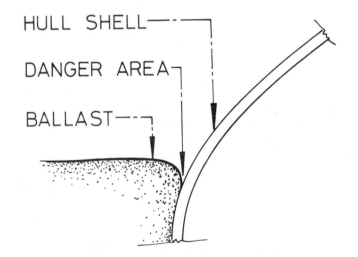

Any type of hull which has ballast inside should be examined very closely around the edge of the top seam. If there is a depression at the edge of the covering over the ballast, water tends to lie and cause trouble. Steel, aluminium and fibreglass hulls all suffer from defects of the shell if water can lie in this type of depression. The cure is to clean out the gutter and fill it with a compound which adheres well to the hull and ensures that any puddle left in the bilge is on top of the ballast sealing and drains away from the shell.

structure. If the boat has not been kept dry it is likely that a wood boat will have rot in the frames where they emerge from the cement.

The only way to be sure what is below the cement is to chip it out, and this is a long expensive job, seldom called for by a surveyor. However, for a prolonged ocean cruise it is good sense to chip out sections of the cement to see what lies beneath.

Occasionally cement or pitch is put into the bilge to check leaks. Neither tend to be successful, even for a short period. The only way to cure leaks is from the outside, because water pressure comes from the outside inwards and seepage between the infill and hull shell is likely. If an infill has to be used as a rather desperate last resort, it should not be the brittle type of pitch, but a kind which stays just very slightly flexible all the time.

Keel Bolts

It is general practice to have some bolts supporting a ballast keel withdrawn. Less often the surveyor may call for the extraction of stem or keel bolts of craft which do not have ballast. If there are signs of corrosion at the bolt heads or nuts, or where there are indications of leaking at these bolts, or where there are signs that the stem may be moving relative to the apron or keel, it is worth extracting random samples.

The surveyor should indicate which bolts are to be withdrawn, otherwise the yard will select the easiest. It is human nature to do this, and thus every time a keel bolt is withdrawn it is always the same one. This may result in one bolt being in excellent condition while the others gradually deteriorate to a pin's thickness.

Where the survey is of particular importance, possibly when the boat is an unusually expensive one or is to be used for offshore racing by a hard-driving owner, it makes sense to withdraw at least two bolts. A very good case can be made out for examining at least two bolts even when the survey is not an extra special one. Where fin bilge keels are fitted it is not unusual for the bolts to be quite small, and incidentally relatively easy to remove. In such a situation four bolts from each fin might be extracted, two from forward and two from the aft end of each keel.

It is common for the buyer of a boat to have a firm quotation for withdrawing and replacing a keel bolt. However, some yards refuse to quote a fixed price. They know from experience that keel bolts can be recalcitrant and the job may take a considerable time, partly owing to the usual inaccessibility of the nut.

Because extracting a bolt is not cheap, some surveyors suggest deferring this work until the rest of the boat has been surveyed. If serious trouble is found elsewhere in the structure there is no point in removing a bolt. The boat stands condemned, at least in the eyes of that potential buyer, so he will not wish to spend further money on her.

Iron or steel bolts are most likely to give trouble, but all types of bolts should be withdrawn, since wherever two metals are immersed in seawater there is a risk of erosion. In practice even a single metal immersed in an electrolyte such as seawater can set up an electric current, with a resulting wastage of metal. One reason for this is that metals are seldom pure, and impurities in the main body of the metal set up electric circuits and hence wastage. It is true that the erosion of the metal may be quite slow, but it continues throughout the 24 hours of each day, all the time the vessel is afloat. The cumulative effect can be serious. For these reasons even the finest bronze bolts through a lead keel, with a good seal at the bottom end, should be examined during a full survey. Stainless steel bolts are by no means exempt from trouble, and where they are fitted samples should be withdrawn for examination.

In general it is usual to renew all bolts if those taken out

A typical corroded keel bolt is shown at the top. When one bolt is found like this the surveyor will recommend that all the keel bolts should be replaced. Bottom left is a bronze keel bolt that has become badly corroded, and broke off short when an attempt was made to take it out. The two small bolts started life in an identical condition and were fitted within a few inches of each other. The wasted one was near a brass fitting and electrolytic corrosion has occurred. This shows the importance of testing more than one bolt in each area.

show 10 per cent wastage. This is not because the keel is about to drop off (the factor of safety is normally of the order of 15) but because bolts with corrosion are likely to cause leaks. When a bolt is taken out and found to have only quite slight corrosion, it is good practice to renew that bolt since the expense of extracting it has already been incurred. The others may be left, but their top and bottom ends should be most carefully looked at.

An interesting technique is offered by X-Ray Marine Ltd of 175 Piccadilly, London W1V 9DB. This firm takes radiographs of ferrous bolts, charging about the cost of a good lunch for two per bolt. The technique can only be used on ferrous bolts and of course the vessel must be out of the water for this job. It is always good practice to avoid disturbing structure whenever possible, which is a particular merit of the radiographic technique. It can also save substantial expense, though this factor will need some balancing, since quite a few yards will withdraw two bolts for the same money. Perhaps its most attractive advantage is that the work can be done in the spring, when many yards are short-handed.

Diagonal Damage

There is a special type of damage which occurs to all types of small craft regardless of the materials they are made of. It is found in every type of vessel from dinghies to the biggest freighters, and can be summed up in the phrase 'diagonal damage'.

Whenever a boat is run into at one corner, it is quite likely that she will show damage diagonally opposite the point of contact. In the same way, if she herself runs into another boat or a quay wall trouble may be expected not only at the point of impact but also on the opposite side and at the opposite end.

This type of trouble is found both in the vertical and horizontal planes. It is easily explained by remembering what happens when a wooden packing case is given a severe kick at one edge. The rectangular shape becomes diamond-shaped as deformation occurs. All four edges change from right angles; two angles become larger than 90° and two smaller (see sketch). The same sort of trouble occurs with boats, where the impact area dents inwards and the basic structure behaves like a box.

Instances have occured of boats falling over on one side with the resultant damage affecting *both* sides. Sometimes the damage on the side which strikes the ground is quite light owing to the cushioning effect of soft mud and water. There have been accidents in which boats have fallen over without any damage at all on the downward side, simply because there

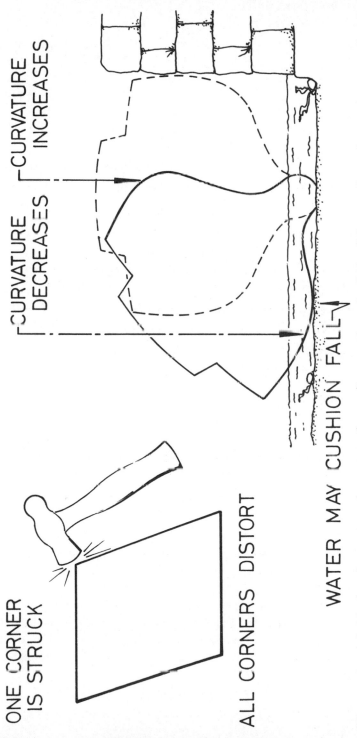

ONE CORNER
IS STRUCK

ALL CORNERS DISTORT

CURVATURE
DECREASES

CURVATURE
INCREASES

WATER MAY CUSHION FALL

Whenever a boat is found to have damage at one edge or corner, the opposite edges and corners should be examined. A structure distorts when it is in collision, and fractures occur at any line of relative weakness such as an edge or sharply curved region.

A typical example occurs when a boat falls over. The side which strikes the ground occasionally has little or no damage because the water and mud cushion the fall. The frames are occasionally found to be fractured at the opposite turn of bilge because they have been jolted into a tighter curve. This trouble occurs particularly when the boat has a tall mast.

was enough depth of water to absorb the blow. At the same time the side which took no blow has suffered broken frames owing to the localised and very sudden increase of curvature at the bilge. A comparable instance has been seen where a dent at one corner of a transom as a result of a horizontal blow has caused star cracking of the fibreglass hull at the turn of the bilge diagonally opposite (see sketch and photo).

Sometimes a stiff member is pushed across so that it transmits a damaging force. A good example of this is a really strong bulkhead, which may cause damage on the starboard side when the vessel is hit on the port side.

The topsides and deck edge of this small cruiser have been badly gouged. When surveying this type of accident it is necessary to remove cabin lining to see the extent of the damage. In practice, the full extent of the trouble cannot always be assessed until damaged parts have been dismantled. When damage at the deck edge of a boat like this is seen it is important to check at the chine angle for frame fractures and leaks along the chine.

Because of this effect it is important to check for diagonal damage every time repairs are seen. Where a dinghy is found to have signs of repair round one edge of the transom, the opposite shoulder should be carefully examined for broken planks, frames and distortion where the thwart meets the topsides. If the boat is of GRP the gunwale edge should be carefully examined for cracks running downwards from the top. Damage is rarely confined to impact point.

Leakers

An aircraft company had to buy a launch for one of their projects, and decided to get an aluminium boat because they were familiar with the material. The boat lay on moorings for a number of months, and then without warning sank. She was salvaged and taken to the company headquarters where engineering experts examined her, using all sorts of advanced electronic equipment. They were quite unable to find out why the boat sank and called in a boat surveyor. He was offered every assistance, technical and manual, but declined all help apart from asking for one labourer and a large bundle of clean rags. He got the labourer to clean off the inside and the outside of the boat very carefully and then examined the whole of the bottom. He could find no signs of leaks and so he had the boat filled with water quite slowly after making sure that she was properly chocked up so that the extra weight could be supported. He lay under the boat with bright lights shining upwards and eventually detected four quite tiny pinholes. There was a moderate sensation when the surveyor claimed to have found four holes whereas the aircraft technicians had been unable to find one.

This trick for finding leaks is by no means infallible. A boat may hold water if it is put inside, and yet let water in once she is afloat. One reason for this is that a boat ashore lies in a different way, with the load supported in quite local areas. Once she is afloat the whole of the bottom is fairly evenly supported, and so the weight of the craft is spread over the major part of the bottom of the boat. It is not only wooden boats, or lightly built fibreglass ones, which move quite appreciably when ashore. I recently surveyed a 9 m (say 29 ft) auxiliary cruiser built quite substantially in steel. At one stage the rudder would not move and it was found that the boat's keel had twisted sideways very slightly as the craft lay

Leaks often give themselves away. The driblets from this bolt show quite clearly where the water is coming in and suggest that the bolt is rusting and should be renewed, with plenty of bedding round the replacement.

The breasthook above has been painted, but rust is breaking through and regalvanising is overdue.

suspended in a crane sling. Once the boat was afloat the rudder pivoted quite easily. The amount of movement of the keel was tiny, but it was enough to bind pintles which fitted tightly into their gudgeons.

Detecting leaks by putting water into a boat is a good trick provided it's not overdone. A great weight of water inside will distort almost any craft. Boats are built to withstand pressure from the outside, so filling the bilge to detect leaks should not be done to excess.

A boat which is a regular leaker gives herself away to an experienced surveyor. The bilge has a series of well-established high-tide marks. The paint in the bilge is overlaid with a pattern of mud, nails lying loose in the bilge are rusted almost away, scraps of paper have a saturated and dried out and bleached look. The whole bilge has a sort of bland dirty look, with general lack of contrasting colours. Sometimes the floorboards and floor bearers have a sogginess about them. Another sign is a high-tide mark of oil, but this can be misleading because the boat may have been flooded once but not be a persistent leaker.

Other warnings are the presence of power-driven bilge pumps which have a well-worn appearance. If the hand bilge pump is bright and chafed with constant use, this is a suspicious sign.

Quite a different type of leaking is downward through the deck or through hatches. This is shown by runnels where the incoming water has left little tracks of dirt, rust and sometimes salt crystals.

Tracing leaks is a rare art. It is particularly difficult in wooden boats which have complicated cabin top joins. Sometimes water will enter at a forward corner post of the wheelhouse and run down the carline which is sloped aft to follow the sheer. The water may finally drip down onto the cabin sole many feet from the original point of ingress. To find this type of leak it may help to have a hose played quietly over the general area, remembering that water will run down sloping scantlings such as shelves and beams. This kind of leak detecting has to be carried out with the boat properly shored up so that she is in the same attitude as she would be afloat.

When looking for leaks in the hull the first thing to remember is that trouble almost always occurs at joins. The places to search for initially are around seacocks, at propeller shaft glands, at butts and seams and scarphs, where the rudder tube meets the shell, and where the echosounder transducer is fitted.

This is where the main trouble was on the launch belonging to the aircraft company. Because the boat lay near a main fairway she had to have her anchor light permanently connected up. It had an electronic eye which switched it on each evening and turned it off every morning, and for this the power supply had to be permanently connected. It was impossible to turn off the batteries at the main switch and still have the light coming on each night. This boat also had an echosounder which did not have its own source of electrical energy. Instead of using dry batteries it was connected up to the ship's circuitry. In normal circumstances, of course, the crew would cut off the electrical supply from the battery every time they went ashore. Because they could not do this, tiny stray currents leaked out of the echosounder transducer, corroded the adjacent shell and let water in.

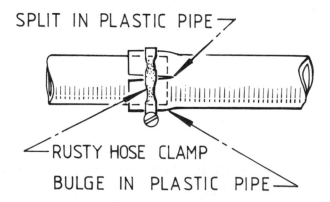

SPLIT IN PLASTIC PIPE

RUSTY HOSE CLAMP

BULGE IN PLASTIC PIPE

Plastic pipes forced over metal pipes sometimes split causing subtle but dangerous leaks. If a plastic pipe has a bulge where it joins a metal one, this is a danger sign. Likewise rust on hose clamps is a sign of trouble because sooner or later the clamp will break.

Wood Construction

Rot

Rot spores travel in the wind and on people, so if a boat is stored on rotten keel chocks, or supported by wood shores which have rot in them, the surveyor is warned to expect trouble on board. If he knows that adjacent boats have rot, he should be doubly suspicious.

Certain types of boat seldom have rot on board because they are open from end to end and air can circulate freely. Few boats in the Dragon class suffer from rot, partly because most of these boats are built without bulkheads and partly because the majority are stored in dry sheds during the winter. Timber with less than 20 per cent moisture is unlikely to decay through fungal attack, and the lower the percentage of moisture the smaller the risk. The age of the timber has little to do with the matter, which explains why some brand-new boats have rot in them. As with human beings, a disease will attack young or old provided the conditions are right.

Salt water is a mild antiseptic, the accent being on the word mild. This explains why rot is more often found in cabin tops than in planking. It also explains why a boat kept in fresh water needs an extra careful survey. But of course plenty of harbours have freshwater streams running into them, so it is never safe to assume that rot does not exist in planking just because a boat is kept permanently afloat in the sea.

The rot in this cabin coaming was easy to detect because of the discoloration. The aft beam of the cabin top is so rotten that parts have actually dropped out, as is seen just above the spike.

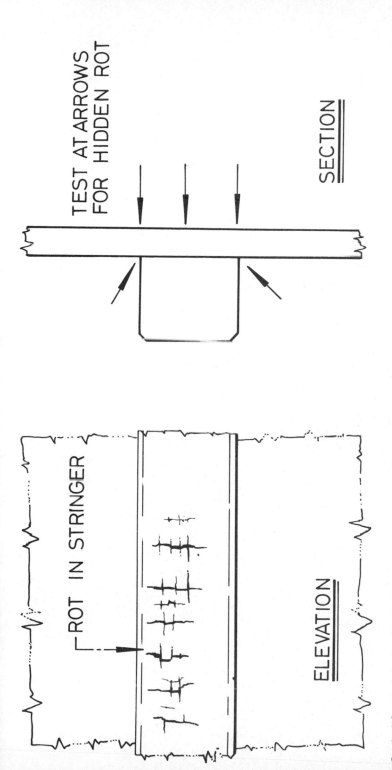

TEST AT ARROWS
FOR HIDDEN ROT

SECTION

ROT IN STRINGER

ELEVATION

On the left, a typical area of rot is shown in a stringer. Its characteristic is the cubing which results from cracks both across and with the grain. When rot is found in one piece of wood the surrounding scantlings should be examined to see if the trouble has spread. If the bulkhead has not been infected it should be well treated with a chemical preservative when the stringer is being repaired.

Sapwood in all species of timber rots more easily than the harder, older, inner parts of the tree. For this reason the surveyor's spike should always probe into any sapwood. Cheaply built boats are much more likely to have white edges to the red mahogany, the white being the sapwood. In oak the colouring is reversed, with the whiter wood the hard core and the reddish timber sapwood.

Surveyors should always insist that rot is treated promptly because of the speed with which trouble can increase. A tiny speck of rotten wood will grow at the rate of about 1 cm per week in normal conditions. But of course the growth is towards the bow and the stern at about the same rate, so what starts as a patch of rot a millimetre or two across can be 8 cm long after one month of neglect.

This frightening speed of advance is one reason why sur-

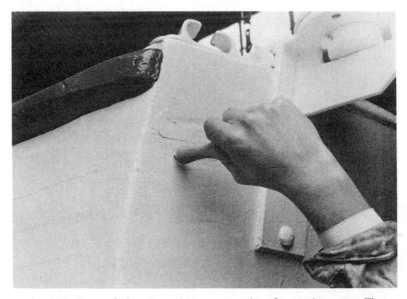

A usual place to find rot is at the top outer edge of a wood transom. The surveyor had plenty of warning of trouble here since the paint was undulating and a graving piece had already been let in.

Since the spike has gone in right to the hilt this rot is severe, and probably plank ends as well as the transom framing and possibly the deck will also be affected.

veyors are reluctant to recommend remedial treatment rather than total replacement. If chemical treatment is suggested it has to be made absolutely clear to the owner that complete drying out and ventilation of the affected area is also important. The strength of the structure in the rotten area also has to be restored by fitting doublers or some similar technique. Above all, the areas which are infected should be re-examined every three months or so by somebody who is both experienced and has full knowledge of the history of the trouble.

Dry Rot (*Merulius lachrymans*)

Quite rightly, this is the most dreaded disease found in small craft. Under the worst conditions it can spread at the rate of about $\frac{3}{4}$ cm per day. Fortunately this type of rot is relatively rare, and it tends to give itself away by a musty smell. Provided it is established in an area which can actually be seen, it is usually relatively easy to detect, although this is not universally so. The external signs are cracking along and across the grain of wood. When the wood has been painted there are undulations and even cracks in the paint. Testing is by spike, and there is virtually never any doubt about the condition since the spike sinks into what was wood with no resistance at all. It is not unusual for the spike to go right in up to the handle.

Once rot has been found, every effort has to be made to stop it spreading by burning the infected timber. The wood should be cut out well beyond the signs of rot; ideally the whole component should be taken out. All the wood removed and all shavings and adjacent parts which are taken out should be burned at once. In some yards, if a boat is known to have dry rot on board, disinfectant trays are put at the foot of the ladder up to the boat so that everyone going aboard and coming off automatically treads in the chemical decontaminator.

Once all the rotten wood has been cut out the whole area should be treated chemically with a substance such as

Cuprinol. All the new wood which is put in should also be liberally treated. During repairs it is very important that the whole area is examined carefully to make sure that the rot has not taken hold in adjacent scantlings.

Wet Rot (*Coniophora cerebella*)

This type of trouble is more common than dry rot, but does not seem to be quite so virulent. It is found particularly where there are leaks above the waterline. It thrives where there is a lack of ventilation and so is found at the bow and stern, particularly where these areas are enclosed. The signs are similar to dry rot in that the timber splits along the grain and eventually cracks occur across the grain as well, almost as if the wood has been crazed but not blackened by charring. However, instead of the blackening which comes from burning there are sometimes thin brown strands. The trouble extends lengthways along the grain and often shows up under paint. Undulations in a well-painted surface are frequently the first indication the surveyor has of trouble, and when he tries the wood with his spike he meets little or no resistance. The wood is totally without strength and therefore has to be entirely cut out and a new component fitted. Again it is important to slobber a rot preventive not only on the new parts being put in but also all round the incised region.

Rot Prevention

Wet and dry rot thrive on the presence of moisture and lack of ventilation. Deck and cabin top leaks are prime harbingers of rot. In practice any such leak which is into an important part of the accommodation is generally cured promptly because of its inconvenience. It is those hidden leaks which infiltrate into lockers which are seldom opened, or behind panelling, which give the most trouble.

Once the leaks have been stopped the next part of the cure is

A search should be made for rot wherever water can become trapped, and particularly where rainwater can seep in. This sketch shows typical vulnerable areas and suggests other comparable danger spots. For instance, stanchions work loose so that rain and spray gets down through their bolt-holes. The same trouble occurs at other deck fittings, especially those which take a lot of punishment.

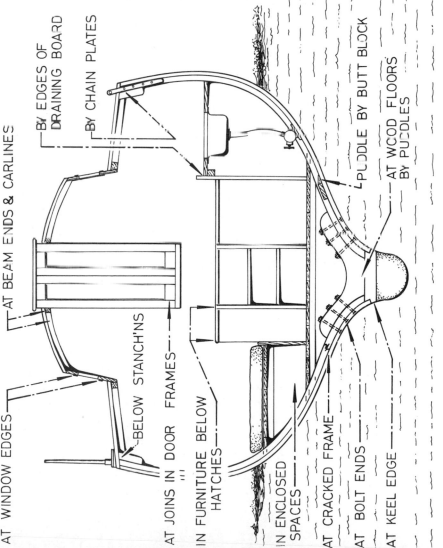

AT WINDOW EDGES

AT BEAM ENDS & CARLINES

BY EDGES OF DRAINING BOARD

BY CHAIN PLATES

BELOW STANCH'NS

AT JOINS IN DOOR FRAMES

IN FURNITURE BELOW HATCHES

IN ENCLOSED SPACES

AT CRACKED FRAME

AT BOLT ENDS

AT KEEL EDGE

PUDDLE BY BUTT BLOCK

AT WOOD FLOORS BY PUDDLES

introducing ventilation. This should be done wholeheartedly, and there should always be two slots or accesses into every closed compartment. If only one vent hole is made the air has little inducement to circulate in and out again. As a basic rule the surveyor should call for an air inlet at the top forward corner of a locker and an outlet diagonally opposite at the aft bottom corner, or call for some similar arrangement with widely separated inlet and outlet. Best of all, of course, are large vent slots at the top and bottom of each side, as well as on the front of every enclosed space.

Worm

Wood vessels, or vessels with wood components fitted beneath the waterline, are sometimes attacked by ship worms. These parasites are found principally in warm waters, and their incidence in temperate climates is relatively rare. In north-western Europe, for instance, it is probably true to say that less than one small craft in two hundred has worm. However, when worm gets into a ship it often causes really devastating damage, sometimes totally destroying the hull within a few months.

Surveyors keep records of their discoveries of ship worm because they know that if a boat in one particular harbour has this trouble, then subsequent surveys in the same area are likely to show the same defect. There is a rumour that any craft kept near the cooling water discharge of a power station is particularly likely to have ship worm. The argument is that the electricity generation plant raises the water temperature very slightly and this encourages worm. It is difficult to get any firm facts about this situation, but it seems a logical line of thought and the story comes up again and again, suggesting that it has some foundation.

Though teredo and gribble, two common types of worm, *prefer* warm water, they keep eating away winter and summer. This means that a boat left afloat for long periods is more likely to have worm. The probability is more than doubled if she does not have a new coat of antifouling every six months. In fact, a general lack of antifouling, or indication that cheap antifouling has been used, is a warning to look for worm.

The first indication of worm may be odd small leaks which are hard to explain. Signs of weeping seen on a plank not at a seam or butt could be significant. A spike should be pushed in nearby, particularly up and down the grain from the leak. The spike at first meets a fair amount of resistance since the surface timber is probably quite hard, and if worm is there the spike then penetrates easily, and then comes up against resistance again. This indicates that the point of the spike has jumped across the tunnel made by the worm and is now into a layer of sound wood again. It takes relatively delicate handling of the spike to detect this condition on occasions. The next thing to do is to prod on either side of the first spike hole, again working along the grain. The result will be the unearthing of a tunnel just below the surface, extending with the grain.

Just occasionally, worm is strongly suspected but spiking produces no definite results. One technique is to shave off about a third of the thickness of the planking. This cutting away will be done over two-thirds of the full width of the plank, and over a length of perhaps 15 cm (6 in.). The same process is repeated in several places, at bow and stern and port and starboard. Assuming no trouble is found, it is reasonable to suppose that no worm is present provided that plenty of spike testing is carried out at the vulnerable areas. The areas shaved away are repaired by graving pieces, and the examination should not noticeably weaken the vessel. However, the owner's permission has to be obtained before carrying out tests of this nature.

The most likely places for finding worm are in those areas

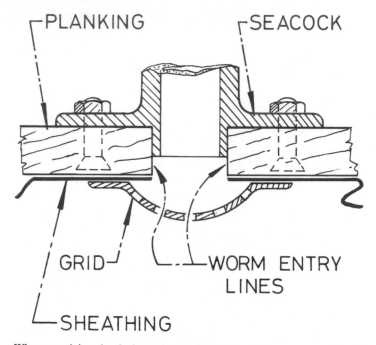

PLANKING   SEACOCK

GRID   WORM ENTRY LINES

SHEATHING

When examining sheathed wood boats it is important to remove grids and gratings over seacock inlets to examine the ends of the planking. Antifouling paint is seldom put on the plank end-grain round the seacock apertures because the grid has to be taken off before the painter can do his work. To prevent worm getting in, the seacock spigot should extend right through the planking or the sheathing should be curved in to meet the spigot.

where the antifouling is least effective. For instance, plenty of craft are put afloat with no antifouling on parts of the underside of the exposed wood keel and deadwood. Boats which are sheathed with copper or plastic often have defects in this overall skinning. If the boat has run aground the chances are that the sheathing will be damaged, probably at the toe or heel of the keel. If the rudder is wood it should be examined all over for faults in the sheathing, particular attention being paid to the heel and the area round the stock. The surveyor should look for lifted edges of the sheathing since this is where worm will penetrate. By stern tubes and echosounders the sheathing may not completely cover the wood, and worm can enter a gap only

1 mm ($\frac{1}{32}$ in.) wide. One location which it is most important to examine is the area round seacocks, particularly if the end grain is not entirely covered by the spigot (see sketch).

Plywood

Whether ply is used for the whole boat, or for the large parts such as the bulkhead and decking, or whether it is just used for a few local pieces of furniture, the problems and testing techniques are the same.

Trouble with ply occurs at the edges, and the butts should be examined with particular care. When two pieces of ply are joined on a curve, such as occurs when this material is used for topsides, a straightedge should be held across the join. There should be no signs of a kink down the joining line, and indeed from outboard the actual join of the two panels of ply should not be detectable.

Much depends on how the butt is made. A butt which is simply two pieces of ply meeting on a frame is seldom successful. Butt straps should be quite 6 in. across, and in many cases 12 in. is no more than adequate. In addition the butt strap must be fully glued in place, possibly with a pattern of through-fastenings as well. The edges of the butt strap must be held tightly down on both pieces of ply, not only to form a strong join but also to prevent water getting in. This is the sort of place where a foot placed firmly against a join and pressed with determination should not reveal any weaknesses.

Because ply is generally used to save weight (among other advantages) it is usually fitted in fairly thin sheets. This means that there should be doublers at high-stress points. Where chainplates are bolted on, where rudder fittings are bolted through, at seacocks, in fact wherever a bolt passes through a sheet of ply or there is a hole of any sort, it is almost axiomatic that there should be a doubler to restore local strength.

The size of an unsupported ply panel depends largely on the standard of seaworthiness of the craft. Some types such as racing dinghies have virtually unsupported ply skins. At the other end of the scale there are miniature ocean cruisers which have the ply panel supported by stringers and frames so that there is never more than a 12 in. gap in the reinforcing. It is important to examine the edges of each stringer and frame to make sure that it is properly joined and lying close to the ply it is intended to support. Particularly at the bows, it will be found that in shoddily built boats the stringers sometimes jump the gaps from frame to frame without lying tight against the ply. Even when the stringers do touch, they quite often only meet along one edge instead of having a full faying surface.

High-speed motor boats are regularly built with very strong bottoms but almost unsupported topsides. For deep-sea work this is not acceptable, because in severe weather these craft have to slow right down. This results in waves breaking against the topsides so that fractures occur. Part of the trouble is that this type of craft is often beamy and full-bowed, so the impact of waves against the bow is particularly severe. In this respect some of the best and most famous builders are at fault.

Ply, like other wood, is tested with a spike. The point should be pushed firmly through the top layer of the wood as it is quite usual for ply to rot inside leaving the top and bottom laminates intact and apparently in good condition. If ply is tapped with a hammer it should give out a ring, but where the core has become rotten the sound will be dead. This is a particularly useful clue, because once the spike has been pushed through a piece of ply the area of the rot can be determined fairly accurately without puncturing the surface all over.

Plywood bulkheads should always be examined in the bilge, since it is quite usual to leave the wood unprotected so that the bilge water soaks it frequently.

Any edge moulding or other protection on the ply edge

should be treated with suspicion. Often the strips along the edge are not continuously tight, and water gets into the crack and remains trapped there, doing all kinds of damage. An exposed edge of ply is almost always unsightly, but from the point of view of reliability it is sometimes safer than an edge moulding. Water can admittedly get at the edge, but it can also dry off easily.

If the surface of the ply is rumpled, this indicates that delamination has occurred. Of all the things that can go wrong with plywood, probably delamination is the most serious, because it means that the ply used is not suitable for marine use (BS 1088). This means that the whole ply panel must be taken out, whereas if rot is found often only a small area needs to be cut out. When delamination is noticed the surveyor has to decide whether the trouble is slight or serious. In general, true delamination extends in long streaks towards the centre of the panel, working rapidly inwards from the edge. Mild delamination can occur even in marine plywood, but the trouble tends to work along the edge without extensive inward penetration. Marine ply which has become wet and then frozen in bitter winter weather occasionally has signs of delamination along the edge, but this is sometimes more unsightly than weakening.

Rot Resistance of Different Timbers

Before surveying it is sometimes possible to obtain a specification of the boat. This will give a useful indication of the probable soundness of timber components since each different species of wood has a known, characteristic resistance to rot.

Because timber has this graded and well-proven standard of

durability, it is important to learn how to distinguish different types of wood. When in doubt samples can sometimes be taken and sent to the Forest Products Research Laboratory at Princes Risborough, Aylesbury, Buckinghamshire, England. This organisation is useful for all types of advice on timber and its condition. Other major timber producing and using countries have their own research laboratories, and I recall obtaining useful help from the Canadian equivalent of the FPRL in British Columbia.

Teak   By far the most satisfactory wood as far as resistance to rot is concerned. It is also more immune to electrolysis than other timbers, but this does not mean to say that it never rots.

African Mahogany, or Khaya   Does not stand up to rot very well. However, it gives plenty of warning since it often goes black before softening. If a mahogany cabin top has been painted over, it is probably an indication that blackening has started and an attempt is being made to keep the boat looking smart in spite of the discoloration. The blackening starts at corners and joins which have become moist. Water works its way into the end grain and trouble builds up, extending along the grain horizontally or vertically, according to the way the wood is used. This type of mahogany is called 'moderately durable' but where it is pithy, as in the centre and the sapwood, it is non-durable. Light-coloured streaks are a sign of poor, soft, unresistant wood.

Mahogany is also frequently attacked by electrolysis. The wide use of this timber is due to its easy working, the fact that it holds fastenings well, its relative light weight and cheapness. However, when it is used externally on a boat laid up in the open it virtually always gives trouble after three or five years unless the craft is kept very well covered and protected against the weather.

Oak   In general, stands up to ship conditions well and does not rot easily. When it does go, it often gives clear indications in the form of a dark blue colour, almost black, which chips off in short semi-soft lengths. Quite often this defective timber is only on the surface, and the oak $\frac{1}{2}$ in. or even $\frac{1}{4}$ in. down may be incredibly hard.

Iroko   Designated 'very durable', but there is a mistaken impression that it is virtually as good as teak.

Oregon Pine, sometimes called Columbian Pine or Douglas Fir   Has a reputation for being a treacherous timber. The indications are that when rot starts it travels very fast, and if it is used in a risky location (such as a beam shelf, where there are stanchion bolts passing through and consequently a risk of deck leaks) rot is to be expected. Just occasionally it is used for masts, and these should be looked at with acute suspicion under mast coats and in similar locations where water can be trapped.

Spruce   Has the reputation of standing up to small boat conditions well and seldom rotting. In practice, its resistance to the maladies of wood is not very good, but it tends to be used for spars and for scantlings in *open* boats, where there is comparatively little risk of rot occurring due to the good ventilation. One trouble with this wood is that it is so soft that an inexperienced surveyor may think that it is beginning to rot when in fact its natural softness allows the spike to sink in without much effort.

Rock Elm, sometimes called Canadian Rock Elm or CRE
Used for bent timbers and has a poor resistance to rot. It used to be favoured by the Royal Navy for their small craft, and conversions of boats built for the Services should be treated with suspicion so far as the condition of the bent timbers is concerned. These bent frames must be spiked extensively since the rot is found in isolated patches and not just in the usual danger spots at the top and bottom.

English Elm   Found on the rubbing strakes of work boats, steel barges, etc. It stands up to bashing well, but has very little resistance to rot, particularly where it is against a steel structure and water is trapped. It is occasionally used for members such as keels, on the principle that these are permanently wet and therefore not likely to rot. This is a mistaken idea, since a well-kept boat is dry when laid up and not permanently wet inside.

Parana Pine   Has a poor resistance to rot, and to make matters more difficult, the sapwood is not easily picked out from the fully grown wood. As a result the sapwood is often included in scantlings and black flecks soon grow on the wood.

Afrormosia (sometimes called African Teak)   Nothing like as durable as teak, though it certainly is durable. Whereas teak goes white with weathering and looks rather nice, afrormosia goes black and looks unpleasant. Blackening is a useful indicator to the surveyor that trouble is developing, and this discoloration commences at the end grain and grows inwards down the grain. Because this wood is cheaper than teak it is sometimes used on fibreglass boats for toerails, handrails, etc. It is a useful pointer that the quality of the boat is probably moderate or poor, since this is just the kind of cost-cutting technique used by boatbuilders trying to turn out cheap craft.

Utile   More durable than African mahogany, and in some ways resembles it. It is about 25 per cent heavier, and confirms the general truth that the heavier a wood, the more likely it is to stand up to decay. However, this principle is only a very broad generalisation, with a number of important exceptions.

Agba   Similar to African mahogany in its general properties, but much more resistant to rot. However, the sapwood has a great propensity to decay.

Western Red Cedar   Considering its light weight, this wood is durable. However, any metals in contact with the wood need protection. This is particularly important because

Western red cedar is occasionally used for decks, and as a result deck fittings and their fastenings need proper ventilation.

Honduras Mahogany   Much more expensive than African mahogany, and also more durable. Because of its high price it should be carefully selected, and the sapwood not used.

Red Meranti and Red Seraya   These woods look a little like African mahogany but are more durable.

Makore   Silica is found in this wood, as it is in teak. Makore has a good resistance against rot and is a fairly hard timber, so it should stand up to spike testing well.

Yellow Pine (sometimes called White Pine)   Classified as 'non-durable'.

Port Orford Cedar (sometimes called Yellow or Alaska Cedar)   Classified as having a good resistance to decay. It is also reputed to be resistant to teredo attack, but this is probably wishful thinking, since no wood except teak appears to have very good resistance against this most malignant of worms.

Test Borings in Wood

A series of large holes drilled in a boat is to a certain extent destructive even if these holes are subsequently plugged carefully and the area neatly painted over. For this reason test boring is not generally undertaken except on larger craft of the rougher type. In any event it is usual to ask the owner's permission before carrying out this type of semi-destructive testing. Also, the borings should be done with as much care and forethought as possible to minimise the damage and loss of appearance. Whoever commissions the survey has to pay for the repairs, which generally consist of plugs glued in place to fill the holes.

Borings are carried out when there is doubt about the soundness of some scantlings, after testing the surface with a pricker has shown little or no trouble. A typical example is the beams of a heavily built fishing boat. Tapping with a hammer may induce a dull noise, a sound which has no ring or echo or cheerfulness about it. This suggests that water has got down through the fastenings, or possibly through deck seams and caused rot to start on top of the beam, the one face which cannot be seen because it is covered by the deck. The surveyor may try pushing his spike in hard, but meet good resistance simply because the sides and bottom of the beam may be sound.

Another place where borings may be taken is in the backbone. For instance, the top of the stem may be found rotten and it will be important to know whether the rot is quite local or extends far down. It costs little to renew the top foot or two of a stem, but it costs hundreds to take out a whole stem and put in a new one.

Borings should be made with a wood bit, not a high-speed metal bit which some shipwrights use. The largest possible shavings are wanted. Good wood produces crisp, brightly coloured shavings which smell pleasant and have a clean, dry appearance. If the bit cuts into rotten wood, among other signs the drilling should become easier, and the shavings will have a musty smell, be dark, friable and often at least slightly moist. Rotten wood powders when rubbed between the fingers and generally speaking is quite easy to identify. If in doubt, samples can be sent to a suitable laboratory such as the Forest Products Research Centre at Princes Risborough, Aylesbury, Buckinghamshire, for an opinion.

Borings will be taken in the area where the wood gives subtle signs that it may be defective. In a beam there are occasions when a considerable length seems to be defective, and it is best to take the borings well clear of the shelves but towards the ends. The drillings will be about $\frac{1}{2}$ in. in diameter in a $2\frac{1}{2}$ in. beam, and about $\frac{3}{4}$ in. in diameter in a 5 in. beam. In practice, many shipwrights do not carry wood bits larger than 1 in. in diameter, and in any case very large holes are not necessary to assess the quality of the wood.

So far as possible the drillings should be carried out below deck, or in from the protected side of the structure: there is less risk of water getting in during subsequent years. Though the minimum number of drillings should be carried out, it is generally advisable to make at least three. The work should be carried out with a newspaper or polythene sheet spread below so that all the chips are carefully collected. As in so many aspects of surveying, this is a situation where the help of an experienced shipwright is worth having.

Plank
Seams

Caulked Seams

A boat with conventional carvel planking should have no seams visible from outboard when she is new. As she gets older it will become increasingly difficult to hide the seam lines, just as old people become lined.

A poorly built boat often shows her seams from the first week. Bad maintenance will make the seams show sooner, and a superbly built boat remains flawless much longer than one less well-born. A hull painted a dark colour but exposed to hot sun almost always cracks her seams even though she is well built, properly maintained and quite young.

Any open seam should be examined to see if the stopping compound is hard or brittle. Because wood swells and contracts with both change of temperature and varying moisture content, it is essential to make allowances for this variation in volume. The use of a slightly flexible stopping in the seams is one way in which swelling is handled. A hard stopping cannot change shape with the wood, so all sorts of troubles ensue. The filling material sometimes crumbles and drops out, or it may crush the edges of the planks. Sometimes it is pinched flat as the wood expands, but stays flat when the wood contracts, leaving a long thin gap through which water flows at the first and every subsequent opportunity.

It is unforgivable to use common house builder's putty on any boat, but there are a lot of unforgiven, unforgivable people about. Common putty is made soft with linseed oil which leaches out into wood, leaving the putty hard and brittle. Putty is an unsatisfactory material even for house building, where the shoddiest materials and workmanship are usual. Sometimes a handful of putty is mixed with a walnut volume of mineral grease, in the principle that the grease will stay with the putty and not wander off into the wood, the way linseed oil does. Perhaps this theory is sound, but like many shipwrights before me, I would ask 'Does the putty know what it's supposed to do?'

Many non-hardening synthetic stopping compounds are coloured, so if the stopping is seen to be white it should be suspected. If it is found to be hard it must be condemned, but care is occasionally needed not to confuse trowel cement with putty. Cement in this context means the filler compound laid on the planking after the first undercoat or primer, to flatten the surface. It goes all over the planking in the form of a very thin layer, with frequent bare patches where the wood is smooth and no filler is needed.

Stopping is put in the seams over caulking. At no point should the caulking show: if it does, it suggests that leaks have occurred and someone has hammered in extra caulking to try to staunch the inflow. Caulking showing on the *inside* may be due to bad planking during construction or to over-hammering the caulking. It is a defect which is acceptable over say 1–2 per cent of the total length of the seams in the topsides, and for a craft used on sheltered waters might be accepted over a similar proportion of the underwater seams. But numerous lengths of caulking showing through are dangerous because in bad weather leaks will start, get worse in vicious conditions and even result in the caulking falling out of the seams. Small craft in extreme conditions are sometimes totally inverted half a dozen times by breaking waves. The crew still expect to get home, a little battered perhaps, but still breathing, and it is up to the surveyor to see that they survive.

Caulking visible on the outside is most common at the garboard, because this is the plank which gives most trouble and so gets the most frequent treatment with the caulker's mallet and iron. Wherever caulking is visible from outside, assuming that the cotton bulges out of the seam and it is not just a case of the stopping having fallen out, radical cures are needed. Almost certainly the surveyor should insist that the caulking is removed. It is not enough to take out a few feet of the material: at least a third of the seam and often the whole length should be hauled out on most boats. If inspection then shows that the seam is a gaping groove, possibly letting in daylight, the time has come for a new plank to be put in. To the almost inevitable protests about high costs, the surveyor should remark that one or two new planks are vastly cheaper than a new ship.

Most caulking is done using a white fluffy string which looks rather like tough angora wool, in the form of a sort of soft rope made by twisting up cotton fibres. It goes dark as it rots. It should not be soggy, or easily broken, or hard or brittle. Any of these conditions indicate that the caulking has served its useful life and is due for renewal.

Nor should it be bunched up, like entrails. Where a wide seam has to be caulked the correct procedure is to twist together several strands into a thicker rope. In practice large seams, such as are found on fishing boats, are often caulked with oakum. This is brown and whiskery, almost like tobacco or moss. It should be twisted into a crude rope, and again not looped in bunches to fill a wide seam. Oakum is tarry and has some slight strength when new. As it rots it loses its springiness, becomes brittle, and is often smelly, friable, sometimes saturated. This is time for renewal.

There are various synthetic materials in use. They tend to be oily or greasy, have some clearly noticeable strength, are usually 'clean' as an engineer understands the term and not water saturated when they are in good condition. If they fail to come up to this standard they are suspect. Recaulking is not expensive, and is in any case necessary every few years, so if in doubt it is common sense to recommend recaulking.

Splined Seams

A few small craft are built with wood splines in the seams instead of stopping. The splines are long thin pieces of wood, wedge-shaped in section, which are glued into the seams. They are made too wide, and once the glue has set hard the excess wood is planed off. Splines tend to last between four and ten years, but some go sooner and some last longer. As with so many things in small craft, there is always some mute, unsung modern Michaelangelo whose work is superb, whose natural skills surpass others. His splines outlast normal experience, just as his planking has that magic smoothness, his frames are so even that they seem to be laid in by machine. At the other extreme there are those ten-thumbed monsters masquerading as shipwrights whose splines do not last a season. Most experienced yard managers know these men. They should be making cars, not boats: they have no feeling for their craft. They call for firm surveying because sometimes it will be argued against a surveyor's report that 'This work *must* be all right. It was only done last season (or last month, or even last week).' However, just because renewal was carried out recently is no reason for saying that the repair is satisfactory.

Splines naturally last a long time if the boat has a sedentary life. If a boat is thrashed, or tends to flex, her splines will work loose sooner. Renewal is carried out by punching the old spline inwards, fracturing the glue lines. The loose lengths of wood are hooked out, and after cleaning the seams new splines are glued in. It is a bad idea to try to gun in glue, to resecure splines which have become loose.

Close-seamed Planking or Glued Seams

It is rare to find a boat with no filling material between the planks. A small number of boats, usually built to a high standard, have their plank edges glued or put together with no material between plank and plank. Probably the best-known example of this type of construction is the International One Design, built of pine in Norway. Incidentally, they kill the old tale that softwood boats cannot have glued seams. There was also a substantial batch of Folkboats built in East Germany having glued seams.

Where this type of planking is seen, the frames should be examined with particular care to see if there are short fractures right across. In some cases the planking swells relentlessly, building up enormous pressures. These forces are enough to pull frames apart, causing short breaks which look as if a fine saw has been used to cut across the frame at right angles. A comparable defect is the 'lifting' of frames, which remain their normal length while the planking expands and bows out to a greater curve than is formed by the frames. To compensate for the difference, the frames come away from the planking.

Faults in close-seaming are hard to cure. If the boat is small enough, consideration should be given to rolling her over so that open seams can have glue run in under ideal conditions, with the seam upright and horizontal.

Double Diagonal Planking

Triple diagonal planking is occasionally met, and it may be taken that the troubles of double diagonal are similar, if not worse, in triple skin planking.

There are two basic types of diagonal planking: the usual one has an inner and outer skin at right angles to each other and each at about 45° to the waterline. A more sophisticated type of double diagonal has the inner skin at 45° to the horizontal and the outer planking fore and aft, more or less like conventional planking. In this case the outer planking tapers towards each end and is therefore more difficult to do: it is indicative of a higher standard.

Because double diagonal is strong and akin to moulded wood, it is usual to have the frames wider spaced than is usual with conventional planking. Occasionally the frames are omitted entirely, or there may be a combination of frames and stringers. Whatever form of internal stiffening is used, there should be no signs of plank movement. In practice, double diagonal planking does occasionally move in severe conditions and it is broadly true to say that this type of construction is normally more flexible than conventional planking. It is designed to stand up to high stresses and as a result is found in fast power craft and in some refined racing yachts.

The seams are likely to show on the outside if the boat has been poorly built or if she is old. An old boat which has been badly built with double diagonal planking tends to look dreadful. This bad appearance is particularly difficult to cure, especially when the outside planks are capping (curving or warping across the width of the plank).

Signs of leaking are serious because the point where the water penetrates the outer planking is seldom opposite where it filters through the inner planking. Normally, if a boat leaks all the surveyor has to do is to get her put afloat, make sure the bilge is dry before she is put in, and then see where the water seeps through. If the boat is already afloat, then it is necessary to dry out the bilge and work outwards from the lowest point of the bilge till the source of the leak is discovered. This technique does not work with double diagonal planking because it is rare for the water to pass through both layers in a straight line.

Signs of caulking, or any widespread form of filling, on double diagonal planking are bad news. They show that leaking has occurred and remedial measures (which are unlikely to be successful) have been tried. No one caulks a double diagonal boat unless they are ignorant or desperate. Essentially, double diagonal planking is a close seam system. The only place where caulking should occur is along the rebate.

The outer planking should be checked for rot, particularly at the hood ends and where the plank ends are cut to long diagonal points. The area at the waterline, particularly right aft, should also be tested since this is a high risk region. If rot is found on the outside, planking immediately adjacent on the inside should be tested. Rot tends to travel wherever it can, so there is a possibility of rot transferring from one layer of planking to the next.

Rot or any form of defect in an outer plank need not be particularly serious because it is often easy to repair. In contrast a defect found in an inner plank is extremely serious. To renew one inner plank, *every* outer plank crossing it must be taken off. This is a desperate business since an inner plank can easily be crossed by twenty outer ones.

Between the two layers of planking it is usual to lay some form of cloth impregnated with a rot-retarding fluid such as linseed oil. The cloth tends to rot sooner than the planking, and this is one reason why leaks occur.

Double diagonal planking should be very fully clenched, with four fastenings round every intersection between the inner and outer seams. The rooves should be tested by inserting a spike beneath them and twisting sideways. With ageing, some copper nails and rooves become brittle and crumble. They often give themselves away by going green and throwing off one or two rooves.

It is broadly true to say that a small defect in double diagonal planking is very easy to repair but a major defect is more difficult than the renewal of a section of conventional planking. Refastening tends to be very expensive and time-consuming because of the large number of fastenings. All the interior furniture and fittings have to be taken out to allow the shipwrights to get at every part of the inside of the shell to clench up. In these days when labour costs are so high in most parts of the world, it is seldom worth stripping off all the outside planking to renew the cloth between the planks when this has become rotten. It is small wonder that so many double diagonal boats are found to have patched areas where short lengths of plank have been let in. Mends of this type look a mess and are not to be trusted in a severe gale at sea.

Beam Shelves and Stringers

Longitudinal structural members can be very difficult to repair, and it is important to detect trouble in them as early as possible. A major repair to a beam shelf is almost always difficult without taking off areas of deck, possibly the whole deck. Even a stringer repair can be awkward, although the job may be considerably eased by laminating and gluing in sections.

Trouble is usually found in areas where rain drips through, such as by chainplates, hatches and deck fittings. At the fastenings there are often signs of electrolytic trouble. This can be checked if it is not serious simply by cleaning off the area, washing away any traces of salt water with warm fresh water.

treating with a rot preventive like Cuprinol and finally repainting or revarnishing. This checks the trouble since it prevents water getting at the fastening, but of course it does not put back

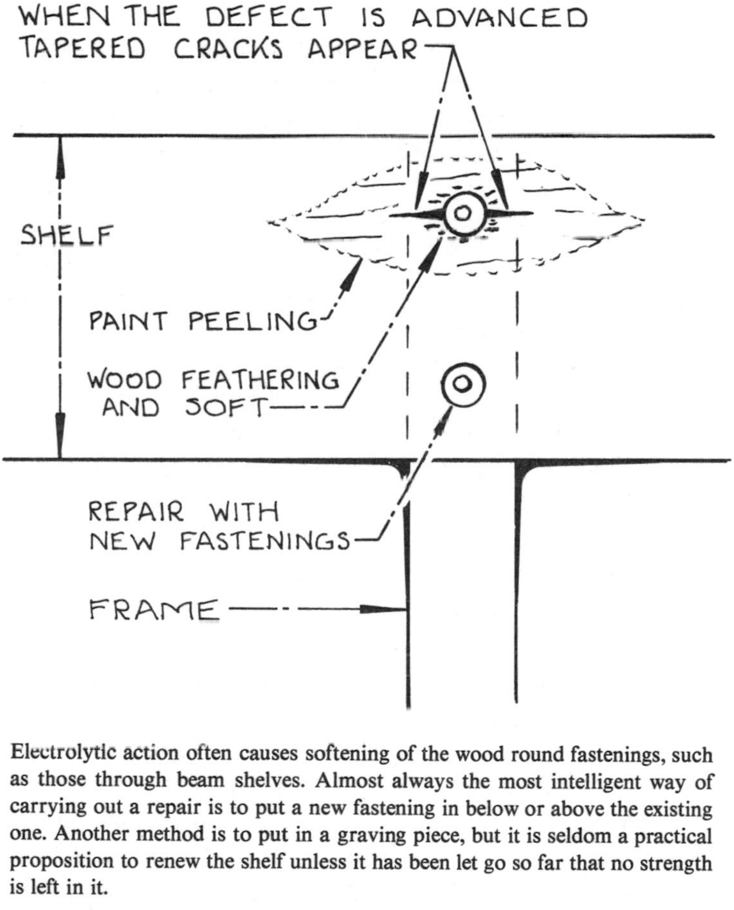

WHEN THE DEFECT IS ADVANCED
TAPERED CRACKS APPEAR

SHELF

PAINT PEELING

WOOD FEATHERING
AND SOFT

REPAIR WITH
NEW FASTENINGS

FRAME

Electrolytic action often causes softening of the wood round fastenings, such as those through beam shelves. Almost always the most intelligent way of carrying out a repair is to put a new fastening in below or above the existing one. Another method is to put in a graving piece, but it is seldom a practical proposition to renew the shelf unless it has been let go so far that no strength is left in it.

lost strength. Probably the best way to do this is to fit extra fastenings in the intervals between the existing ones. Another procedure is to put graving pieces in way of the soft wood. This is not easy to do neatly and it can be a slow, expensive game.

A check should be made that the shelves and stringers are adequately fastened. Ideally there should be a fastening at every frame, but quite a few builders secure the longitudinals at alternate timbers. In any case the fastenings should not be more than about 40 cm (say 16 in.) apart.

Where the shelf and stringers are massive, such as in traditional inshore fishing boats, quite vicious-looking longitudinal cracks and splits are not too serious. However, on lighter types of craft this sort of split is less acceptable and often calls for some form of doubler to bridge the trouble.

Any serious cracks *across* the shelf or stringer should be viewed with the gravest suspicion. The structure all round should be examined since it suggests there has been a thundering great collision, or possibly the craft has been squeezed between the quay and a bigger ship, or some other grave trouble has occurred.

Sometimes longitudinal scantlings are slit vertically with a saw to make it easier to bend them into the ends of the vessel. This cut cannot be painted and the best builders run glue into the slot. Others make no provision against the ingress and lodgement of water, and so this becomes a particularly vulnerable area for rot.

Another popular technique is the tapering at each end of these longitudinal members. This is both to ease the fitting and to reduce the weight at the ends of the craft. On a sailing boat the taper should not extend back anywhere near the chainplates because this is where maximum strength is required. The extreme ends of both beam shelves and stringers should be secured to the backbone, to the transom and so on. However, it is fairly common practice not to tie the ends of stringers on craft under about 13 m (say 40 ft). Even craft quite a bit bigger than this which are not heavily stressed can get away with stringers which simply die away, unsecured except to the frames, at each end. This is yet another situation where the quality of the ship shows up, and the surveyor has to assess whether she is likely to be asked to withstand severe stresses or whether in future she is going to lead a relatively sedentary life. A certain amount depends on the plank thickness, since each plank is in effect a longitudinal stringer. If the planking is rather light and the frames spaced far apart, then there is every reason for fitting breasthooks at the ends of the stringers.

Just occasionally stringers are responsible for frame fractures since the longitudinal strength member forms a fore-and-aft hard spot. The curve of the bilge is held down a fore-and-aft line and when the craft is badly bumped the frames may fracture in line down the stringer. If the fractures occur behind the stringers they are not always easy to find, detection sometimes being easier by touch than by sight.

Cracks in Bent Timbers

Most bent-timbered boats have at least one or two cracks in the framing. It is not unusual for boats which are brand new to have three or four minor cracks in the timbers, caused during construction. The best builders replace any frame which is seen before launching to have a crack in it, but many boats which have steamed timbers are built by people who do not claim to be in the top flight; they specialise in economical rather than superbly finished craft.

When looking at certain types of boat it is often virtually certain that a batch of broken frames will be found. For instance, Folkboats built in some East European countries suffer from broken timbers because the close-seamed planking, which has no caulking, expands when wet. The frames cannot stretch longitudinally in the same way and short fractures occur straight across the grain. Some of these are such sharp breaks that they appear to have been made with a tenon saw, and they are normally easy to detect because the adjacent frames as well as the one broken are usually away from the planking, sometimes as much as $\frac{1}{2}$ in. This is because the frame has tried to straighten across the turn of bilge before rupturing.

Boats like 6 Metres which were built with a mixture of grown and bent frames regularly have fractured timbers. That generation of rather lightly built carvel launches which grew up just before the popularity of hard-chine planing motor boats often have narrow frames which are found to be fractured. If the original fairly low-powered, light, petrol engine has been replaced by a diesel, then the chances of frame breakages are greatly increased.

If a yacht is sitting on a road trailer, or if she is far from her own element, there is a good chance that some of the frames will have been broken during transport. The trouble is particularly likely if the trailer supports are located *beneath* the turn of bilge, and especially if the rise of floor is small so that the trailer side supports are pushing nearly vertically upwards. Where the palms at the end of the supports are relatively small and not softly padded the chances of frame breakage are increased. Under these conditions the frames in way of the side supports should be examined first, and those adjacent also scrutinised meticulously.

Once the damage to the boat has been recorded and repairs recommended, it is pertinent to point out the source of the trouble. It may not be the surveyor's job to recommend alterations to the trailer, but he should at least warn the owner that unless the vehicle is changed trouble will recur.

A likely place to find broken timbers is at the reverse turn down towards the garboard, particularly if this turn is sharp. This defect is most often towards the stern. In sailing yachts with auxiliary engines, trouble should be expected beneath the engine. If a boat has been put ashore and bumped by passing waves the keel will be forced upwards as the mass of the hull is dropping down into a trough, and this causes frame fracture, particularly aft, and especially at the reverse turn.

Where one broken frame is found the chances are that there will be others. Adjacent frames should be very carefully examined in line with the known crack because these breakages occur in the same way that toilet paper tears—across a line of weakness. In the same way, if a crack is found at the twenty-third frame on the port side, the twenty-third frame on the starboard side as well as the twenty-second and the twenty-fourth on the starboard side should be scanned for trouble.

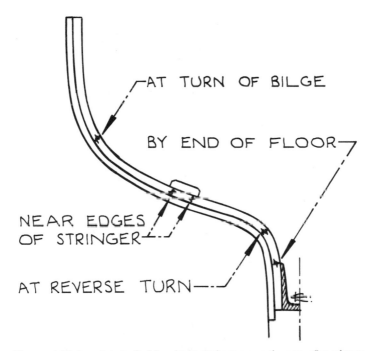

The most likely points to find breaks in timbers are at the area of maximum curvature and at high stress points where other potent structural members abut. If floors do not taper away gradually, they make hard spots at the ends of the floor arms. In the same way, the bilge stringers hold the boat rigid and flexing occurs clear of them, putting an unfair local strain on the frames at the edges of the stringers.

Sometimes the crack is only on the outboard face of the frame, particularly where it is at the turn of bilge. Because only the outer fibres have parted, the crack cannot be seen when the frame is viewed from directly athwartships, which is one reason why each frame must be viewed from forward and aft, and with a really powerful light.

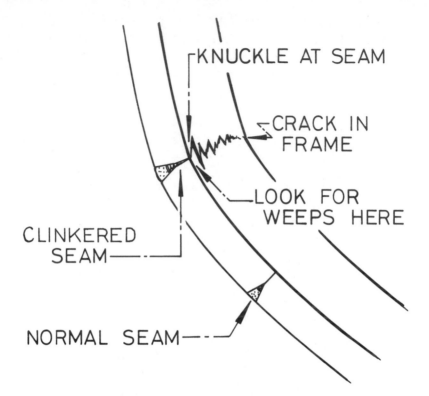

KNUCKLE AT SEAM

CRACK IN FRAME

LOOK FOR WEEPS HERE

CLINKERED SEAM

NORMAL SEAM

A clear angle along the seams in a carvel-built boat is sometimes called 'clinkering'. The defect can look almost like a very tiny chine, and may be more visible on the outside, although sometimes it looks worse on the inside. It is occasionally caused by a row of broken frames, and on other boats it is the clinkering which causes the frames to crack in line. The bad appearance is secondary; what matters is that leaking is likely all along the seam.

Another place to look for trouble is where the planking has clinkered. (The word 'clinkering' is used to describe a sharp knuckle between adjacent planks along a seam, almost like a chine. Clinkering can be inwards or outwards, that is to say the sharp angle at the seam may be an included or excluded angle (see sketch).) The knuckling may cause frames to crack by putting a local high stress on them so that the most severely stressed gives first and others are likely to follow as they are asked to carry an extra unfair load. Alternatively, the clinkering may be the *result* of a series of frame fractures which leaves a seam unsupported.

A usual way to repair broken bent timbers is to put in new timbers, quite often leaving the existing ones untouched. This is partly to save the expense of taking out the defective wood and partly to save disturbing the structure of the vessel. The new frame should be made at least slightly stronger than the ones

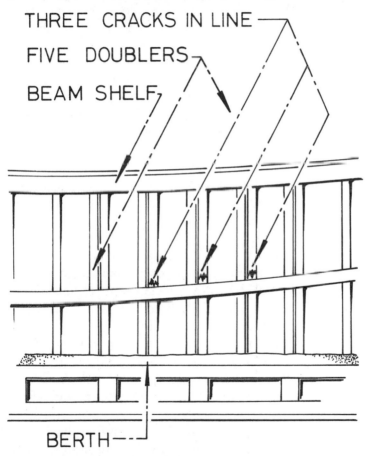

THREE CRACKS IN LINE

FIVE DOUBLERS

BEAM SHELF

BERTH

When recommending repairs for cracked frames, it is good practice to specify additional doublers when a series of cracks are in line, in order to prevent a recurrence of the trouble. The doublers are carried up to the beam shelf and down to behind the berth, so that their ends do not show and in order to extend the doubling well beyond the fracture line.

which have broken: since the broken frames have proved inadequate in the scantling, it is illogical to put back just the same strength. In practice it may be impossible to increase the moulding (the athwartships dimension of the frame) and so the fore-and-aft dimension should be put up, in my opinion by at least 30 per cent. By the same token, it often makes sense to double up more than just the broken frame. Certainly, if three frames are cracked in a line it is only common sense to double them up and double up the intact frames adjacent, so that the three fractures are repaired and reinforced with five doublers (see sketch).

One useful way of repairing fractured frames is by laminating in new lengths. This can be done using the hull as a form, and it sometimes has the advantage that no heating is needed.

The new lengths of frame should be ended with care. For instance, the top end might be under a stringer or the beam shelf and the bottom might be down at the keel or at berth level. The aim is to hide the ends, for neatness; where possible they should be terminated at a high-strength region. When laminating is done, it is good engineering to taper away the ends so as to avoid hard spots.

To make a neat job the crack must be cut out, and in this case the new frame will either be put in from keel to gunwale or scarphed in. The scarph should have a taper of one-in-eight or thereabouts, and should be glued and through-fastened with a minimum of three fastenings in the join.

Whatever type of repair is made, the new piece of timber should extend at least three planks above and below the crack. It should also have two fastenings to each plank, except right at the ends of a vessel, where the planks may be too narrow due to tapering.

In way of a fracture, rot is likely because water lies in the rough, jagged edges of the fibres, without drying out for long periods. This sort of place is akin to unplaned timber, in being prone to rot.

Grown
Frames

It is not unusual to find that grown frames have warped and 'moved' even on relatively new or well built boats. If this movement is up to about 10 per cent of the moulding or siding of the frame, it is generally considered not serious, and on fishing boats it sometimes amounts to as much as 15 per cent without responsible surveyors becoming perturbed. Naturally the survey report should mention this type of movement.

A more serious trouble, which is found particularly on roughly built craft, is a shortage of fastenings. At each futtock join there should be at least three bolts, and to space these reasonably far apart there must be an overlap quite six times the siding or moulding, this figure being considered a minimum. It is also not unusual to find that the wood is softening round the fastenings. A recommended cure is to put in additional bolts rather than try to remove and replace the existing ones.

Grown frames tend to become soft where two futtocks are edge to edge, since water lodges there, dirt collects and the resulting mud is a potential place for trouble.

The join of the bottom futtock to the floor is especially important. It is near the bilgewater so it is often wet. It is probably adjacent or below the sole, so that dust and dirt gets into the slightest opening at the join and this encourages moisture to stay, as well as forming a good breeding ground for rot. It is also likely to be one of the most highly stressed of the joins.

One class of builder claims that provided all scantlings are thick enough, all will be well forever more. This sort of optimistic wood-butchering is particularly found in small fishing craft, and one of their characteristics is all grown frames. These frames are massive, but there is often a line of sapwood down one edge of the futtocks. Sapwood rots sooner and faster than heartwood, and is easily detectable because it is a different colour (usually lighter) than the good wood. In extreme cases, I have seen strips of bark along frame edges. At least this is fair warning: it shouts aloud of shoddy building; it states unequivocably that there is either rot there already, or that rot will soon strike because it is being given every facility.

Laminated Members

Thin strips of wood glued together in laminated scantlings are often a sign of good building, particularly if the laminations are quite thin, say around 3 mm ($\frac{1}{8}$ in.).

When examining a laminated stem the top should be scrutinised, particularly if it is weathered or if there is no protection on top. This is where the initial signs of glue failure are likely to be seen. For instance, a large number of the Loch Long class have suffered from this trouble, with the top of the stem opening out as each laminate in turn has suffered glue failure. The result, from the side, looks like some monstrous shaving brush.

The cure here, as in most cases of glue failure, is to clean up the laminates and get rid of as much of the old glue as possible, then run in new glue. To complete the repair the laminates are bolted together, ideally using thin but numerous bolts well staggered. Sometimes bolts cannot be fitted in, in which case screws have to be used, but these tend to be rather less satisfactory. If only a few bolts can be worked in, a combination of bolting and screwing is needed.

If one laminated scantling has failed the chances are that others will have followed. Members built in frosty weather tend to suffer from glue failure unless some form of heating is used during the gluing process. I have noticed that glue which resembles a clear uncoloured glass seems to fail more often than other types, but this may be a series of coincidences.

Laminated frames are relatively rare and are often a sign of good building. Glue failure is most likely at the base of the frames, particularly where there is a sharp reverse turn down towards the garboard. If there are no floors, or if the floor fastenings are driven fore and aft through the frames, delaminating should be suspected.

Delamination in beams is most likely at the ends and where carlines run in to join the beams. It is not easy to introduce fresh glue to a delaminated beam, partly because of the difficulty of up-hand work. It is probably best to fit entirely new beams.

Splits should be expected where fastenings have been put in along the same plane as the laminates. A good example is a laminated tiller where the layers are horizontal: look for trouble at the aft end where the athwartships bolts go through the rudder stock joining plates. Total renewal of the component is often the only full cure if this trouble occurs, and certainly a tiller is too important to merely patch up.

Laminated components occasionally have cracks on both the inside and outside at the sharpest bends. In theory the whole point of using laminates is to avoid cracked timber, but sometimes shipwrights are too ambitious, or the component may have been overstressed. Rot in laminated parts is unusual, though it may grow from a crack. Rot spores, together with moisture and dirt, collect among the jagged fibres and deterioration extends along the grain.

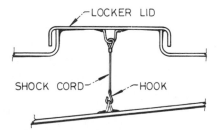

Production builders try all sorts of tricks to save money. Hatches which are only held in place by shock-cord can be dangerous in rough weather, and should at least have a back up, preferably two metal clasps.

Wrought-iron Floors

This is a generic name given to steel and iron floors made of ferrous strip material. Characteristically these floors have a moulded dimension which is usually about one quarter of the siding, with no flanging. The true wrought-iron floor was worked by a blacksmith and given tapered arms, which were intended to prevent high stresses at the tips. The increasing use of welding and the passing of traditional smith work has resulted in floors which are of constant section right across, so that they are often weak at the knuckles and too strong at the ends. This gives rise to broken bent timbers in line with the floor ends.

A particular fault is found in wrought floors, especially in the region of an engine: localised electrolytic action, which results in pitting. However, the floor looks all right, in the dim light in the bilge, because the pitting in the metal is covered by a black mud. The floor sometimes appears to be in reasonable condition even when hammered or scraped, unless the whole length is very carefully examined. This can be impossible beneath an engine, especially if a low-set drip tray covers the floors.

The defect occurs particularly at the knuckle, so wrought floors should be chipped there with a sharp spike which will pry off the semi-loose surface muck, and show up the pockets of local erosion. An ordinary flat scraper will ride over the holes, suggesting that the floors are sound. As with other types of defect, where one component has a particular trouble, the surveyor should at once go to the similar adjacent parts to see if the trouble has occurred.

If the bilge is kept dry there is no chance of this particular electrolysis occurring, because one of the essential ingredients which causes the trouble is missing. There is a school of thought which holds that a few gallons of water in the bilge is a good thing because it keeps the bowels of the ship 'sweet' (whatever that may mean). This attitude was never held by the best builders and surveyors, and probably stems from the world of badly built fishing boats. It's no longer a popular theory; it may well have started because a large proportion of cheaply built fishing boats used to leak from a few months after they were launched.

Repairs to damaged floors should be carried out so that the trouble does not recur. An obvious precaution is to make the

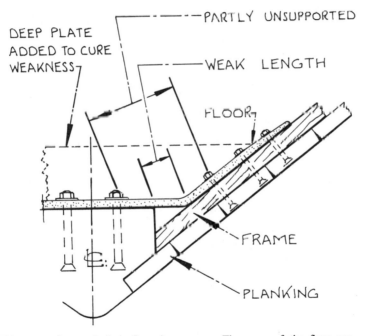

This type of wrought-iron floor is common. The arms of the floor are relatively thin in a vertical direction, and spread fore and aft for approximately the width of the frame. As a result they are weak in the direction of the main stress. The gap where the floor jumps from the backbone across to the frame is particularly vulnerable, although in fact the weak region extends from the fastening into the backbone across to the first fastening up the frame. There is very little resistance against bending in this type of floor and as a result the garboard is likely to leak. A cure is the fitting of a deep plate (shown dotted). This plate should be carried as high up as possible, the limitation to depth usually being the sole.

new floors thicker, just in case the source of trouble has not been eradicated. Another approach is to use a 'nobler' metal, but this is a pricey business. Whatever material is used, the floors should be drilled for fastenings before being very fully painted all over before installation.

It is always good practice to use existing components when making a repair, because it saves time and money, and presumably the original parts fit precisely. Provided the floors are not too far gone, they can be made as good or even stronger than new by welding across the base a deep vertical bar which must be at least 40 per cent welded along the bottom, and fully welded up each side. Welding *in situ* cannot be recommended because the surrounding structure is virtually bound to get burned, though some skilled welders seem to achieve miracles.

Wrought floors are laid across the hog and extend up the inner faces of the frames (see sketch). Sometimes the top of the hog is well above the inner face of the planking, so that part of each floor, on each side, is unsupported. This condition is exacerbated if the floor fastenings into the hog are near the ship's centreline. If these fastenings are only short coach screws, then the situation is usually worse still. Under these conditions the floors do not do their job properly; they cannot tie the ship's sides to the backbone structure, so the job has to be done at least in part by the garboards. As a result, these lower planks work and leak.

Any experienced surveyor will spot chronic leaking within seconds, and he will look at the floors before he recommends recaulking the garboard. If the floors have to 'jump the gap' excessively, they should be stiffened. A deep vertical plate welded right across is again a good answer to the trouble, since it gives the floor tremendous strength and prevents it flexing at the knuckles.

It is always a problem to know when to call for renewal and when to mention a defect but recommend no immediate remedial action. The factor of safety has to be considered. The majority of parts of small vessels are built with a safety factor of about 4. This figure is often exceeded, but in racing boats it is reduced; it is current practice on highly competitive racing boats to design components with a safety factor of 1·5. With a factor as low as this no deterioration can be tolerated, and any slight sign of trouble means that renewal or repair must be carried out before the craft can be used again. This is akin to aircraft construction and usage, but it is not the general case in small craft.

With a factor of safety of 4, a 50 per cent loss of strength is tolerable, as the scantling should still be twice as strong as need be. In the case of a plate floor $\frac{1}{4}$ in. thick we can accept widespread pitting down to $\frac{1}{8}$ in. thickness before insisting that the time has come to renew the defective parts. But if the vessel is to make a prolonged deep-sea voyage, it is common sense to insist that repairs are carried out when only 30 per cent corrosion has occurred. A vessel going offshore can expect to encounter more severe weather than one working in sheltered waters, and if the voyage is long, the next chance for inspection and repair is a long way off in time and distance.

Incidentally, a surveyor works on the basis that every small ship receives annual maintenance. This should include full inspection of components known to be deteriorating as well as the whole structure. It has to be admitted that far too many ships of all types do not get anything like full annual maintenance.

A plate floor is not much of a test of the surveyor's skill because the strength is more or less proportional to the thickness, assuming that the fastenings are in good condition. A wrought-iron floor is a different case, because the throat is the critical point. (The throat is the juncture of the bottom and side part.) Here the strength of the floor is dependent on the stiffness at the throat, so a 50 per cent loss of thickness means far more than a 50 per cent loss of strength. Just to complicate the matter, wrought-iron floors are also dependent on their through-fastenings. Quite a small amount of rust in way of the bolts is likely to mean that they no longer hold the metal tight, and this is a case where renewal or repair is needed after quite a small amount of wastage has occurred.

Fibreglass Construction

Surveying Fibreglass

Early in a fibreglass survey it is important to look for the builder's nameplate and also the plate put in by the moulding company. It is not always easy to find the moulder's badge, but a typical place to search is on the inside of the transom, high up. This location may be masked by the aft deck so that viewing it can be difficult. The reason for discovering who has made and completed the hull is that *full* fibreglass testing by a surveyor in the field is difficult, often impossible. The correct procedure is to take samples and send these to a laboratory, but this very often cannot be carried through. Owners object to pieces being cut from their boats, and buyers seldom have the time or inclination to wait for a report and pay extra for tests.

Fibreglass is like any other material; it needs skill and knowledge not just to work but to check, to handle and to store. There is even skill in buying correctly. A careless or inexpert moulder may make a mistake when producing a boat, but the defects may not show until the hull has been completed and sent to the owner. This is just one reason why the reputation of the moulding company and that of the firm who complete the craft are valuable guides to the surveyor.

Where there is no nameplate, the surveyor will naturally be suspicious. If he does not recognise the name, he will look for cost-cutting techniques. A few short-cuts to keep down the price of the finished boat may be acceptable, but if the whole boat is a seething mass of gimmickry designed to produce the cheapest possible craft, the surveyor's normally suspicious nature should be particularly wary. The sort of indicators

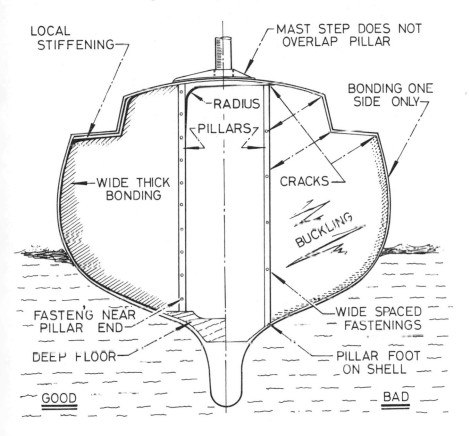

Good and bad mast step construction are shown here. On the left-hand side are the correct techniques. The pillar has close-spaced fastenings with bolts near the top and the bottom into the bulkhead. This in turn is very fully glassed on both sides to the hull, to the cabin top, to the deck, etc. Perhaps most important of all, the foot of the pillar lands on a floor which spreads the load down to the keel and well up round the reverse turn. The mast step itself extends beyond the pillar, and the underdeck doubler has no sharp angles. On the right-hand side these precautions have been omitted, and the signs of trouble will be in the form of a buckling bulkhead, cracks at high stress points, possibly signs of distortion and even leaks.

which shout out a warning are: the use of afrormosia instead of teak for trim, widely spaced stanchions, a fin keel designed with a strong bias towards easy construction and fitting but little thought for the water flow round it, fore hatches without hinges, portable bilge pumps, screws instead of bolts in deck fittings and so on.

In fibreglass construction a sight of the construction plan is important. It is not easy to obtain hull construction plans from fibreglass moulders, but the better-quality builders are often co-operative. A moulder who claims that the plans are no longer up to date should be treated with some suspicion. If the plans are not current it is pertinent to ask how the men on the job are supposed to know exactly what procedures to follow, who dictates the amount of material and its location, and what happens when the foreman is away ill?

Armed with a plan, the surveyor should check that such items as the floors have been put in exactly as designed in size, thickness and numbers. One moulding company found it was losing money, and so having built a series of eighteen boats according to the designer's plan, the next fifty or so were fabricated with *no floors at all*. As a result the fin keels moved disconcertingly in bad weather. The company then went broke and was taken over by a new firm who restarted production, putting in the correct number of floors. However the new regime had also underpriced their product and so they cast about for methods of saving money. Presumably they were still employing the same chargehands, because the new management also decided to leave out floors. It is no consolation to a hard-worked surveyor to know that the new management also eventually went bankrupt.

The point is that in this series boats Nos. 1 to 18 inclusive were quite good; the next fifty not only had a serious defect but were extremely difficult to put in good seaworthy condition. Production of the next batch was again reasonable, since floors were fitted, but subsequently further boats were built in a dangerous condition. There would have been little problem if the floors had been fully visible. However, below sole level, but above the top of the floors, there was a full glassing-in to form tank tops. Without some fairly advanced surgery it is impossible to tell whether one of these quite popular boats is sound or not. Unless, of course, the surveyor happens to be one of the few people alive who knows exactly where production was adulterated and which hull members are safe!

The surveyor has to look over the whole of the moulding inside and out. Trouble is most likely in the areas which are difficult to mould, such as deep down inside a narrow skeg or at the bottom of a hollow fin on a keel boat. Indications of good workmanship and supervision in the awkward areas confirms the standard of construction throughout the boat.

Frames and stringers as well as spray rails and other bottom stiffeners should be tapered out, not stopped suddenly. Where a structural stiffener is not tapered at its end, it should be joined to some form of stress dissipator. For instance, a glassed-in berth front which acts as a deep vertical stringer should not end abruptly on its own. It may be joined to a bulkhead (see sketch) or continued to form a galley front which in turn links to the engine case siding. This component in turn is then fastened to the deep cockpit well sides which are extended down to the shell, and so on. Where any stiffener does appear to end rather abruptly, the whole area should be scanned for indications of trouble such as separation of the glass laminates or tearing off of tape in the fillets, or cracks which radiate from one point.

When surveying a GRP boat which is intended for some particularly tough job, it is best to get the owner's permission to cut out samples and have these sent to a laboratory for testing. The cost of cutting out the sample and making good the damaged area is a charge against the person commissioning the survey. Likewise the laboratory tests will be charged to him and will be extra to the normal survey costs. This laboratory testing can be expensive, which explains why it is only carried out when the craft concerned is particularly large or is intended for high-speed service, or where there are special considerations, as for instance in lifeboats.

Another instance where tests might be carried out is where

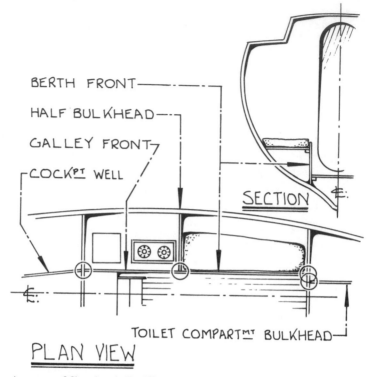

BERTH FRONT

HALF BULKHEAD

GALLEY FRONT

COCKPT WELL

SECTION

TOILET COMPART^{MT} BULKHEAD

PLAN VIEW

Any part of fibreglass hull stiffening should be tapered away at the ends, or should butt onto another stiffening member. The aim must be to avoid hard spots where a stiffening member stops suddenly. The surveyor should look closely at the way the hull is stiffened and very carefully check round any potential hard spots.

This sketch shows how the berth and galley fronts are butted onto bulkheads, with the partial bulkhead forward of the galley linked to the galley front. The toilet compartment bulkhead does not line up exactly with the berth front, but this is not important because it does butt onto a main bulkhead.

the boat has widespread indications of defects, and confirmation of her quality and condition is needed. It is good practice to get permission *in writing* to cut out samples. The work should be done only by experts and in a properly fabricated shed, so that repairs are carried out without delay under proper, controlled conditions of temperature and moisture.

Samples may be sent for testing to the major suppliers of glassfibre, or to Southampton University in Hampshire, England. Before despatch it is important to label each sample, noting which part of the vessel the pieces were taken from.

Just occasionally a new seacock has to be fitted to a boat; this offers a good chance to get a small sample from the hull without causing any damage. The hole for the seacock should be cut with a hole cutter because this tool produces a piece of waste like a disc with a hole in the middle, whereas a drill only produces granulated swarf. The trouble with this technique is

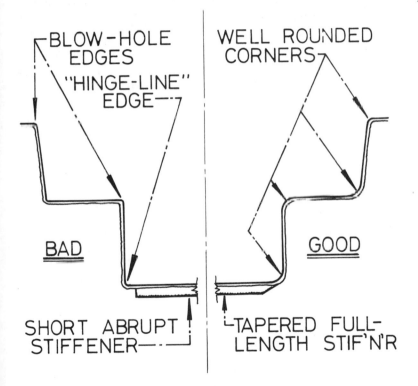

Edges and corners on fibreglass hulls should be well rounded, both for strength and to avoid blow-holes. A well-rounded edge is also less likely to chip or be damaged. On the left, poor practice is shown, with indications where trouble is most likely. The right-hand side shows how these high-risk areas should be treated, with regard to both corners and stiffeners.

that a single sample is not fully representative. This applies to all sampling, so some discretion has to be used when taking pieces from a hull. Samples may be cut from the floors or engine bearers, or even from the edges of bulkheads where glassing-in has been carried out. However, these pieces are not really very valuable as indicators of the quality of the *main hull shell*. Such pieces can be quickly and easily repaired, and the damaged area can be made good quite inexpensively, often leaving only the subtlest signs of the sampling.

When using a hole cutter on fibreglass an electric drill is needed, otherwise the job will take a long time. The drill should not be pushed too hard against the fibreglass because this will cause separation of the laminates, particularly in the final stages of the cut when the blade is nearly emerging. Almost always the cut will be made from the outside so as to penetrate the gel coat first. As a further precaution against delaminating the shell in way of the cut, a wood block should be held against the inside of the fibreglass.

The Surface of Fibreglass

So far as possible, the whole of the outside and inside of a fibreglass hull should be scrutinised. In practice it is not usual to scrape off antifouling, because unless this is done most carefully part of the gel coat is taken off too. Loose antifouling is taken off in sample areas.

On a sound, well made GRP hull the whole of the outside and inside is even, without changes in the surface appearance: the general impression should be that the hull has been made by a machine which works at precisely the same rate throughout construction. There should be no patterns or pimples or dimples, no roughness on the outside, and on the inside the same standard of 'smoothed roughness' all over. The colour should not change in tone; there should be no suggestion of bleaching or darkening.

A fault which is easy to detect is yellowing. This may be caused by oil scum on the sea's surface getting at the fibreglass shell. Unless the oil is taken off promptly the scum is liable to work into the shell and the indications are that the only full cure is to paint the hull.

Some of the older white hulls turned yellow through age, and here again the only cure is painting; coloured hulls tend to fade or bleach. A more serious trouble is blistering caused by osmosis. This may be the result of poor moulding conditions, continous immersion in water and/or chemical reaction; whatever the cause, the effect is for remnants of styrene under the outer skin to become mixed with water passing through the gel-coat (in osmotic action) to form blisters, which eventually burst. Local patches can be treated by cutting out the defective area, drying out and filling in. If the hull has trouble all over, the gel-coat must be stripped right off, washed with water to disperse acids, followed by surgical alcohol to dry the surface; the boat is allowed to dry thoroughly—a matter of weeks, even in hot weather. Finally the surface is painted with three coats of epoxide paint followed as necessary by antifouling.

Bubbles are easy to see when they pierce the surface. A good quality moulding has no bubbles anywhere, and a good boat should be entirely free from this blemish. However, cheaper craft and boats used for 'commercial' purposes may have something like 5 per cent of the moulding surface in the form of small bubbles without being condemned. In special circumstances up to about 8 per cent might be accepted, on components which are not structurally important. Acceptable bubbles will be about 1·5 mm ($\frac{1}{16}$ in.) in diameter, evenly spaced. If there is a collection of bubbles, and especially if they are near a high-stress location such as a rudder gland or chainplate, the defective area should be cut out and fully repaired. Bubbles which penetrate more than about a fifth of the depth of the laminate are serious, particularly if they are closely spaced.

Apart from visible bubbles, there are those which are covered by a thin layer of gel coat. These are discovered by gently tapping with a pricker handle. They are most likely to be found along edges such as the top of cockpit coamings, the deck-edge of a cabin top, the jutting edge of any upstanding component such as the chocks for handrails, and so on. If the handle of a pricker is rubbed along one of these edges it will collapse bad bubbles. The cure is to fill the cavities with a resin putty, but of course a large number of holes is serious and suggests that a new moulding or a new section may be required.

This trouble is particularly common on imitation clinker boats. If the edges of the lands are not well rounded they are likely to contain a large number of hollows, and a simple way to find the condition of the hull is to lay it on a clean grit-free

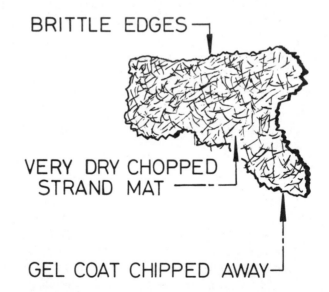

BRITTLE EDGES

VERY DRY CHOPPED
STRAND MAT

GEL COAT CHIPPED AWAY

If the gel coat on a fibreglass hull has become chipped away, exposing an area of dry chopped strand mat, the condition is likely to be serious. The surrounding hull should be tapped with pricker handle to discover the extent of the defect. It is likely that the cure must be the cutting out of the defective area and reglassing, as for damage.

wooden floor and *gently* roll it from side to side. The boat should first be picked up at the bow and then at the stern, first on one side and then on the other. This will test the lands on each side and for a fair distance fore and aft. Naturally only boats up to about 18 ft can be tested in this way, and care must be taken. It must not be carried out on a rough, stony or abrasive surface, which will damage any hull, or cause good moulding to look doubtful.

An internal dry patch is seen where the gel coat has cracked

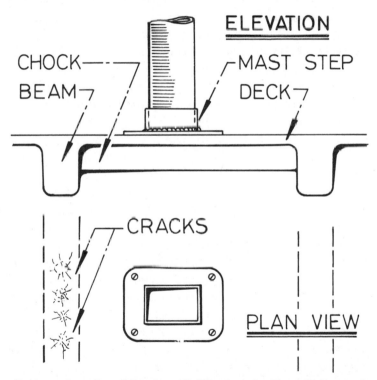

ELEVATION

CHOCK

BEAM

MAST STEP

DECK

CRACKS

PLAN VIEW

Cracks on the surface of fibreglass tell different stories. Near a deck-stepped mast a row of cracks is sometimes seen. Careful measuring is likely to show that these cracks occur over the mast support beam, suggesting that in heavy weather the bridging arrangement between the beams is inadequate. One cure, which is particularly attractive because it is so simple, is to extend the sides of the mast step well fore and aft so that they overlap the beams. The mast step then forms a bridge and helps the chock under the deck to carry the load onto the support beams.

and come away. The glass, seen from the outside of the hull, is in the form of a dry random mat (see sketch). In my experience this is a serious defect, because when it is found in two or three areas it is a sign that large parts of the hull suffer from the defect. Tapping the hull with a pricker handle fractures away more of the gel coat, which usually peels off like eggshell. But the hull underneath is not smooth like an egg's interior; on the contrary, it is an area of weak glass strands with no reinforcing of resin. The trouble occurs if a moulder tries to wet more than one layer of cloth at once, or if there is insufficient rolling of the glass and resin, or where the resin has gone off very quickly and cannot penetrate through.

Cracks in the gel coat are rather a worry for a variety of reasons. A very narrow crack, so tiny that it cannot be seen, is just as serious as a large crack since the structure has been fractured through; the width of the gap is immaterial, as the loss of strength and watertightness has occurred. A very fine crack will draw in water by capillary action. This water is unlikely to be dried out by a warm wind and so the water will stay inside, doing its worst. A wider crack may take in water but discharge it quite easily when the atmospheric conditions encourage drying. Another reason why cracks are serious is that they can be hard and sometimes downright impossible to see. Searching for them should be done in a good light and preferably with a powerful magnifying glass. The hull surface should be looked at from different angles because the way the light falls on the surface results in cracks showing up from one aspect but not from another. Far and away the best method of detecting cracks is by using a flaw detection process. There is a convenient one made by Ardrox Ltd, of Commerce Road, Brentford, Middlesex. This company has a kit comprising a penetrant, a remover and a developer in their 996 process. The fluids are in aerosols so that they can be very conveniently carried from boat to boat, and used quite easily except in the rain. Oil, dirt, paint and so on first have to be removed from the surface, and the three aerosols used in turn. They show up cracks by fine red lines, so there will be difficulty using this process on certain types of red hulls. Ardrox also supply an alternative system, their 92 process, which is in some ways better for fibreglass but is not sold in the rather convenient aerosol packs. Ardrox dyes are also excellent for revealing fine cracks in metal fittings.

A general inspection of the surface, without using either a crack detection kit or a magnifying glass, may suggest that there are quite a few cracks whereas in fact the trouble is scratching. A magnifying glass shows that cracks are deep, tiny little canyons reaching right through the gel coat to the glass below. Old cracks have weathered edges. Scratches do not always penetrate the gel coat, but when they do they are as bad as cracks. When there are indications that the cracks have been present for some time, for instance if their edges are weathered, the surveyor should take a great deal of trouble to find out how much water has got in. It is also important to find out what has caused the cracking. Exhaust pipes, cabin stove chimneys and other sources of heat will crack the GRP. A more common source of cracking is some form of excessive strain. It may be a collision, a bumping dinghy, a stanchion wrenched inwards or outwards, the forcing of one part of the boat into a fit with another, and so on. A good example of cracking trouble occurs when a hull topsides flange is forced inside a deck moulding flange which has been made too tight a fit. Various forms of 'panting' also cause serious line cracks and these are dealt with in a separate chapter on the hinge effect.

Minor cracks should be filled, and where the trouble is serious the surveyor should recommend that the damaged area should be cut out and repaired as for full-penetration damage.

Occasionally a bright light is used to test the quality of fibreglass. The light is held outside the hull and the surveyor works inside, or vice versa. The trouble with this technique is that it can be extremely misleading, even when the surveyor is experienced. In general the light should show that the shell is even and consistent throughout. But of course there will be variations in this; for instance, the shell will probably become progressively thicker working down from the topsides towards the keel. There is likely to be thickening from just below the sheer up to the deck and further thickening towards the stem, and again towards high-stress areas such as in way of the mast. These increases in thickness are naturally misleading.

However, if a light shows local sharply defined changes in the texture, this suggests that there is trouble present. It may be

The vertical deck edge flange of this fibreglass boat has cracked right through. It has been repaired and then cracked again, suggesting that there is local overstressing. Possibly the forestay fitting is not properly secured and is causing the damage. It does not look as if the defect is caused by a head-on collision since the stemhead roller fitting seems to be unblemished.

delamination due to a severe bump, in which case the affected area has to be totally cut out and renewed. Alternatively, the powerful light may show up air bubbles. If they are so bad that the light shows them up clearly, then either the shell is thin or the bubbles are particularly bad.

Just occasionally, when an important survey is being carried out, it will be necessary to discover what the hull thickness is in various locations. This can be carried out by simple drilling. Naturally, the owner's permission has to be obtained first and each hole must be filled after examination. There is a typical surveyor's dilemma here in that the drilling should be carried out at low-stressed points so as not to weaken the hull; on the other hand, it is only in the highly-stressed areas that the hull thickness is likely to matter very much. Another difficulty is that repairs can only be carried out when the weather and temperature are satisfactory, and in extreme cases it may be necessary to seal the holes at least temporarily with bolts pulled up on watertight washers. In general the drilling technique will not be used except in rather special circumstances.

Where a fibreglass hull has been repaired, the join of the new and old material should not be visible from the outside. The edge should also be a perfect bond inside, with no place round the perimeter of the join where the spike can lift any part of the repair, or penetrate the edge of the join.

A surveyor will normally recommend repainting when the hull surface has become dull or badly scratched, or where there is a repair which is clearly visible. As a general rule painting will be carried out right round the vessel, though just occasionally there may be situations where one side only is repainted. It requires a great deal of skill to make a reasonable match of the painted and unpainted surfaces, particularly at the transom, and total repainting is almost always the correct recommendation.

Some hulls have fire-retardant paint in danger areas such as near the engine, round the fuel tanks and over the galley. If this paint film is broken or peeling its protective effect is reduced, if not totally lost.

Just occasionally on the inside, black speckles like a mildew

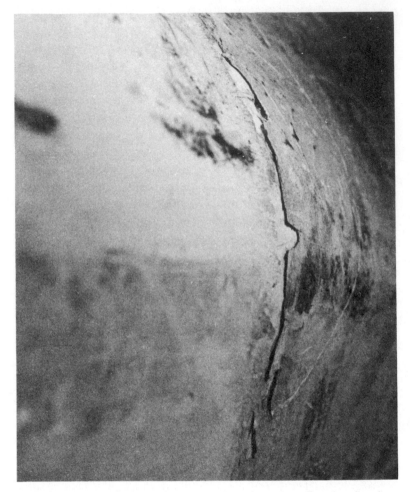

An example of a bad fibreglass repair which is peeling off at the edge. A surveyor seldom gets such a clear-cut warning of trouble; this type of defect is usually quite subtle in the first stages, extending over one or two inches at first.

growth are seen. It may in fact be that this is a damp area, possibly where there is a leak between an internal scupper drain and the main hull. Just because there is no dampness present does not mean that the defect is not there. Leaks of this sort are not consistent; they may only make their presence felt in bad weather or when the boat heels over.

Tapping with the pricker handle may give the classic dull sound of partial delamination; alternatively, firm pressure with hand or foot may show up the very slightest movement of the surface laminate relative to the rest of the moulding. This defect is sometimes found round the edges of a badly made repair, on the inside of the hull. On the outside, the edge of an inefficient repair may be detectable by a crack in the gel coat which extends discontinuously round the renewed area.

Painted Fibreglass

What looks like a superb fibreglass moulding may be a defective one that has been painted. I've been told that some years more than 50 per cent of the boats at the London Boat Show are painted. It is argued that a really fine paint finish is needed to give the best possible appearance, because virtually no moulding is as good as the best paintwork. The suggestion that half the boats in the show are painted should be taken with a pinch of salt, because few builders or moulders will admit even to their best friends that they have dolled up their show boats. However, a lot of boats are found to be painted, often so well that it is hard to detect that a covering layer has been put on over the original gel coat. If the moulder takes the trouble to do a first-class job of the painting he can probably be trusted to cover only *minor* defects which are on the surface of his mould. But if the paint is obvious, if there are even the faintest signs of brush marks or the subtlest of curtaining, the surveyor has grounds for suspicion.

On a boat which is not newly painted there are likely to be at least two or three small patches where the paint has been chipped. A little delicate probing with the spike may show that the paint is ready to flake off quite easily. Tapping with the spike handle may result in paint falling away. With average luck the exposed fibreglass will have a tale to tell. In most circumstances a surveyor is not justified in removing well-applied paint on smooth topsides which externally appear free from defects. He has to be unusually suspicious, or have a special reason for spoiling a good finish. It will normally be advisable to get the owner's permission to remove intact good-quality paint because it is an expensive business repainting a hull to a fine standard.

Below the waterline fibreglass boats should always be painted, even when they are afloat in fresh water, to minimise the effects of marine fouling. It is said that on badly polluted rivers the toxic materials in the water are so vicious that nothing will grow, but I know of only one river where there is evidence that this condition applies, and the local authorities are beginning to clean up even there. So on balance, there should always be antifouling on the bottom. If this paint is seen to flake off easily it is likely that no etch primer has been put on prior to the antifouling undercoat. Some of these special primers are colourless so that it is easy to miss patches. This results in certain areas losing their antifouling right down to the moulding.

If crustaceans get a grip on the fibreglass it is essential to remove them slowly and painstakingly, otherwise the gel coat will be scoured, or ground or chipped off. Rock-hard barnacles well entrenched on the gel coat should get an adverse report, and perhaps a recommendation that removal is to be carried out cautiously.

Bulkheads in Fibreglass Construction

Generally these are of ply, glassed in round the edge. Some of the best authorities lay down that the hull should have doubling all round on the inside in way of the bulkheads, fitted before they are put on. In addition they consider that the bulkhead

TOPSIDES ⌐ ⌐-- ─┐ CORNER
FILLETS

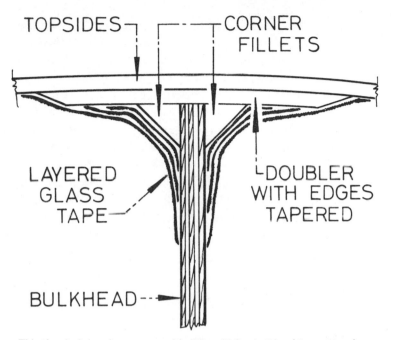

LAYERED
GLASS
TAPE

└DOUBLER
WITH EDGES
TAPERED

BULKHEAD ---

This sketch shows the way a good builder will fit a bulkhead into a fibreglass hull. The doubler is to prevent the bulkhead from imposing a high local loading on the shell and the fillet wedges are to avoid sharp angles for the glass tape to bridge.

Not all boats have all these details at each bulkhead edge, but the more the builders have departed from this arrangement, the lower the quality of construction and the more likely are resulting defects.

should have triangular fillets on both sides, so that the glassing-in does not have to fit inside a tight included angle (see sketch). These back their arguments with sound logic, but in practice few builders follow this ideal. In practice even respected builders simply lower the ply into the fibreglass shell and glass in as in sketch on page 118. Where this is done the surveyor must look for high spots on the outside of the shell, particularly where a bulkhead is highly stressed, as in the case of the under-mast bulkhead(s) on a sailing yacht.

In practice many builders, especially those who are working to a small profit margin, fit the bulkheads quite carelessly so that there are appreciable gaps in places. This may have a fortuitous effect, with the fibreglass tape acting as a spring so that hard spots are avoided. But of course the ply must touch somewhere, so there may be one or two serious hard spots with all the stresses concentrated in a very small area.

Bulkheads are sometimes checked for trueness, though this can be surprisingly difficult since two adjacent bulkheads may both be put in at about the same angle to the centreline. Measurements fore and aft between bulkheads would not throw up such angling off the true athwartship line. What is serious is a bulkhead which has become distorted or bent. This is most likely to be found in a highly stressed under-mast bulkhead, especially where a big doorway has been cut, and insufficient stiffening or pillars added.

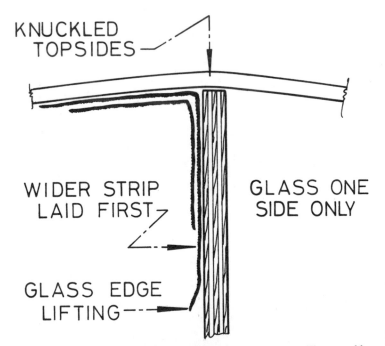

KNUCKLED TOPSIDES

WIDER STRIP LAID FIRST

GLASS ONE SIDE ONLY

GLASS EDGE LIFTING

Typical defects of a badly glassed-in bulkhead are shown here. These troubles will not extend right round the perimeter of the bulkhead except in really bad instances. Trouble is most likely where the work is most difficult of access, namely high up under a deck edge and deep down in a confined bilge space.

All round the bulkhead edge the glass should be examined carefully to make sure it is adhering well. Cheap builders occasionally leave out the glass entirely in awkward places. For instance, the fore side of the forward bulkhead may lack glass tape round its edge, and as this area sometimes holds pockets of water, inevitably moisture attacks the edge of the bulkhead. Dampness will also penetrate at bolt-holes or where fastenings pass through fibreglass and wood. Every piece of wood used should almost always be coated all over otherwise mildew starts. Its black specks are a useful guide that trouble is in the offing.

While looking at the bulkheads it is worth thinking about the ship's general ventilation. It is relatively rare to see ventilation slots through bulkheads, but without them, where there are tight-fitting doors at the bulkhead aperture, there is little chance of any through-ventilation from bow to stern.

Enclosed Wood in Fibreglass Construction

Wood scantlings are put in GRP boats for a variety of purposes, such as engine bearers, local stiffening for chainplates, to form floors and so on.

It is generally considered poor practice to leave any part of the wood exposed, because water should be kept away from the wood. If the wood does become damp it will swell and later shrink. This is likely to cause separation from the GRP, so that the wood no longer properly contributes to the local or general strength. As this is one of its main purposes, the defect is serious. In addition, any relative movement between the wood and the GRP may let in a film of water, which will freeze in very cold weather and result in further structural damage because the wood and the GRP are forced apart.

Some authorities claim that marine ply should be used if any wood inclusion is needed, since it is dimensionally stable and unlikely to absorb much water because of the high glue content. This seems an intelligent line of thought, because even where the wood is fully sealed all round there is still the risk that water will penetrate at bolt-holes and similar points where drills or fastenings are passed through both fibreglass and wood.

In practice the surveyor will come across a large number of situations where wood is used in GRP boats without total enclosure. Some factories turn out great numbers of boats every year using what can only be called poor techniques. The surveyor will normally draw attention to this second-rate practice without actually condemning the boat. However, he will probe around the exposed wood ends very carefully to see if separation between the wood and the fibreglass has started.

There are, of course, certain situations where the wood is glassed in round the edge only. Bulkheads are a good example, and here there is generally no question that the glass should cover more than the outer few inches all round.

Just occasionally engine bearers are fitted like bulkheads, being glassed in round the bottom edge. But even here the builder should make every effort to exclude water. He should glass in the whole of the bottom edge on both sides of the bearer and extend the bearer between two bulkheads, glassing onto the bulkhead right round the butt ends.

Fibreglass Decks

The join of a fibreglass deck to a fibreglass hull is worth giving very special attention. It is usually relatively easy to examine, and in the early days of fibreglass construction this region gave trouble, the consequences of which are still around.

Not so long ago I surveyed an apparently well-built fast motor cruiser. I became suspicious when I noticed how the deck-to-hull join was uneven and that in places the 'want' seemed to be rather large, and as a result a great deal of stopping had been ladled in. Right up in the bow the join seemed to be particularly poor, so I climbed forward and pushed a small coin up the aft face of the

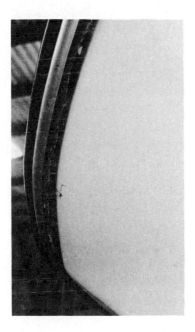

The deck flange of this motor cruiser is so badly fitted that water can easily get between it and the hull moulding. The fibreglass flange had been bolted to the top of the hull, but long lengths of the bolts are visible from below, where the stopping is missing.

stem right up to near the deck. The coin never reached the deck but disappeared into a cavity at the stemhead, and I heard it fall with a clink on the concrete outside. The deck-to-hull join was so poor that the stopping had either fallen out the extreme bow, or the join had never been properly filled.

The join, where visible, should be even. In practice a certain amount of tapering in and out (owing to the slightly varying thickness of the hull shell and the deck edge flange) is permitted. The join must be 100 per cent watertight, and if in doubt a powerful hose should be turned on the join from the outside while someone inside, armed with a powerful lamp, looks for driblets of water getting through.

Various techniques are used for joining the shell to the deck, such as upturned flanges, downturned flanges, a horizontal outward turned flange in the hull and a flat deck flange, and so on. Each has its advantages and disadvantages, and should be judged on its merits and the visible result. Whatever system is used there should be nowhere for water puddles to lie. This applies particularly where the deck is given an upward turning flange and mated to a vertical or near vertical upstand along the

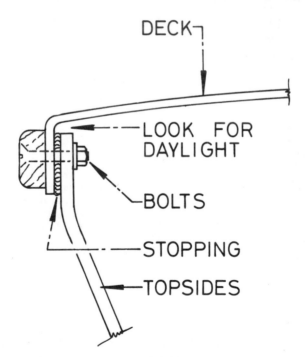

Fibreglass hulls are joined in many different ways to GRP decks. A typical method is shown here, with stopping between the two flanges. This stopping sometimes hardens and drops out, or dries and cracks. Occasionally the stopping is not used in sufficient quantity, so that there are gaps where water can get in. Hose testing from outboard and below is not always possible, but the surveyor can look all round the deck edge for slits of daylight coming up through gaps in the stopping.

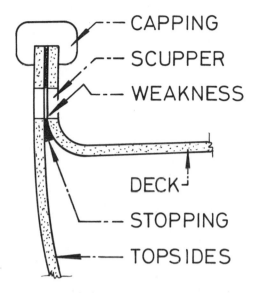

CAPPING

SCUPPER

WEAKNESS

DECK

STOPPING

TOPSIDES

Scuppers cut through an upturned fibreglass deck flange can be a source of leaks. Where the hull and deck flanges are secured and bedded over a reasonable width, no leaks occur, but below the scuppers the depth of stopping is often quite limited. The stopping forms a wedge, and if the deck moves relative to the topsides this wedge may drop out beneath the scupper, letting water into the hull.

top of the hull shell. Everything is normally all right provided no apertures are cut in the upstand, for sheet leads or more usually for scuppers. Scuppers are likely to cause leaks since they are right down at deck level and the filling material is thin, and often badly supported (see sketch).

The flange edges may be covered by rubber or plastic extrusions, or wood edging pieces may be used. Whatever the material it should be well secured, continuous, free from damage, scratches, tears at fastenings or splits. Where repairs are needed a completely new length should be put in, except in very special cirumstances where a short length might be tolerated. In some instances a special extrusion may no longer be available, in which case a new extrusion has to be specified, or possibly a wood moulding made up and secured in place of the plastic.

Deck and hull flanges are secured by rivets or bolts. In practice, few builders use rivets on craft larger than about 8 m overall (25 ft). I do not subscribe to the view that these fastenings are only temporary, necessary until the glassing-up of the hull-to-deck join has hardened. The fastenings are part of the overall structure and should be spaced accordingly. This is a minority view; it is usual to find bolts spaced 0·6 m (2 ft) and more apart, so that they cannot be expected to do a lot of useful

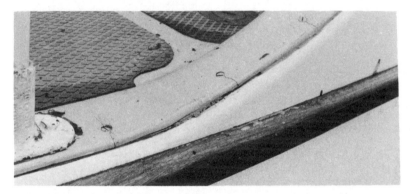

The fibreglass deck-edge flange has cracked at each fastening. Stopping below the flange has fallen out, so leaking here seems inevitable. Before recommending repairs the surveyor has to determine the reason for the cracks. It may have been overtightening of the fastenings, but the indications are that the deck flange never matched the hull, so the cracking occurred when the two were pulled together.

work throughout the main life of the vessel. They are indeed temporary fastenings whose work is largely over once the deck edge glassing-up is complete. By the same token, these bolts should be commensurate with the size of the vessel. I do not like 6 mm ($\frac{1}{4}$ in.) bolts joining the deck flange to the shell of an 11 m (36 ft) yacht.

It is usual practice to glass over these bolts, and this should be done very thoroughly so that no water can possibly get at them. If either the head or the nut on the bolt are not glassed over, each one should be carefully examined for the beginnings of corrosion, and signs of movement.

When examining the mating of the deck to the hull shell, it should be remembered that a join which is hard to make will be poorly finished. A good join tends to look right, and it will not incorporate any harsh or sharp flanges.

There have been cases where chainplates have been secured to a deck and as a result the deck has been pulled right off the hull. A surveyor told me about an instance he came across of this trouble. The yacht had gone to sea and it was noticed that the mast lent over alarmingly. As soon as the boat was back in harbour the surveyor was called for and he stood on the deck, giving the shrouds a hearty pull upwards. The chainplates seemed secure enough until he had the idea he should be standing on the *quay* and not on the yacht at all. He jumped ashore and grabbed the shrouds, pulling them vigorously upwards. The deck curved up towards him in an interesting and surprising way!

The 'Hinge Effect' in Fibreglass

As the surveyor walks about on the deck or cockpit sole of a fibreglass boat he is likely to feel the structure 'give' with his weight. This phenomenon is widespread in small craft, but is also found on medium sized and even some big boats. It is argued, plausibly enough, that provided the deck continues to carry the load of the crew walking about, all is well. The surveyor may accept this argument for a boat intended for use in sheltered waters, but for deep-sea work a flimsy structure is suspect because it cannot support the weight of a breaking sea coming aboard.

Even inshore craft, however, cannot have flexible panels if the 'hinge effect' begins to show itself. This condition gives rise to a series of approximately parallel cracks along the edge of a panel where the repeated bending to and fro cracks the gel coat.

A common place to find this trouble is along each side of the bottom of a cockpit well. It is found if no cockpit grating is fitted, or if the grating is so flimsy that it does not distribute the crew's weight evenly over a large area. It is widely found where the cockpit sole is weakly supported or where the bottom beams are not carried to the full width of the well. It is sometimes seen when these beams are spaced too far apart, or end too sharply.

If the hinge effect is allowed to develop, eventually the whole panel will drop out. This is admittedly rare, but it is occasionally found in the bottoms of high-speed motor boats where the whole hull surface pants in and out at each impact with the sea's surface. The reversing strain, occurring thousands of times each day, soon cracks through the gel coat and then sets about fracturing the glass fibres.

This situation can arise in sheltered waters where the waves are quite small but closely spaced. The impact with each individual wave may be quite modest as compared with the crash into a big sea offshore. However, the frequency of the reversal of loading on the bottom of the boat is so high that the glass cracks through more quickly than when the vessel is used offshore. This particular trouble is found especially with sandwich construction. If the outer skin does not continue to grip the foam plastic core the trouble may develop very quickly. The first indications of the hinge effect are of course the roughly parallel lines of cracks along the 'hinge line'.

On racing dinghies the hinge effect is seen along the inside edges of the buoyancy tanks where they meet the hull bottom. Another location is each side of the centreboard case, with extensions aft along the backbone stiffener. The cause of trouble here is the flexing of the bottom of the hull. As the boat pounds over the waves the bottom can be felt moving in and out appreciably. In addition the crew push the shell down as they move about on board. I have seen this trouble on a batch of racing dinghies less than a month old. These boats were of a well-known class with sail numbers above 34,000. We detected the trouble early on, but recommending the cure can be surprisingly difficult. Owners of this type of boat do not take kindly to fitting any structure which increases weight, such as floorboards which would have checked the development of the crack lines. In practice floorboards are a rather poor idea since they do relatively little to prevent the upward bulging of the shell as the dinghy hits a wave, and they only check the trouble, not cure it. They do not even fully prevent the downward bulge due to the weight of a foot on the shell unless the floorboard bearers perfectly match the shell and are spaced closely. Besides, floorboards are considered so old-fashioned by dinghy racing owners that the surveyor is probably reduced to quoting the Belloc rhyme,

> There is no cure for this disease
> they say as they take their fees.

In the case of a racing dinghy, there may indeed be no cure except to strip all the fittings off the boat and put them, with mast, sails and rigging, onto a new shell. This new hull should have the buoyancy tanks and centreboard sides brought into the hull bottom with a radius of at least 50 mm (2 in.). There should also be some local stiffening along the line of the join, all to prevent the hinge effect.

Fastenings in Fibreglass

It is broadly true to say that fibreglass dislikes metal fastenings. A bronze or steel fastening is a harsh, hard piece of metal which has a nasty habit of imposing high local loadings on the moulding. As a general rule it is therefore advisable to have washers which are twice the bolt diameter, or better still, three times the diameter. The same big washers ought to be put under bolt heads where they bed on glass, but this practice is seldom seen. Another basic principle is that bolts should not be used through laminates which are less than 3 mm ($\frac{1}{8}$ in.) thick. All fibreglass should be well reinforced in way of bolts, and the stiffening should taper away at the edges. Where the surveyor finds trouble due to bolts passing through fibreglass, he can sometimes suggest that a well-bedded wood pad and longer bolts are the required cure. The pad must be large enough in length and breadth to spread the load. Ideally the edges of the pad should be tapered away, and its thickness must be adequate so that it does not bell up when the bolt is tightened.

If bolts are a source of trouble, screws are a thousand times worse. In handrails they prove inadequate. Holding even small bollards with screws is beyond the bounds of morality. Those builders who fix their mooring posts to the foredeck on even the smallest outboard runabouts should be consigned to an early unhallowed grave. On second thoughts, perhaps this is too harsh a judgment: after all, surveyors depend for their livelihood on vessels getting into trouble. Nothing enhances a surveyor's prosperity like a builder who only screws his deck fittings down.

The area close round each chainplate should be carefully examined for cracks, particularly on the inboard side. It is hard to get chainplates to line up exactly with shrouds, and even when there is ample local reinforcing there is a tendency for the chainplates to pull inboard. They try to cut across the deck and the result is cracking and very often leaks. This trouble is not easy to cure. At least one famous builder who annually modifies and improves his standard production craft has recommended that the latest type of chainplate should be fitted where this cracking is found on his older boats. Fitting the new style ('hair-pin' type) chainplate involves relatively radical alterations. An alternative might be to remove the chainplate and fair away the cracked area. Then fill the cracks beyond the holes and replace the chainplate at a better angle, with wood chocks or metal plates on deck bedded down on a rubbery flexible compound to prevent further leaks.

When removing a keel bolt from a GRP boat it is just as important to look at the fibreglass under the washer and the structure round the bolt-hole as it is to examine the condition of the bolt. It is not enough to have washers which extend well fore and aft and athwartships. They must also be thick enough not to dish downwards when the bolt is tightened. Also, these washers should be bedded either in some glass and fresh gel coat, or on a flexible non-hardening material like Sylglass tape which will spread the load evenly.

Leaks in Fibreglass Boats

Everyone knows that fibreglass boats are homogeneous and leak-free. When one of these boats does start to leak, the first reaction is incredulity. The impossible appears to be happening, and the situation is vastly unpopular.

The logical way to find the source of leaking is to first assume that the fibreglass shell itself is entirely watertight and work on the principle that the water is getting in at one of the apertures.

A seacock is sometimes the culprit. The fitting itself may be defective or loose so that water gets in at one of the mechanical joins. Alternatively the trouble may be at the flange. Almost always the flange is perfectly flat, but the GRP shell seldom is. This means there must be ample bedding under the flange because no amount of tightening of bolts will pull the flange and the hull shell together. The various waterproof beddings used suffer from different drawbacks. Some are sticky and rather unpleasant to use, so that workmen putting the goo on do so without sufficient enthusiasm. Just occasionally the bedding gets washed out; sometimes it becomes brittle, and either drops out or cracks in such a way that water can seep in. Sometimes the bedding is entirely forgotten; and on other occasions it is put in but not right round the flange, so that there is a gap at one side.

What applies to seacocks can also apply to other fittings, such as the palms of A-brackets. Other A-brackets have no palms but instead the legs pass right through the shell, where they are glassed over. Sometimes the legs are bent outwards before being glassed over, but in any event there is relatively little strength fore and aft, only strength athwartships due to the spread of the legs. What occasionally happens is that the A-bracket gets bumped in a forward or aft direction and since there is little resistance against this type of accident the legs move slightly. The resulting leak may be difficult to detect since water may emerge inside the hull quite some distance from the A-bracket. This trouble is particularly likely to be found if the hull is complete and the A-bracket installed some time before the propeller shaft is put in. A protruding A-bracket is particularly vulnerable if the hull is moved in a factory or by road without the propeller shaft in place.

An externally fitted keel gives the same kind of trouble as seacocks. The trouble is magnified because not only is the fibreglass skin uneven but also the top of the keel may not be perfectly flat. Here again, bedding can become hard, or get washed out, or be put in unevenly, and so on. The surveyor may recommend curing a leak past a keel bolt by specifying ample soft bedding under the big plate washer inside the boat. This is perhaps adequate in some instances, provided the boat is used in settled weather and sheltered waters. However, leak curing from the *inside* is never satisfactory, and should only be recommended in a few special cases.

Some fibreglass boats have deck scuppers which are piped down to exits at or below the waterline. These pipes also serve as frames, and they are almost always glassed in after the main hull has been completed. Leaks here start for several reasons.

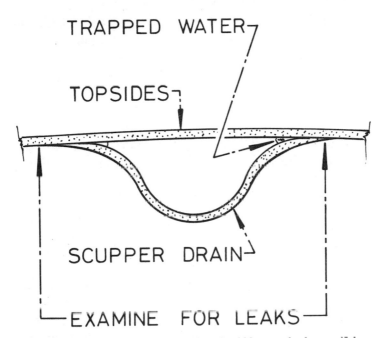

TRAPPED WATER

TOPSIDES

SCUPPER DRAIN

EXAMINE FOR LEAKS

On fibreglass shells the drain scupper edges should be examined to see if the top-hat section has been forced away from the topsides, either by a bump alongside or by frost. Sometimes the drain scupper has an internal pipe, but this is not always 100 per cent watertight at top and bottom, so water can get between the pipe and top-hat section and become trapped.

Sometimes the pipes are made in the form of a 'top-hat' section, so that each side of the pipe meets the hull at an acute angle. Water may lodge there and freeze, forcing the pipe away from the shell (see sketch). Alternatively, the leak may be at the point where the scupper in the deck joins the pipe down the inside of the hull. Unless the deck is put on most carefully, and the scupper well glassed round, there is a good chance that the join will not be perfect, particularly on the outboard side.

Both GRP and wooden decks suffer from leaks if stanchions are overstressed so that the stanchion flange and its bolt are moved. The same applies to mooring cleats and other strong points secured to the deck. This type of leak is usually fairly easy to find because as the water runs down from the source of trouble it leaves a dirty mark. A variety of repairs can be recommended; for instance the fitting can be rebolted, with a teak pad on deck and another below the deck. Both pads should be well bedded in a compound which will take up the unevenness of the fibreglass. Wherever possible new fastening arrangements should be stronger than the ones that have failed, though the failure will normally result from overstressing and not normal usage.

If a GRP boat leaks, most people immediately suspect the stern gland. This is logical enough, but if this fitting is found to be well packed it is worth investigating the way the stern tube is fitted. If it is glassed in, perhaps the bond no longer holds and water is seeping in between the glass and the tube. If the engine has vibrated a lot, or if the propeller has become unbalanced and caused shaft vibration, the chances of the stern tube being loosened just the tiniest bit are enhanced.

The rudder tube and its gland should be treated with the same suspicion as the stern tube. Just occasionally a boat is found to leak inconsistently; she may leak one week but not the next, causing a great deal of dismay. The reason may be that the rudder gland is at or just above the waterline so that in calm weather there is no pressure against it and no water gets in. In severe weather, as the boat pitches the rudder stock gland may become immersed and water may trickle up the rudder stock.

I met a similar case on a high-speed motor boat which had cockpit drains. This boat was fine until the seas became about a foot high, when the cockpit drain flanges let in water. These flanges were not properly bedded in, and during a gale this boat sank on moorings. The manufacturers hotly denied that they had allowed a production fault to slip past their notice, claiming that they had built six hundred boats and this was proof of their integrity. They were subsequently shown to be wrong in a rather sensational way, when sister ships suffered a similar fate.

Foam Sandwich Construction

A farmer friend of mine bought a dinghy of GRP foam sandwich construction. He pointed out the advantages, since this boat had the usual inner and outer layers of fibreglass with a thick enclosed layer of buoyant foam plastic. Unfortunately the boat only lasted two seasons, and separated into the inner GRP shelf, the sandwiched foam, and the outer GRP layers. I pointed out that he had only bought one boat and now had three, and asked if this was not what all farmers aimed at: a clear case of breeding from an initial single purchase. Since his boat was quite useless and the money all down the drain, he took the joke rather badly.

But this does highlight the biggest problem with this type of construction. Unless the GRP adheres strongly and continuously to the inner foam plastic there is serious loss of strength which can quite soon condemn the structure.

If possible the ship's plans should be studied to see what precautions were taken during construction to prevent separation of the layers. Next the hull and deck should be carefully examined for signs of distortion. Anyone who does not have a good 'eye' should take a long batten, say, 2 by $\frac{3}{4}$ in., and lay it along the hull and deck to detect any unfairness. Next the inner and outer layers of GRP should be pressed, to see if they move. It should not be possible with ordinary hand or foot pressure to get any sensible movement of any of the GRP.

When testing GRP sandwich construction a steady, firm pressure should be applied to a large number of points. While the load is being put on, the ear should be held close to the structure and if a noise is heard, something like a scratching or crackling sound, it is likely that the core is not adhering to the facings, and is being sheared. If this is found, permission should be obtained to take cores in unobtrusive places. These must be big enough to allow the surveyor to see whether the fibreglass is tight against the foam. Any air gaps are totally unacceptable, because if the fibreglass is $\frac{1}{16}$ in. away from the foam sandwich it is not adhering and might just as well be 2 in. away. Sandwich construction should also be examined along the full length of all edges since this is where breakdown or separation is likely to start.

A light hammer or pricker handle is used to tap all over the hull, and the resulting noise should be a cheerful ring. A dull sound indicates either an air cushion or water absorption. In extreme cases the water can actually be heard to make 'soggy' sounds. Around strong points such as chainplates, and also in way of the seacocks, there should be solid pads which will give out a different, deeper echo when tapped. These pads should extend well beyond the fitting or strong point. Since they are hidden once the inner layer of fibreglass has been applied, siting the fittings is critical. In practice, anyone working carelessly or without a detail plan is likely to position a seacock so that it extends over one edge of the built-in pad.

For a chainplate the internal stiffening should extend well out in all directions, because the stresses here are so high. This is sometimes a good place to do drill testing on the inside, since renewing the fibreglass skin in this area is relatively easy. It is a sign of good building if the inner fibreglass skin is thickened up in way of any fitting. Naturally, it must be extensively reinforced in way of stressed fittings.

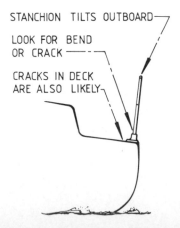

STANCHION TILTS OUTBOARD

LOOK FOR BEND OR CRACK

CRACKS IN DECK ARE ALSO LIKELY

Stanchions should be vertical, otherwise they will be forced inwards when the boat comes alongside a quay wall. Either the deck should have a horizontal area to take the stanchion base flange, or there should be a tapered wood wedge fitted under each stanchion base to ensure the stanchion stands upright.

‖ Metal Hulls

‖ Steel Craft

There is a great gulf between large steel ships and small craft built of this material. There is another gap between steel boats and those built of wood or fibreglass. In many ways steel is a good-tempered material. It seldom splits like wood, or gives way under quite moderate wear and tear like fibreglass. It tends to be much stronger than needed for the usual day-to-day service. Its main trouble is corrosion, but this takes place regularly, at an even rate for the most part, and in a fairly predictable way. The same cannot be said of deterioration in wood or fibreglass. (For a fuller understanding of steel construction as it relates to small boats, there is my book *Small Steel Craft* published by Adlard Coles Ltd in UK, and International Marine in USA.)

The surveyor's basic problem when looking at a steel boat is to discover where the corrosion is and what depth of wastage has occurred. A secondary set of problems concerns denting, etc., but the troubles here are almost always less severe and easier to find, though admittedly not always particularly easy to repair economically.

A good deal can be learned about the steel structure simply by hammering. The hammer has to be used with energy, except on very light craft where plating 3 mm ($\frac{1}{8}$ in.) thick will buckle even when new, if subject to over-enthusiastic battering. Hitting frames, floors, stringers, the keel, the rudder and so on with the

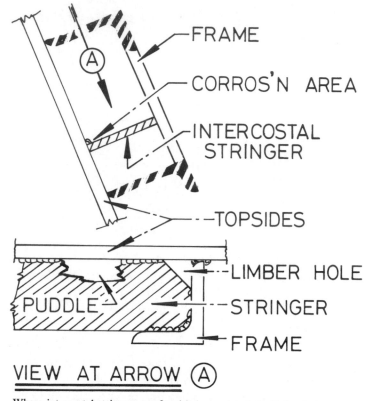

FRAME

CORROS'N AREA

INTERCOSTAL STRINGER

TOPSIDES

LIMBER HOLE

STRINGER

FRAME

PUDDLE

VIEW AT ARROW Ⓐ

Where intercostal stringers are fitted it is usual to have limber holes at each end to let water drain away. Sometimes these limber holes become blocked with dirt and paint so that water sits on top of the stringer and causes local corrosion. On other occasions the intermittent welding collects puddles of water between each run of welding and again local corrosion occurs. Limbers are equally necessary in wood, fibreglass or aluminium construction.

hammer has two effects. It chips away the layered rust, and reveals excessive weakness since the scantling being tested will dent or bend if it has become too thin.

As with all types of survey testing, if a weakness is found in one place, then all the comparable areas should be tested in the same way. For instance, if No. 7 floor is found to be flimsy on the starboard side, the port side should be tried, and the adjacent floors ahead and astern should be given the same treatment.

A more sophisticated method of testing steel structure is by drilling. The holes should be at least 6 mm ($\frac{1}{4}$ in.) and better still 8 mm ($\frac{3}{8}$ in.), or even larger. The important thing is first to obtain special steel plate measuring calipers before specifying the size of hole to be drilled by the shipwright, since the caliper head diameter will govern the minimum hole diameter which can be used. When the surveyor is working between tides it is

This steel skeg is near a bronze propeller and stainless steel propeller shaft. Extensive electrolytic action has corroded the skeg badly. No sacrificial plate was fitted on this boat.

essential to make arrangements for the holes to be welded over before the tide rises. Where welding facilities cannot be obtained, bolts with watertight washers are fitted.

It is easy to miss some of the holes when closing them over after the survey, so special precautions should be taken to make sure that every hole is sealed. Before drilling a hole, the area should be marked with a bold chalk circle by the surveyor. He should try to follow some sort of pattern; for instance he might mark different locations in batches of three, so that whenever bolts are being put in or rewelding done, the crafts-man will have a cross-check that he is not missing out any aperture. These precautions are just as important if the vessel is on a slipway, because the holes can just as easily be forgotten prior to relaunching.

On small craft it may be necessary to have a right-angle drill to get into awkward corners low down. An alternative is to have a flexible extension drive with a chuck on the end and driven off an ordinary electric drill, to get into deep confined spaces such as the fin keel of a sailing yacht.

As a general rule the drill holes should be low down, because corrosion takes place where puddles lie. However, drilling should not be so near a corner that there is difficulty getting in a bolt and washer.

The third and in many ways the most effective method of testing steel scantlings is by ultrasonics. The testing device is small and portable. There is no reason why it should not be used up masts or down in confined double bottoms. It is very thorough; there is no reason why every square inch of every plate and frame should not be tested, if time and patience are available. Paint, rust, grease and dirt have to be cleaned off the steel surface so that the transducer has good contact, but otherwise this testing procedure has few disadvantages.

Typical of the ultrasonic testing meters available is one made by Wells-Krautkramer Ltd, of Blackhorse Road, Letchworth, Hertfordshire, England. With various extras, it costs well over one quarter the annual salary of a junior white collar worker. It is extremely handy to use, being battery operated, and weighs only 2·5 kg (5·5 lb). The version used on small craft has a range of 1·7–15 mm (0·07–0·6 in.). Anybody prepared to spend roughly twice as much can get the Ultrasonic Flaw Detector type USM 2 from the same company. The attraction of this instrument is that it can not only be used for measuring plate thickness and corrosion but also for testing welding, plate quality and so on.

For anyone disinclined to buy an ultrasonic tester, one can be hired from firms like Rank Precision Instruments Ltd.

When making drilling tests or using an ultrasonic tester it is important to work to a pattern. It may be worth obtaining a dyeline print of the vessel's construction plan and marking the locations and results of each test on this plan. Anyone interpreting the survey will have an easier job if the results are set down visually in this way. Using a plan also prevents missing areas, and by using different colours a single view showing one side only can be used for both port and starboard.

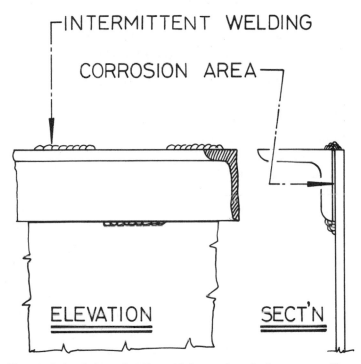

If an angle bar is intermittently welded to a plate, for instance to stiffen a floor, there is always a risk that water will get between the plate and the flange of the bar. In theory a bar should be toe-welded, but the ideal practice is not always followed.

Steel craft deteriorate to a well-established pattern. The bottoms of compartments are always in far worse condition than the tops. Floors are almost always more seriously corroded than frames. It is not unusual to find a frame in perfect condition except for the bottom 2 per cent of its length. Floors and frames should be heavily chipped before their thickness is measured. Where an ultrasonic machine is not available calipers can be used without drilling on scantlings of this sort.

The garboard plates would normally be markedly corroded, since puddles in the bilge lie on them. However, in practice almost all well-built craft except the smallest have heavier garboard plates. This extra thickening at the bottom is less often found in bulkheads and as a result these are vulnerable to corrosion. Here again it is not unusual to find the whole bulkhead in reasonable condition except for a few inches at the bottom, where corrosion may have penetrated right through.

Exposed plate edges out in the weather or down near the bilgewater are always vulnerable; for instance, the scupper holes in bulwarks where no doubling or reinforcing has been fitted usually show wastage.

Trouble is also likely externally at the waterline, since this area is constantly wet and also well aereated. Particularly aft and round the rudder stock, the steel will be found to be corroded. Another troublesome area is by seacocks, or anywhere near different metals. Just occasionally a steel seacock is welded to a steel hull but a non-ferrous pipe is linked to the seacock. In this case there may be trouble inside the seacock.

It may be necessary to cut away plating to gain access. For instance, if a double bottom is too shallow for a man to climb through, the only satisfactory way of finding the condition in this space is to cut away the top plates. Sometimes access has been partly blocked by recent additions of equipment on the ship, and this is another occasion when cutting away plating may be the only method of making a thorough inspection. The surgery should be carried out intelligently so that replacement can be made neatly with the maximum amount of down-hand welding and the minimum disturbance to furniture and other equipment. When looking in tanks it is important to examine the striking plates under sounding tubes. On cheap craft these striking plates are omitted so that local corrosion is probable (see sketch in Tanks section).

Corrosion will be found where water can be trapped in narrow interstices. Beneath wood decks which are on top of margin plates and other deck plates there is often serious corrosion. The trouble multiplies here, since the rust crushes the wood and forces it upwards, allowing more water to get in so that more rust is generated, and so on.

When looking for places where puddles have been lying, it is important to remember that a boat's attitude varies. She may be laid up with her keel horizontal, in which case she is likely to be down by the nose. A fishing boat may spend some time laid up afloat with ballast out and no nets or fuel aboard, so that she may trim to a different angle, and possibly lie heeled into a quay wall when she takes the ground.

Corrosion is regularly found where vent trunks and tubing

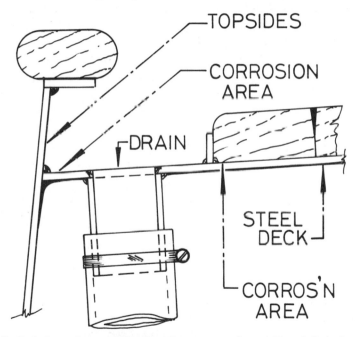

In deck depressions, puddles lie and cause corrosion troubles. A drainpipe cannot be put right against the topsides because a welder would not able to get round the outboard side of the pipe spigot. As a result a tiny quantity of water can lie outboard of the drain, and this causes rusting.

Between the edge of the wood sheathing and its steel boundary bar there should be a watertight seal. However, this sometimes has faults in it, maybe only a centimetre long but enough to let the water get in. This moisture cannot easily dry out, and corrosion starts. Once it gets a hold it tends to force the wood away and let in more water.

meet the deck, round the bottoms of the steel skylight coamings, and under the gratings, particularly those fitted over quadrants and tillers. Wherever chafing takes place corrosion advances fast. Anchors and chain rub as they run in and out, and a ship which regularly goes aground will corrode fast at the heel of the keel, on the underside of any bilge keels which regularly touch the ground, etc.

Mild buckling of plates and frames is generally not significant on commercial craft. However, it is unacceptable on yachts, directors' launches and other prestige craft. A serious dent may call for immediate repairs because welds or riveting may be fractured. On commercial craft the owner may simply ask for the strength to be restored by local welding. The appearance may not be restored, but very often the owner is more interested in getting the craft back to work and he is unconcerned about the look of the hull. With yachts and similar craft the reverse applies, so it will be necessary for the surveyor to arrange for the dent to be hammered out or cut out, and a major repair completed.

Dents may give a clue to the way the ship has been handled and treated. There is a class of middle-water fishing boats which all have buckled bows because their reverse gears are slow to react and they tend to hit quay walls before the propeller has had a chance to take way off the ship.

Aluminium

Aluminium alloy craft have to be examined notably for corrosion. Paint should be removed in small patches all over, to reveal the condition of the metal beneath. Wherever the paint is crumbling or uneven, a wire brush or scraper should be used to get down to the metal and discover the condition under-neath.

Just occasionally a particularly unpleasant type of corrosion occurs with this metal: the paint remains intact all over except for one little area, which is then subject to intensive local attack because it is the only area which has no guard against the flow of electric current. There have been cases of electrolytic cor-rosion acting like a drill, penetrating inwards over a tiny area, right through the plating.

Inspection should be very careful all over, but particularly around the waterline, at apertures near the rudder, propeller and brackets, and wherever two different metals are adjacent. It has to be remembered that aluminium alloy comes in a wide variety of specifications, and the stem band could be different to the stem plate and adjacent shell plating.

Rivets should be inspected carefully because they have a tendency to become loose, partly through stress and partly through corrosion. They usually give themselves away by fail-ing all round the edge. This leaves a small crack which fills with dirt, a rare instance where grime is a surveyor's friend. Faulty rivets have to be drilled out and replaced, and generally speak-ing it is advisable to replace ten faulty rivets by fifteen new ones. Extending the line of replacement each side of the known defects ensures that rivets which may be on the verge of going are included in the repairs.

Welding needs much more attention in aluminium craft than on steel vessels. Hair cracks are more common, and it may be necessary to use a dye detection system in special cases. Sur-veyors not having their own facilities can use companies such as Rank Precision Instruments to do this part of the survey on a sub-contract basis.

Because aluminium is a relatively soft material, it is probable that there will be dents in the craft under survey. The edges of the dents should be searched for fractures, especially near adjacent riveting and welding. Mild dents are probably best left alone, particularly on commercial craft where appearance is not generally important. Even quite large dents which are watertight can be left alone on the principle that hammering out may cause hardening or cracking and cost money. On boats where appearance matters, much can be done with filling provided the composition can be persuaded to adhere to the surface. A problem with aluminium craft is the shortage of skilled technicians who can carry out repairs. Surveyors have to be practical in their recommendations, so there are times when it is better to fill dents than repair them, simply because of the difficulty of getting the necessary manual skills.

Aluminium superstructures tend to give trouble at the corners and at flanges secured to the deck. Wherever an aluminium structure is joined to a hull or deck of different material there is likely a corrosion risk, especially at the fastenings.

The same applies to deck fittings. For instance, cadmium-plated steel bolts are sometimes used to hold down aluminium stanchion base flanges. Corrosion pitting may occur round the head of the bolt, but this will not show if repeated painting fills the holes. It is important to scrape away the surface paint to see if there is trouble beneath. Similarly, it is quite usual to secure aluminium hatch frames with stainless steel bolts, and here corrosion may be found in the countersinking in the aluminium flange, since small puddles tend to lie in the depression.

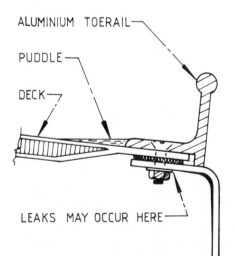

ALUMINIUM TOERAIL

PUDDLE

DECK

LEAKS MAY OCCUR HERE

Where an aluminium toerail is bolted down to a fibreglass deck there may be leaks at each fastening, particularly if the toerail traps water in a puddle and if the toerail has been bumped inwards in such a way that the bolts are slightly loose. All the bolts should be put in with bedding round them and if self-tapping fastenings are used here, leaks are likely.

Major Components and Fittings

Rudders and Steering Gear

Boats built on what might be called 'traditional' lines are probably over ten years old, as most boats built in the last few years have come from production lines rather than boatyards. 'Traditional' building includes fairly large factors of safety in the rudder and steering gear, but old boats almost always suffer from wear and tear in the moving parts and so defects must be expected in the steering equipment. This is particularly so since rudders tend to move slightly the whole time a boat is afloat, even though the craft is not underway. Fishing boats and work boats in particular get insufficient maintenance and poor lubrication, so that steering defects are regularly found in these craft.

What may be loosely described as 'production line' boats are almost always built to a very competitive price. They have lightweight fittings with a much smaller margin of safety than was usual ten or fifteen years ago. These boats cannot be passed as sound unless rudders and all their fittings together with the linkages and steering equipment are in first-class order. All types of racing craft must have perfect steering equipment because any backlash or play is unacceptable.

A surveyor therefore starts out with the certain knowledge that the majority of small craft examined are bound to need attention to their steering equipment. Whenever possible the rudder should be dropped and the whole steering linkage taken apart. In practice dismantling is seldom carried out *before* the survey, unless the ship is over 20 m (65 ft).

Some small mass-produced fibreglass boats are so assembled that the rudder cannot be taken off without cutting away structure. Occasionally quite serious surgery is required to get at the bearing surfaces for examination.

Rudders should be tested for wear in both the athwartship and fore and aft directions. This is done by seizing the blade and trying to move it backwards and forwards. On craft over 20 m (65 ft) this cannot be done easily by hand, but a foot placed against the blade will sometimes show up wear. Alternatively, a heavy screwdriver may be used as a lever.

When wear is found, whether at the bearings or the glands, it is important to try to assess how fast the trouble is developing. It may not be enough to simply fit bushings: there may be unsatisfactory materials in contact. For instance, white nylon is no good for bearings because it is too soft, and ovalises, as well as swelling. If Ferrobestos or Tufnol are found as the rudder bearings then just a little movement or working clearance is acceptable because these materials swell when immersed in water. The situation here is a little clouded because different types of these plastics swell different amounts. This is yet another case where manufacturers' recommendations have to be followed.

If the rudder stock is stainless steel it should be examined for crevice corrosion, particularly where it disappears into the gland or tube. Mild steel stocks also tend to rust at this point.

If the gland itself is inaccessible, then repacking is infrequently carried out. When it is done, the workmanship is likely to be poor; it is only human nature to send a second-year apprentice into the dark, cramped, aft peak to do an awkward job. Gland bolts should have some form of locking arrangement, especially if there is any· risk that the rudder will vibrate. This is most likely where there is a long light stock and a large single-plate rudder. If a big propeller is in front of this rudder the chances of vibration are enhanced.

The heel of this rudder is touching the deadwood, presumably because the gudgeons and pintles have worn. Alternatively, there may have been washers on the pintles which have been removed because a new propeller has been fitted and adequate tip clearance is needed. The tip clearance at the bottom is too small, being less than $\frac{1}{12}$ of the diameter of the propeller.

Almost always the heel fitting shows the greatest sign of wear, particularly if the boat is being used in shallow gritty water. Wear here is at least twice as fast when the heel bearing has to carry the whole weight of the rudder, especially if it is a massive steel one. Some wooden rudders float, so that the loading at the bottom is reduced.

Rudder hangings should be examined for misalignment; this trouble exists where one bearing has a lot of wear on, say, the starboard side, the next one has wear on the aft side, and the next one maybe has wear on the port side. The trouble can, of course, be a bent stock. Provided the stock is found to be straight, the cure may be to fit bushings with fair holes biased on one side, or fore and aft.

Rudder straps seem to 'eat' their screws. It is surprising how often screwheads shear off when an attempt is made to withdraw them for examination.

Metal rudder blades should be examined for hair cracks by the stock and where the blade meets the top and bottom flanges. Poor builders omit the welding between the flanges and the blade. Steel rudder blades corrode particularly at the bottom edge and sometimes at the aft edge. A hammer should be used vigorously against the blade to make sure that it is not heavily corroded and also to ensure that it is well secured to the stock. A double-plate rudder may need drilling to confirm that there is plenty of metal left. These test holes are normally made in the bottom and in the side plates near the bottom.

Quadrants, crossarms, double tillers and all the other devices fitted at the tops of rudder stocks need careful examination for weld fractures, which are shown by hairline cracks. Any bolting or riveting should also be subjected to hammer testing and the most critical inspection. The reversing strains caused by putting the helm first to one side and then to the other, as well as the vibration from the water flow over the rudder blade, result in all sorts of damage. It has to be remembered that the flow from the propeller may mean that the rudder is constantly vibrating at a high frequency. In addition, when the vessel lies on moorings, rolling and pitching will cause the blade to struggle to and fro. All these strains are taken by the linkage at the top of the stock.

The lead of the wires onto the quadrant must be exact. If one or both of the wires do not extend to precisely the right angle and at the right height there is always a chance that a wire may drop off the quadrant. There will certainly be wear on the wire and possibly on the guide plates of the quadrant, not to mention wear at the sheaves. Sometimes little heaps of powdered metal in the bilge below a sheave cage will be a warning that wear is taking place. Sheaves which lie flat are particularly prone to this trouble.

Each sheave cage should have at least three bolts securing it to the hull structure. On small boats it is occasionally permissible to use screws to secure sheave cages, but only if the screws are in *shear* (see sketch). If screws have to be used they should be strong, with at least four through the flange of each cage.

Where the wire meets the quadrant or tiller there are often shackles and rigging screws. These should be fully wired up to prevent accidental loosening. The shackle pins and the clevis pins in the rigging screws should be tested for wear. Rods which are linked to tillers and crossarms take a great deal of punishment and wear fast (at the pins and forks), so here again some dismantling is needed.

Steering wire which is beginning to strand should be condemned. Stranding is the condition which occurs when the individual thin wires which make up the rope break due to fatigue. Occasionally the steering wire is made very thick, on the principle that it will be strong and last for a long time. What happens is that the extra thick wire does not render easily round the sheaves and so fatigue is accelerated. I have seen *plough* steel standing rigging wire used as steering wire. The result was that the steering was so stiff that nobody could stand at the helm for long, and it was lucky that the trouble was detected before fatigue failure occurred.

Some steering wires are plastic covered. The skinning of plastic has the advantage that it protects the wire, but once the plastic is even slightly damaged the wire has to be totally condemned. It is important to find out why the plastic has become damaged since there may be a sharp edge at a sheave cage which is going to cause future trouble, even with uncoated wire.

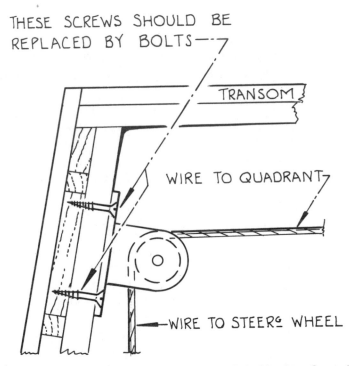

Sheave cages for steering gear should always be bolted in place. On small craft an argument might be raised for using screws in shear. There is never any excuse for putting screws in tension, as shown in this sketch.

There should be splices or some reliable endings on the steering wires. The join of the wires to the quadrant or tiller is often found to be a nightmare. Otherwise reliable riggers take leave of their senses, knotting the wire or merely seizing it back on itself. Sometimes they use wire clamps—notoriously unreliable fittings, especially when used singly. If these clamps have to be used, then they should be at least in pairs, and for deep-sea work there should be three on each wire, with the middle one reversed. There used to be a certain amount of excuse for not splicing the wire ends because the job often has to be done on the ship, away from the riggers' shop where special wire splicing vices are kept. But nowadays Norseman terminals can be used instead of splicing, and there is no reason for treating steering wire less seriously than ordinary rigging.

If the steering wire is rusty, this is a good indication that renewal is due. After all, most steering wires are fitted below decks and they work through sheaves which are heavily greased or oiled. The rust indicates that there has been neglect, and suggests that the wire is old and therefore very probably suffering from fatigue. Particularly bearing in mind how inexpensive steel wire rope is, the surveyor has every justification for condemning rusty wire.

On fishing boats, work boats and tugs, some of the steering linkage may be on deck. Chains running in channels down the side scuppers or rods extending along the sides of the aft deckhouse are seen on older craft. All this equipment is hard to keep properly lubricated because rain and seas coming aboard wash away grease. If the channels containing these steering linkages are covered over it is important to have them opened up for a full inspection. A quadrant on deck with a grating over it is another feature seen on these types of ship. The gratings have to be well secured to prevent them being washed overboard, and the result is usually an unpleasant mechanical mess redolent with rust, wear and grime. The whole area tends to be vastly inaccessible and usually merits a page of closely spaced writing in the surveyor's notebook.

A simple tiller might seem a pretty safe piece of equipment. In fact, the history of ocean cruising is littered with cases of tillers breaking off short. For deep-sea work a tiller has to be truly massive, and if in doubt steel stiffening plates on top and bottom or on each side should be specified.

Tillers tend to chafe on the underside where they rub against the cockpit coaming. They should be checked for sloppiness, particularly on racing boats. It is quite usual to see weathered and blackened tillers, and in theory this is not a serious defect, but a tiller is a particularly prominent part of a boat and it is a sign of poor maintenance if this item is neglected. It is easy to look after, and if it has been neglected it is a good indication that the whole boat has not been given her fair share of kindness.

Steel tillers should be checked at the neck where the fork is secured, especially if there is a weld there. Aluminium tillers have a poor history, particularly offshore. If there is any doubt about their strength the rudder blade should be secured and the tiller lent against with a degree of firmness which simulates a bad sea breaking against the rudder blade.

Emergency tillers tend to be forgotten for years on end. As a result, when they are needed they sometimes do not fit because of rust or damage to the stock head or the tiller end. If there is a screwed plate over the stock this should be removed and the tiller tried. As the key for removing this plate is often lost, the whole emergency steering system is in jeopardy. On power-driven craft it is not unusual to find that the helmsman cannot see when using the emergency tiller, and there should be arrangements in this case for a compass to be mounted near the aft steering position.

Deck Fittings

Equipment on a small ship's deck gives a further quick (but not always entirely reliable) idea of the general condition of the craft. Defects in deck equipment are generally fairly obvious, and they should be seen by crew and maintenance staff almost immediately. For the most part they are easy to put right, so there is little excuse for not carrying out repairs. As a result the condition of deck fittings gives an indication of the standard of past maintenance. It also is a guide to how hard a boat has been used, this being very clearly seen on inshore fishing boats and ocean racers. For instance, I have seen a seine-netter with wooden bollards cut three-quarters of the way through by the constant wear of warps, yet the crew appear to have ignored the growing danger that the wood post must any day break and as a result probably injure somebody, and certainly cause damage to gear. This just about sums up deck fittings: in themselves they are often relatively unimportant, but when one of them fails it can start a sequence which leads to disaster. An example is the fastening of a mooring bollard. If it is not secured through an underdeck pad, it is likely in the end to tear out. This will almost certainly happen when the weather is bad, and the craft will then go ashore to leeward. Unless she is pulled clear without delay she can become a write-off, for want of a single wood pad.

All deck mooring points should have a minimum of three fastenings, and these must be *bolts* right through the deck and through some substantial structure beneath. On small quantity-produced craft there is a tendency to use screws through cleats and this is wholly unacceptable. Cleats and bollards need to be sensible and practical in both size and shape; the surveyor is letting his client down if he does not point out that a sharp cleat can very easily cut through a warp. Where Samson posts and wooden mooring strong points are fitted the design must be such that warps, even if made of wire, and anchor chains cannot cause damage. Samson posts should generally have whelps to take the wear and chafe.

By the same token, the stemhead roller and other fairleads must not be merely adequate for moderate weather. Trouble arises in hurricane conditions. So far as possible, everything that floats should be designed to withstand force 12 in her own particular waters. A hurricane in a sheltered harbour will cause a 20 ft boat to plunge about very severely, and if she has no proper ears each side of the stemhead roller the mooring cable will jump out. Long before the gale subsides the mooring may cut through the deck edge and eventually saw down to the waterline. The boat will sink just as surely as if she had been caught out at sea. Stemhead mooring rollers should have keep-pins or some other locking arrangement across the top of the side ears so that the mooring cable cannot ride out. It is not unusual to find chafe on the side deck, very often reaching a maximum by the first obstruction (possibly the first stanchion or the forward legs of the pulpit), indicating that the mooring cable has previously lifted off the stemhead roller and ridden back along the deck edge. When this evidence is seen it is not enough to call for the repair of the deck edge: the basic cause must also be rectified.

Stemhead rollers in at least six cases out of ten are inadequate and badly planned. The majority are designed with the sole object of being cheap to manufacture, little thought being given to the crew who have to haul in the anchor chain, working on a wildly pitching foredeck, short-handed and tired, while the boat lies back on a bar-taut anchor chain. One of the penalties we are paying for cheap, mass-produced boats is a rash of minor components which are barely adequate for their job. They work as long as the weather remains moderate.

Stemhead rollers should be checked for wear at the axle pin and the roller. The securing arrangement to the deck also needs examining, and the whole fitting should be tapped with a hammer, mildly or strongly according to the type and size of vessel.

A surveyor should draw attention to deficiencies in the protective plating and coating of fittings. The surface protection itself is not all that important, but if it is not kept up to a good standard all sorts of troubles ensue. For instance, gal-vanised bolts which become rusty will flake and swell, allowing water to get at the deck edge and cause rot, or delamination or separation of the glass fibres according to the material of the deck and hull. In this connection it is probably worth recom-mending new bolts rather than regalvanising old ones, partly because it is cheaper, partly because it is quicker and partly because regalvanised bolts have to have their threads recut,

Plain steel fastenings were used to hold these rub-rails in place. Moisture has attacked two of the fastenings so that they have rusted and one has pushed its dowel right out; the other dowel is beginning to come out. Cracks have started from both fastenings, and the only proper repair here is to fit new rub rails with non-ferrous fastenings.

which often results in an early reappearance of rust at the threaded end.

It is a surveyor's job not only to prevent the occurrence of accidents but also to preserve the material and quality of the boat he is inspecting. For this reason he must point out defects in chromium plating and galvanising because if maintenance is not regularly carried out the condition and value of the craft will depreciate. Nylon coated fittings do not seem able to stand up to the hurly-burly of an active life afloat, and fairleads in particular tend to shed the nylon coating quickly. For hard-used fairleads the surveyor will probably be right in advising the owner to change to a harder-wearing material.

Stanchions and pulpits should be tested for tightness and strength. Here again we come up against the problem of fashion. It is now the done thing to fit very limber pulpits on craft up to 35 ft, particularly if they are power driven and above average in speed. The builder's excuse will be that he cannot put on heavier fencing round the deck, and in any case buyers would not pay for anything more elaborate. The surveyor should point out that the pulpit is a floppity affair and leave it to the owner and his crew to take full precautions against going overboard either singly or in groups, as assuredly they will if they trust these flimsy fashionable contrivances. A good pulpit is able to stand the surveyor's boot thrust firmly against the top. After all, this is no more than it will get at sea in quite moderate conditions.

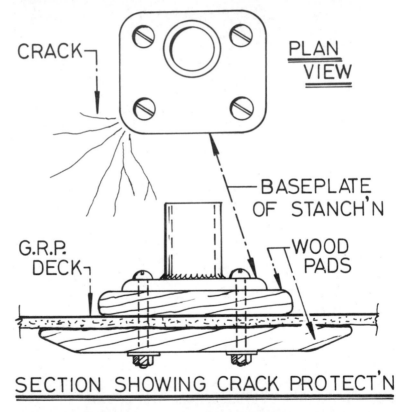

CRACK

PLAN VIEW

BASEPLATE OF STANCH'N

G.R.P. DECK

WOOD PADS

SECTION SHOWING CRACK PROTECT'N

Cracks in fibreglass growing away from a deck fitting tell an obvious tale. At the top is shown a stanchion base which has been pulled inwards so that one corner has cracked the deck. The bottom of the picture shows how this kind of trouble is avoided, with upper and lower wood pads sandwiching the GRP deck. Both pads have to be well bedded in a non-hardening mastic compound to give a watertight seal.

Stanchions should be spaced about 1·8 m (6 ft) or at the most 2·3 m (7½ ft) apart, since they will not offer each other enough mutual support to withstand hard use if they are too widely located. Each base should be examined for looseness at the deck, and checked for a split pin or other fastening holding the stanchion tube into its socket. With stanchions as with so many other components, the surveyor has to assess their size and strength relative to the type and size of craft. For instance a pilot boat should have absolutely herculean stanchions, at least 4 cm (1½ in.) in diameter, spaced no more than 1·5 m (5 ft) apart, each stanchion having a base plate quite 10 cm (4 in.) square with four through-bolts. The stanchions should be joined by rigid steel tubing, preferably in two or even three rows. The whole fitting should be quite massive even on the smallest pilot boat intended for inshore work.

Lifelines need to be inspected particularly at their ends, since this is where most of the trouble arises. Their rigging screws should be wired up or locked with split pins, not held by locking nuts, which cannot be relied upon to hold under all conditions. End shackles should also be wired up. Lashings at the ends of lifelines must be of Terylene (Dacron) or nylon, and need to be in multiple turns to ensure that their strength is comparable to that of the main wires.

Lifeline wires tend to fail due to fatigue, which occurs where the wire meets a stanchion. The frequent bending of the wire causes failure, particularly if the lifelines are made to turn sharply, for instance at transom corners. Galvanised lifelines are sometimes a happier choice than stainless steel, because they give warning of intended failure. As soon as rust shows, new wires should be fitted. The wire itself is so cheap, and these items are so important, that it is advisable to recommend renewal whenever rusting or crevice corrosion has begun.

If the plastic sheathing on a stainless steel lifeline wire is cracked or chafed away, there is a chance of crevice corrosion. The trouble with this type of metal sickness is that a very tiny area under attack is often more serious than a big region. If there is only a 1 mm square area open to electrolysis, the metal is eroded away just as fast as if there were a square metre under attack. Corrosion rate is proportional to the current flowing, and if the accessible area of metal is tiny the depth it is eroded can be startling. I have some bolts in my office with 3 mm ($\frac{1}{8}$ in.) holes in them which go right through the 25 mm (1 in.) heads. It looks as if metal-eating teredo have been at work.

When testing components like lifelines some care is needed. I once went aboard an almost new boat, lying afloat. The lifelines looked fine, but I leaned hard on one just to be sure. It gave, and only some quick footwork saved me from a ducking. I called for the yard foreman: 'Look, all I did was to press hard on this lifeline and it failed. Like this. Whoops!' The second one failed the same way, and I just clawed my way inboard without plunging over. We subsequently found that Norseman end fittings had been used with slightly non-standard diameter wire. Every lifeline was apparently strong till it was given a hearty jolt, when it failed with awful swiftness. The boat was just about to depart for a long voyage with an owner who sailed singlehanded.

Some surveyors draw attention to the fact that pulpits and stanchions are occasionally secured by screws. This seems a very reasonable warning bearing in mind that screws here are so much less reliable than bolts. On the other hand, other surveyors feel that this singling out of pulpits and stanchions is wrong, since all deck fittings should be through-bolted. All agree that there should be underdeck pads to take the nuts and washers, almost regardless of what construction material is used. Mass-produced small boats need special checking, since there is a tendency to omit these pads or to locate them carelessly so that some bolts do not pass through the pads. Another growing trouble is the omission of nuts or washers on some of the bolts. Some production lines are notoriously lax in this respect, so that it is not unusual on a particular craft to find two bolts in every ten lacking nuts or washers.

Handrails are often screwed down. They are easily tested by merely giving them a hearty jerk, first ensuring that the lifelines and stanchions will catch the surveyor if the handrails do not stand up to their job! Flagpole sockets too are generally screwed down. As the staffs extend outboard and are frequently damaged in locks and alongside quays, it is not unusual to find that the socket is sloppy.

Sheet leads need very secure fastening. Where a length of track is used, bolts are normally found except in those special cases where the track has to be right outboard and screws must be used since nuts cannot be put on. While it is not unknown for sheet lead tracks to pull right out, a more usual failing is

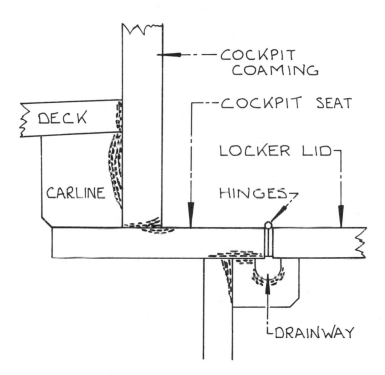

Rot is likely to be found wherever puddles can lie. Cockpit coamings are often subject to severe stresses, particularly where sheet winches are fastened to them, and this may open the joins slightly. Water gets into these small fissures and lies there, causing rot. The trouble is easy enough to detect in a drainway, or at the bottom of a coaming where it is open. But if the trouble has spread to a carline it is very likely to be on the hidden face which is impossible to see. Only drilling will show this up, apart from dismantling some of the structure.

kinking between fastenings. When this happens the sliding fairlead cannot be moved fore and aft because it jams at the kinks and the only cure is to fit an entirely new track. Naturally a larger size must be fitted, otherwise the same fault will occur the next time the same strain comes on the new track.

Mainsheet horses tend to give relatively little trouble except at their end stops. The modern style of X-track with roller traveller is regularly sold with light end stops which cannot stand repeated severe gybing. The slider should be checked to see that the rollers are not jammed and wearing flat.

Steel ventilators should be checked for corrosion, particularly near the bottom and at the junction of the fixed deck tube and the rotating part. A cowl vent which has become seized may be a serious danger, since cowls seldom have any means of closure and if they cannot all be turned away from the weather they may take in a great deal of water. On yachts it is usual to fit a water-box type of vent in association with a cowl, but even here there should be some means of shutting off the ventilator if the craft is intended for offshore use. The weakness of plastic cowl vents is that they become sloppy, and can fall off or get easily knocked off.

Surveyors are not expected to carry out a lot of dismantling work. For instance it is not usual to strip down the anchor winch or the sheet winches. The former will be checked to ensure that the pawls and brake are working, and that the handles are present, that they fit and that the winch works. Sheet winches should be tested for excessive wear, seizure and slipping ratchets. It is also sensible to examine the bases: make sure that these are properly angled relative to the sheet lead; also ensure that there is adequate built-in strength.

By the same token, the deck filler caps to the fuel and water tanks are relatively unimportant but they should be checked to ensure that they seal down tightly. A washer that has become over-compressed or a thread that has become worn or crossed will result in water in the fuel or in the fresh water tank. This could have disastrous consequences.

Deck fillers should be labelled in such a way that no amount of weathering can erase the vital word 'fuel' or 'water'. The sea is not likely to put more than a few gallons of water into the fuel tank, but an over-enthusiastic marina attendant may put in hundreds of gallons of water where only fuel is supposed to go. It may be argued that it is not a surveyor's job to give warnings of this type, but surely the whole purpose of a survey is to protect an owner's interests in every possible way.

Obvious defects in the alignment of light boxes and navigation light arcs should be pointed out. A surveyor cannot be expected to spend a long time making accurate measurements of the arcs through which the various lights shine, but he should draw attention to blatant defects.

Equipment for anchors should be examined, because if there are no chocks the flukes will damage the deck, and the anchor may shift underway. On even the lightest anchor there should be at least two lashings, and on large craft going to sea a minimum of four. These have to be man enough to withstand the craft being hove down 80° or so, because when a vessel is in this kind of trouble the last thing she needs is the anchors galivanting over the side, taking their chains with them! The new style of shallow anchor locker which is being fitted on the foredeck of many production craft needs a thoughtful look. Some of them have lids which are not firmly attached, and chainpipes lead into the locker. If the lid blows overboard the chainpipe is then vulnerable and may let a lot of water below, particularly as the locker will collect and hold a deep puddle of water. The anchor also needs securing in this locker, for safety and to prevent chafe.

Chainpipes are liable to lose their covers. The galvanised type suffer from seized covers which, when freed with too much energy, break at the pivot pin. While it is safe to assume that no boat ever sank simply because her chainpipe had no cover, it could be a contributing factor.

The arrangements for lifting anchors overboard are subject to a good deal of abuse, and it is not unusual to find serious defects in eight cat-davits out of ten examined. In particular there is a tendency to fit totally inadequate tackles, with no arrangements to prevent the davit from rotating when the anchor is being lifted. Without any securing arrangement the davit will swing from side to side, bashing the anchor against the ship's topsides as it emerges from the water.

Chainplates

Chainplates have to be checked to ensure that they have an adequate standard of strength. It is unusual for surveyors to carry out even basic calculations, the usual procedure being to look at the fittings and assess whether they are in line with normal building practice. As a basic rule it is widely agreed that the chainplates on one side of a boat should be capable of supporting the total weight of the craft. This is of course a rough guide, but for a variety of purposes it proves adequate.

Since strength is obtained by using the correct materials and adequate scantlings, the surveyor should draw the attention of his client to brass chainplates since these must be considered risky even on quite small craft. If galvanised plates are used, any serious rusting is dangerous and should be pointed out. With stainless steel there is always the risk of crevice corrosion. If plate material incorporating a bend has been used, fatigue cracking is sometimes found, usually at the fold. Bronze chainplates tend to be reliable except that the cast kind may have blow holes. If an examination of the surface shows the presence of blow holes it is logical to expect that they will occur right through the material, and the plates should be condemned.

The type and situation of the chainplates also require comment; for instance it is essential that they are correctly angled to line up with the rigging wire which is fastened to them. The

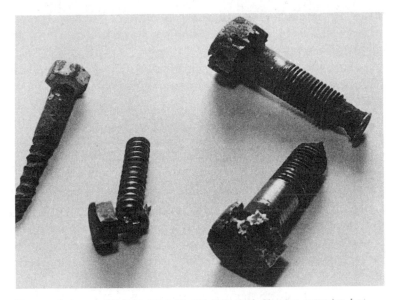

The two bolts on the right are both stainless steel. Crevice corrosion has attacked them so that the heads are honeycombed with holes and the thread ends are heavily corroded, in one case right through. In the middle of the photo there is a bronze coach screw which has a hole down the centre. No survey could detect this type of flaw since it is totally hidden until the break occurs. The coach screw on the left is a typical steel one which has corroded right away at the threads. This coach screw was used to hold down a WC and the usual moisture round the base has ruined this fastening.

'hairpin' type are generally good, but occasionally are fastened without any set-in angle. If there are three each side, it is normal for the middle one (for the main shroud) to be vertical; the fore and aft pairs require tilting in to line up with the lower shrouds. If this is not done, then on a small boat, under 8 m (26 ft), a toggle at the join between the rigging screw and chainplate may be adequate. However, on larger boats the chainplate must line up exactly whether or not toggles are fitted.

One may see a forestay fitting which 'girts' the toggle so that there is a very serious risk of fracture of the clevis pin (see sketch on page 183). Where Norseman terminals are used the chainplates should be sized to match. The limits here are fairly strict, so there may be a smaller allowance for wear. In any case wear should be carefully noted and recommendations made for renewal or repairs.

Where the boat is to be used for deep-sea work, the chainplates should be well spread fore and aft. Examples are yachts used for ocean cruising, or pilot boats with heavy masts which may tend to whip fore and aft in the short steep seas often encountered in estuaries. Unless the chainplates are spread well apart they have to stand up to very high loadings.

To be sure, on a sailing yacht, if the aft lower shrouds are spread well aft from the centreline of the mast the boom cannot square off as much as may be desirable, but a surveyor's job is to ensure the safety of the craft first and foremost. In general he is not concerned with racing results unless he is working on a racing yacht, and has had specific instructions to make recommendations which will improve performance.

The method of securing chainplates to the hull must be up to the best shipbuilding standards, since this is one of the areas where the loadings will be high. It is virtually unforgivable to latch chainplates onto the hull shell without substantial doubling or similar reinforcing. It is not enough to secure a chainplate to a strength bulkhead, because the majority of these bulkheads are less strong than the hull shell. Not only are doublers generally required on the bulkhead, but these doublers should spread the load right up to the deck and well down the bulkhead.

For the same reasons, the fastenings through the chainplate should be at least three in number, even on the smallest craft. If one of three fastenings in any way fails, this leaves only two at work. If reversing loads come on a chainplate with two remaining effective fastenings it will pivot and work itself dangerously loose in quite a short time. In any case less than three fastenings tends to put too high a local loading on each bolt. Where the hairpin type of chainplate is used there are only two nuts, one on each end of each leg. These must be properly locked and good builders fit locking nuts. But of course Nyloc, or a similar safety nut, may be used instead.

The rigging screw has worn away the top of this chainplate and careful inspection showed that there was corrosion here as well. It needs to be renewed or fully repaired.

Chainplates which have become worn, loose, or possibly show signs of fatigue cracking at a bend, need replacing. The method of doing this will often be specified by the surveyor. He has to remember that if a certain type and size of chainplate has failed, the replacement must be in some way better, stronger and more easily able to take care of the stresses involved. Because of the importance of these fittings it is no bad thing to make the replacements longer *and* thicker *and* wider, with *more* fastenings, than the component being replaced.

It is occasionally difficult to remove a chainplate because it may be glassed in, welded in an inaccessible location, or even bolted in place but suffering from severe rust. Under any of these conditions it is worth recommending that new chainplates are fitted without the removal of the old ones. Naturally a lot depends on the size and style of yacht, and the standard to which she has been built and maintained. Since the removal of the old chainplate will inevitably mean some patching up to cover the holes, it is often better to leave the old chainplates, thus saving a great deal of work, since their removal can seldom be fully disguised.

One of the most serious troubles associated with chainplates is leaking through the deck. It is hardly surprising that these fittings, being so highly stressed, cause leaks, especially when there is no guarantee that the line of pull is exactly in line with the fitting. In general it is not a good idea to recommend sealing the leak by using any rigid securing method. One of the most effective techniques is to bolt down chocks bedded in a rubbery compound such as Farocaulk. Using wood chocks and a non-hardening compound results in a flexible seal which is more likely to be effective than any form of rigid patching.

Hinged Hatches

There is a fashion for unsecured hatch tops. It is a natural result of the tendency among mass-production builders to cut every corner to save money. A surveyor may ignore this sort of thing, on the principle that what is common is acceptable, or he can remember that his job is to protect life and property. A hatch with a loose top becomes an open hole in the deck if the top is lost. Such a loss is most likely to occur offshore in a strong breeze, when there will be big seas running. Under these conditions the lack of any cover over a major hole in the deck is inviting disaster. If the top is not hinged, there should at least be a safety line well fastened to the ship and to the hatch cover.

Almost as important is the seal round the cover. A boat used inshore can get away with a leaky hatch, though it will result in an uncomfortable cabin. But offshore, when every wave sweeps down the deck, a poorly fitting hatch can let in as much water as a weeping skin fitting.

Cracks in a hatch may require more than a brief mention, because any repair needs to put in additional strength, since the original structure has proved inadequate. A wooden hatch top with drying-out cracks is hard to cure. Simple stopping is seldom the answer, so even if the hatch is an attractive teak one, it may be sensible to sacrifice appearance and cover the wood with a watertight material which will not react to wetting and drying like timber.

If the hinges are screwed on, test to see if these fastenings are standing up to the job. They seldom do for long. Even bolts are inadequate if they are not well spread out, at least three in each hinge flap, and none too thin. Hinges often fail when the top is thrown back too hard or too far. Some sort of backstop is needed on many craft to prevent the hatch top bashing into the anchor winch, or forcing the hinges beyond their designed opening angle. Sooner or later someone stands on the top of a hatch when it is open, and hinges can seldom stand this sort of abuse. It is a good idea, when pointing out the damage, to suggest a remedy to prevent the trouble from recurring.

To keep out both water and burglars, hatches need hasps or clamps. These are subject to many of the ills of hinges, and if they are found to be loose it is worth recommending that bolts be substituted for screws. On small craft in particular, many of the troubles in this area are due to using small fittings which may be adequate on mere cars, but are incapable of standing the racket afloat.

On hatches which bed down on rubber seals, the clamps need a screwing arrangement to force the seals down tightly. In due course the rubber perishes and needs renewing, as on opening windows and ports.

Locks, to be effective, are best fitted inside. If they are on the outside they should either be Yale-type locks or padlocked hasps. Hasps need to be secured by clenched bolts or concealed screws, otherwise the most inexpert thief will unfasten the hasp in seconds. The surveyor's second duty is to protect property.

Perspex hatch tops become crazed after a few years. The crazing itself has no particular disadvantage apart from its poor appearance, but it seems to be a prelude to brittle cracking. Glass on hatches tends to get scratched, but again this can only be criticised on the grounds of smartness. Cracks call for renewal.

Spars

It is not unusual to find six identical masts in one yard. There may well be sixteen more, closely similar. This makes it difficult to be sure that the mast being surveyed belongs to the yacht under inspection. For this reason the surveyor should always cross-check with the yard that he is looking at the correct mast, and as a further check the maker's name and mast number should be noted. Virtually all aluminium masts have the maker's nameplate, usually near the bottom and on the forward side. Aluminium booms and poles normally carry the maker's nameplate too.

The mast heel fitting must tally with the mast step, and this is a further confirmation that the correct spar is being examined. All this may seem rather elaborate, but there has been at least one instance of the wrong mast being surveyed, which might not have been serious, if only the yacht's own mast had not collapsed within a few weeks of commissioning.

Some light alloy spars have the boat's name 'pop-marked' on the heel casting; others have the name chalked, usually near the heel; and in the best conducted yards it is usual to paint the yacht's name on the heel.

The boom gooseneck fitting must match the fitting on the mast, which is a further confirmation that the correct boom is being examined. In general the shade of anodising on booms will be comparable to that on the mast, though this is by no means a definite identification.

A yacht yard's mast store is seldom a satisfactory place for surveying. The spars are jammed together tightly; many are high up out of reach, in the dark recesses of the dusty eaves of the main shed. Even if the surveyor can get to the spar he cannot see more than glimpses of it. The only way to carry out a full mast or boom inspection is to have the spar lifted down and laid on a proper bench, which is carefully aligned and has multiple supports. The spar is then examined from top and bottom to see if it has any permanent bends. It is next turned 90° to see if it was lying in such a way that the bend was taken out by the weight of the spar. Squinting along the length will also show up other defects, such as the misalignment of the track, spreaders, or fittings.

A highly stressed racing mast is expected to be perfect in every respect, whereas a rugged cruising mast is designed to take a certain number of knocks and may be acceptable even if it shows signs of wear and tear. On craft used for particularly hard voyages, the spars have to be particularly rugged, and in theory can be accepted with defects which would not be tolerated in an inshore racing boat. However, no vessel should set off on a long voyage with any defects which can be put right, and therefore a very rugged mast must sometimes be condemned even though it shows relatively minor defects. This is a typical surveyor's dilemma, and it is often best solved by simply listing the defects and leaving the final. decision to the owner. Some surveyors are prepared to make verbal suggestions which they will not commit to paper, but the more experienced take care that their suggestions, in a difficult situation like this, are neither witnessed nor recorded.

Whatever the type of spar, all fittings should be rigidly secured. This applies not only to the metal tangs but also to winches, and above all the cleats. The base of the mast track should have some device to prevent slides coming out when the mainsail is dropped, while each end of the boom should have a properly designed strong-point capable of withstanding the pull of the mainsail tack and clew. In particular, the outer end fitting should be capable of taking both the horizontal pull when the sail is hauled taut, and the almost vertical pull in service.

Aluminium Spars

In general, the tubes from which aluminium spars are made do not give much trouble. Slight regular undulations across the length of the tube are due to a mild defect during the rolling process, part of the manufacture when a round tube is made oval. This irregularity is usually quite subtle, and though it might be noted it is generally not considered more than unsightly. It does not appear to affect the strength of the spar.

A definite dinge is serious, and it usually indicates that the spar has been dropped heavily across a steel bar or some similar hard material. Because the components and tubes which make up aluminium spars are normally rather thin, and are made with relatively small factors of safety, any really noticeable defect like a dent must be treated as serious and fully repaired. The mast makers are usually the best people to approach for recommendations as to the best repair.

Small masts, such as those fitted to dinghies or day boats, can be bent straight if they have become slightly bent. A bend up to about 5° can be removed by supporting the spar with the bend upwards, on two sawing horses. Gently but firmly, the spar is bounced downwards until the bend is removed. Naturally this is only done with great care, the sawing horses being well padded. It will not normally be done to a spar used in the top flight of keen racing.

Where a spar is made up of two lengths with a sleeve inside, usually the butt joint will be riveted without any welding. Ideally the butt should be perfect, with the ends of the two adjoining tubes mating exactly. In practice, discrepancies which by fine engineering standards are quite serious seem to be tolerable. However, heavily stressed racing spars or masts on boats used for extensive deep-sea cruising should not have this type of defect.

Welds at both joins in tubes and where fittings are welded on should be carefully scrutinised. Aluminium welds tend to fail from the ends inwards. There is a growing practice of welding parts to the masthead using aluminium components where formerly stainless steel was used. Wherever a highly stressed component comes to an abrupt end, it is important to look for welding failures.

The whole length of each spar should be examined for corrosion. Danger points on masts are the heel and at any fitting. However, the most likely location for corrosion of the main tube is under the mast coat. Where a mast is standing, the coat should be removed completely so that the surveyor can get a good view all round. Corrosion is common at the heel fitting, particularly if the mast step has no drain so that the heel stands in a permanent puddle.

When corrosion is seen on an aluminium spar the depth and extent of the attack should be compared with other punctures in the tube. If the corrosion is equivalent to two sets of rivets for cleats, the trouble is not serious, particularly if the mast actually has two adjacent cleats riveted on. But if the fault is twice the weakness caused by two sets of rivet holes the time has come to suck the teeth and make suggestions like 'Do not use this spar outside sheltered waters, or in winds over force 6, or without reefing over force 5 . . .' and similar frightening innuendo.

If corrosion or pockmarks are found in a more or less continuous line right round the spar the trouble is not to be dismissed. Scraping the gritty deposit will show the depth of the erosion, and if it is anything like a quarter of the metal's thickness renewal is essential. On a racing boat quite a modest sign of corrosion is a shrieking warning, calling for a new mast immediately.

Loose rivets should be drilled out and replaced with larger ones. If two rivets in a cleat are loose, all four should be replaced. Of course rivets do not co-operate conveniently. They grow a sandy white deposit, hinting at horrors without actually showing blatant signs to help the surveyor. A few moments delving with a survey spike or some gentle tapping will often show that the rivet is about to become loose, so that it is due for boring out and replacing. It is the old story: preventive maintenance is vastly cheaper and easier than repair work. Maintenance always pays for itself by keeping insurance premiums down, quite apart from conferring peace of mind.

If the anodising has become chafed or been scratched off this should be noted, since it means that the mast's protective coating has been taken off and corrosion will begin as soon as the weather can get at the spar. Aluminium corrosion takes the form of a white grit and pockmarks. The grit itself is not particularly serious but the pockmarks are, especially when they start to penetrate deeply into the metal.

Most aluminium spar troubles are at the fittings, not in the tubes. Each fitting should be examined for cracks and also to ensure that it is tightly secured to the mast. Stainless steel tangs sometimes get bad cracks, particularly at joins and bends. I once came across a sensational case of this trouble when surveying a large motor-sailer in Palma. It was my first visit to the harbour so I had the paid hand pull me up on the main halliard to the masthead. On the way up I admired the view without taking much note of the spar. It was only when I got to the top that I found that every tang had severe fatigue fractures on both sides. I very promptly requested the paid hand to lower me down to the first crosstrees, where I found the same trouble repeated. Likewise at the lower crosstrees, almost every tang had the same trouble—a pair of fatigue cracks at the point where the stainless steel was bent out away from the mast into the line of the shrouds. What had happened was that this boat travelled considerable distances under power. All the time the engine was running, the wire stays vibrated, forcing the tangs backwards and forwards at high speed over a minute arc, just enough to start cracking.

Certain types of tang are supported by a single bolt which allows them to pivot. It is important to make sure that the pivot has not become worn or sloppy.

The track should be checked to make sure that it is tight and straight. Rivet spacing should not be much over 75 mm (3 in.), and there should be some form of stop at the top to prevent the upper slide riding off.

A good motto is 'When in doubt, consult the makers', especially if there are signs of trouble on something like an aluminium mast. There are not many firms making alloy spars, so it is roughly true to say that each firm will be supplying perhaps fifty boatbuilders. As a result each spar maker must have an annual production of about fifty times the number of boats which are produced by the average builder. Spar makers are therefore gaining experience much faster than boatbuilders. This argument applies to other specialist equipment manufacturers.

The industry is tending to have more component manufacturers each year. My experience is that this type of firm is co-operative, and interested in knowing about things that go wrong. If they get a precise description of the trouble, ideally with photos, they can often suggest remedies based on past experience and their knowledge of the equipment.

Wood Spars

Virtually all spars are now made of aluminium alloy. This has been so for several years, and as a result almost any wooden spar which is being inspected is bound to be old. Since wood spars have a fairly well-defined life expectancy, they are all suspect.

The most dangerous condition, rot, is the least common. It is found at the bottom, just occasionally at the top, and particularly at about deck level. Where a mast coat has been fitted, secured by a row of nails, the chances of rot are increased. The nails themselves are of course quite inexcusable since they weaken the mast just at the highest stress point. Rot is occasionally found at mast bands and at cracks and other openings. It is detected by tapping and with the spike, but when examining a hollow spruce spar of immaculate appearance the spike has to be used most circumspectly.

The most common fault on any wood spar is weathering. This usually shows up by discoloration, particularly blackening. It is an indication that the spar is ageing and has been neglected. Weathering takes place when the varnish coating has been allowed to deteriorate.

It is not unusual to find widespread bruising on wood spars, particularly near the bottom on the forward side when the craft has been used for racing. The butt of the spinnaker boom thumps into the mast, making a mess of the surface graining. These dents can be spread over several feet, and provided they are not too deep, also provided the spar has been carefully varnished each winter, a lot of surface bruising seems to be acceptable. Naturally, nowhere on a wooden spar should there be a dinge inwards which fractures the grain to any depth or extent.

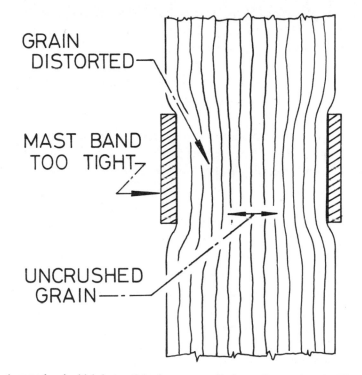

GRAIN
  DISTORTED

MAST BAND
  TOO TIGHT

UNCRUSHED
  GRAIN

A mast band which is too tight does not crush the surface grain only. The outer layers press in against the next layers, almost to the centre. Because the outer grain contributes most of the strength, this type of crushing is serious and often means the spar must be condemned.

Where mast bands are fitted, the grain should be examined to make sure that there is no crushing. This crushing is particularly serious since it extends right round the spar and the outer grains are displaced inwards, in turn distorting the line of the next layer of graining, and so on towards the middle of the mast. This means that in a horizontal plane virtually every single line of grain has a double joggle, one kink at the top and one kink at the bottom of the mast band. This is a thoroughly dangerous condition which virtually always condemns a mast if it is more than slightly serious (see sketch).

Compression shakes can be the most difficult defects to

discover. In a bad light, where the shakes are relatively subtle, it can be almost impossible to find them unless the surveyor knows exactly what to look for. (This is one reason why the experienced surveyor keeps his ear permanently to the ground. He tries to know of every case of dismasting in his own territory, together with as many relevant details as possible.) A compression shake is seen on the outside of the spar as a joggle in the grain. It can be extremely subtle, and it occurs on the inside of the bend, where an excessive strain comes on the mast. As a result it occurs on the starboard side if a port side shroud parts. Assuming that the mast does not break when this occurs, the windward side of the mast is stretched and the leeward side compressed. The mast may spring back when the boat is luffed into the wind, but the chances are that the spar will have a slight permanent bend towards the side opposite the shroud failure. It is this slight bend which sometimes leads the surveyor to find compression shakes.

Bends in wood spars as a result of bad laying up are fairly common. It is the nature of wood to remain in a given shape if set and held in position for long. If, for instance, a mast is laid along a bench with a chock in its middle 1 cm ($\frac{3}{8}$ in.) high so that the mast lies with a 1 cm bow upwards, when the chock is taken away the mast may be found to have a permanent bend if it has rested thus for four months. The bend will probably only be 0·5 cm, and not the full 1 cm, but a bend will be there.

A particularly common fault in cheaply built wooden spars is the excessive spacing of the screws in the track. This applies to both mast and booms. As a general rule, screws should not be spaced more than 75 mm (3 in.) apart regardless of the size of the vessel. When possible, screws should be tested for tightness and a screwdriver run up the track to make sure that no heads stand up. The joins in the track should also be tested for exact alignment.

All fittings should be tested to make sure that their fastenings are tight, that there are plenty of fastenings, and that the fittings are not moving or being pulled into the wood or diagonally sideways by an unfair strain. Fittings should be designed so that they line up with the direction of the shroud which is attached to them.

Another common fault is loose cleats. It is worth recommending that cleats be glued as well as screwed when being resecured. Also the base of the cleat must be curved, where appropriate, to fit the round of the mast.

The sheave axles on the masts seldom get lubricated and as a result they wear away even though the sheaves are not rotating very much. By grasping the sheave and moving it vertically the amount of wear can be detected. Sheaves should not be able to tilt even slightly, otherwise halliards jam down the side. Sheave case wear is particularly dangerous as it also leads to jamming halliards. The surveyor will know from his own experience the best way to cure badly leading halliards, but it is worth remembering that the old-fashioned type of bull's-eye has many advantages. It is easy to fix, and even if it suffers a good deal of wear itself it is cheaply and quickly replaced.

Steel Spars

Small commercial craft have steel spars, and occasionally they are found on fishing boats and yachts. Where possible they should be tested ultrasonically, because this method is quick and reliable. Failing this, drill testing is advisable.

The ends, and hidden areas such as round a mast coat are trouble spots. Anywhere that water can lie should be tested. For instance, above a mast band there may be a fine gap between the spar and the strap. Water which seeps in will corrode the spar just where the stresses are likely to be high.

A fillet or ridge above a mast band may look like a line of welding securing the band to the tube. Hammer the paint away to discover the truth. What looks like a weld painted over may be layers of rust held together by frequent applications of the best ship enamel.

The lifting gear of small commercial craft will sometimes have test certificates. These are likely to be with the ship's papers, and will save the surveyor a lot of worry, always provided they are up to date. Incidentally, a browse through the various certificates relating to the liferafts, radio, anchor chains and so on may reveal a lot about a ship, showing whether the equipment has been examined regularly and recently.

Steel masts are particularly vulnerable when they are in enclosed steps. This is true whether the heel of the mast is on deck or in the bilge. Hearty belabouring with a hammer gives a lot of information, but to examine it completely the mast has to be lifted out and laid horizontal. Very occasionally a steel mast is fitted with a wooden topmast socketed down into the top of the steel tube. This is bad practice, and the wood is likely to have rot in it after even a few months. Extensions of this idea, such as tubular steel stiffeners on wooden spars, are just as likely to cause trouble.

Steel goosenecks and similar moving parts wear fast. Paint or galvanising is ground off the first time they move under load. Rust starts right away, and it is chafed off whenever further movement takes place. For instance, a derrick may seem well secured, but be able to swing two degrees when the boat rolls at sea. This results in constant wear abetted by rusting. The speed with which a metal-to-metal contact can wear is astonishing. I have seen the $\frac{3}{4}$ in. thick steel eye at the bottom of a fishing boat's rod forestay ground away to little more than $\frac{1}{8}$ in. The shackle through the eye was in a similar condition, and these parts had chafed each other away between surveys. This forestay supported the mast, which was used both for fishing and for off-loading the catch. The crew, as usual, worked as a tightly-knit group on deck, so the falling mast could have wiped out the entire crew apart from the helmsman, if it had been left a few weeks longer.

Standing Rigging and Rigging Screws

When looking at standing rigging it is important to consider the type of craft being inspected. Quite different standards apply. For instance, on fishing boats and small commercial craft it is usual to fit very heavy standing rigging and accept lower standards generally. Cruising yachts used to be fairly heavily rigged when built on traditional lines, but the modern tendency is to production-line these boats in factories. This has resulted in a new approach to rigging, the main criterion being cost. As a result a large number of small cruisers are rigged down to a bare minimum, and plenty are not completed with an adequate standard of safety for hard seagoing work.

Racing craft are naturally built with the smallest factor of safety which the designer feels he can get away with. As a result even quite small defects on racing craft means that the damaged component must be replaced.

The rigging should be up to a good standard specification, such as that of Norseman Ropes Ltd, of Bridge Road, Sarisbury Green, Southampton, England.

When examining stainless steel rigging a brown staining is sometimes found. In general this is not important, and it may be either a mild surface corrosion or preservative oil on the wire. Corrosion of stainless steel wire and end fittings in the form of pitting is extremely serious, and even if found to quite a small degree, calls for total renewal. Stainless steel wire also develops hair cracks which are difficult to discover without the help of a magnifying glass.

Galvanised wire has the agreeable habit of giving everyone due warning when it is coming to the end of its useful life. It displays ever-increasing signs of rust, which works up from the bottom. When the rust is quite slight the wire almost always has another year's use in it, and a widespread practice is to turn the wire end-for-end to give it an extra season or two.

When any wire starts to put out 'gashers' it is time to start renewing. A 'gasher' is a strand of wire which has parted and stands out, so that anyone who slides his hand over the wire gets a knife-cut through the flesh. A single parted strand may not be serious, but having found one, careful examination will show that others exist. This is a sure sign that the wire is due for renewal.

Kinks in wire are bad. In galvanised wire a noticeable kink very often means that the wire is weakened but will go on doing its job on a safely rigged cruiser or commercial vessel. This assumes that there are no parted strands at the kink. Stainless steel wire which is kinked should be condemned, although a mild kink on a thick wire might be tolerated on a vessel which only works in sheltered waters. Even the mildest kink in rod rigging is not acceptable and calls for renewal.

It is generally considered part of the normal fitting-out process to strip off some serving from various splices at the ends of shrouds and stays to examine the condition under the covering; it is likewise usual to look inside a sample selection of Norseman terminals. However, a surveyor working under special instructions, possibly from a buyer who wants to go far offshore, may also do this. This is not really a borderline case; it is quite clearly part of fitting out. A really badly made splice can be detected through the serving. It is necessary to differentiate between a splice which is made ineptly, but has ample length with strength, and a splice which is about to fail. Much the same applies to Norseman terminals. Occasionally one is seen which looks messy, but if it has been proved by time and gales it *may* be reliable even if the wires do not seem to lie tidily.

Norseman end fittings are fully examined by unscrewing, to look at the arrangement of the wires inside the main body of the fitting. The wire ends should all be the same length and should lie in a neat circle round the conical core, as shown in the Norseman illustrated guide for riggers. In practice, it is not usual for the surveyor to carry out this full examination, partly because of the time involved, partly because the terminals have to be held in a vice for dismantling, partly because reassembly is critical. If it is done badly, a terminal which was previously satisfactory may be made unreliable. For this reason the dismantling is done by a rigger, and the surveyor carries out a partial examination, looking at the wires where they disappear into the terminal, because this is where fractures are most likely to start. Provided the terminal lies along the same axis as the wire it is highly unlikely that the wire will give trouble by the terminal. But if the fitting has been secured to a chainplate which is not angled in line with the shroud, there must be a tortured bend somewhere, and it is most likely to be at the junction of the wire and the terminal.

The same remarks apply to pressed fittings. They need scrutinising at the top of the short length of sleeve because this is where corrosion and wire fracturing is most likely. Any hint of movement or looseness, pitting or crumbling on a pressed fitting calls for exclamation marks all over the surveyor's note pad. He has hit a jackpot, earned his fee, and should let the matter be made blatantly clear in his report. This is the essence of surveying: a single accident averted more than pays the surveyor's fee. Even a small accident afloat is expensive.

The cost of replacing wire rigging is normally quite a small item as compared with general fitting out. This is one reason why some surveyors give sweeping condemnations of any gang of rigging which does not seem entirely perfect. Another reason is that by tradition, in many small boat spheres, all rigging is renewed at every refit. For instance, thirty years ago, before the coming of nylon and Terylene, it was general practice on top racing yachts to renew every item of running rigging each year. Certainly rigging is so important, and the consequences of even small failures are so serious, that the rule must be: when in the slightest doubt, insist on total renewal.

It is also advisable to call for renewal whenever signs of patching and makeshift work are found. Just occasionally shrouds are found with short lengths of chain to bring them up to length, or there are bulldog clips instead of splices. Sometimes flexible wire is found among the standing rigging, and this should be rejected. The only occasion when flexible wire is used in standing rigging is for runners where these pass round sheaves. Here, of course, flexible wire is essential.

Rigging Screws

Wire rigging which is not allowed to deteriorate very seldom fails. Rigging failures are almost always caused by breaking rigging screws or shackles, or some other component; seldom is the wire itself the culprit. For this reason it is good practice to have all the components of a gang of rigging made one size larger than the actual wire. For instance, 8 mm wire might be matched with 10 mm rigging screws. For deep-sea cruising or on craft which lie jostling in crowded harbours, a further increase in size might be recommended.

In Norseman rigging the various components are designed to match up, so it is essential that the maker's recommendations are followed, otherwise the end fittings will not mate with the rigging screws, and so on.

The rigging screws and all their components should be examined for rust and wear. Clevis pins in particular suffer from wear, especially where the bearing surface of the chainplate is quite narrow. Signs of sharp bends, or fatigue, or one broken arm, are all reasons for calling for new split pins.

Modern rigging screws often have locking nuts, but these are not reliable. In particular, stainless steel locking nuts on stainless steel rigging screws have a habit of working loose, presumably because the material is so hard that even when a big spanner is used with energy, the metal cannot bite in and form a true lock. Rigging screws should be wired up or pinned.

There is one subtle fault which is occasionally found in rigging screws which can have catastrophic consequences because it may cause repeated failures before it is detected. This can be summed up in the phrase 'inadequate swallow' or

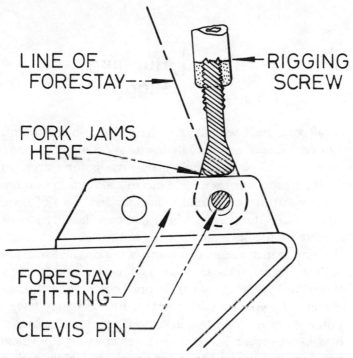

LINE OF
FORESTAY

FORK JAMS
HERE

RIGGING
SCREW

FORESTAY
FITTING

CLEVIS PIN

If the distance from the top of the clevis pin to the underside of the rigging screw fork is too small, girting occurs. The rigging screw cannot lie back at the correct angle, so it bends, or distorts the clevis pin, or gouges the forestay fitting.

'girting'. It is sometimes found on mass-produced boats, so presumably every single boat in such a class has this defect! Almost certainly the best way to cure this trouble is to buy or make up a specially long-jawed toggle, since most standard toggles have the same size of swallow as the rigging screw they are designed to mate with. The trouble is not easy to detect if the vessel is not rigged, but the signs are seen on the forestay plate and in the jaws of the rigging screw.

Running
Rigging

Natural cordage is seldom seen these days, on small craft. Its low price does not compensate for its short life and unreliability due to rot. The principal current use is for warps. Ropes made from grown fibres should be twisted open to examine the inside for shortness, internal breakages and signs of discoloration or rot. Natural rope which has been heavily stressed is elongated in the lay, and a pale washed-out look indicates weathering, which means that some of the original strength has been lost. Hemp, manila, sisal and cotten ropes might be summed up by saying that their presence on board or in the store should warn the surveyor that the boat may have been run on a shoestring, or may have been poorly fitted out.

It is usual to use Terylene or Dacron or an equivalent for sheets, for most halliard tails, for downhaul tackles and so on. For warps, modern usage recommends such cordage as staple polypropylene or monofilament polypropylene. Chafes and cuts are the main enemies of these ropes, and any serious signs of this type of damage calls for total condemnation of that particular rope. Polypropylene also weathers, a trouble which can be found by scratching the surface: where little pieces come away, the rope can no longer be trusted.

Sometimes rope receives a reverse twist, producing 'crow's feet', which are miniature loops in the individual strands. This reduces the strength by half and again total condemnation is called for. Sometimes the 'crow's feet' have been carefully removed, but they leave an unusual sloppiness or local softness in the rope.

Ropes which have been subject to excessive heat will melt and the fibres become damaged. The indications are signs of smoothness and flattening, troubles which sometimes occur when rope passes very quickly over metal so that friction heating results. Accidents like this have occured on winch drums.

Terylene and similar synthetics become fluffy on the outside, but this sign of surface chafing is not serious, and it appears to minimise further wear. Just occasionally three-strand rope will be found to have a 'long' look. This results from rope which is badly made up in the first place, or possibly from overstretching. In either case the rope is likely to be unreliable and should be written off.

For yacht use, ropes which have become heavily soiled with oil or dirt are generally unacceptable but on many commercial craft inevitably the warps get dirty and remain so throughout their life.

All splices should be examined, if necessary the serving being cut back to expose the tucks. Every splice should have at least a mating tuck and two subsequent tucks for *each* strand.

When examining the running rigging it may be desirable to distinguish between what is adequate in size for racing, and what is good practice for cruising. Small racing boats use very light ropes in order to cut down weight and windage, but this sometimes results in the crew needing gloves in moderate or bad weather. On cruising yachts, where a big factor of safety and easy handling are important, thicker ropes are generally favoured. For ocean cruising purposes a factor of safety between 20 and 50 per cent over normal cruising usage is good practice.

On all ropes the end thimbles must be tightly held. In itself a loose thimble is not important, but it soon comes adrift in service; the rope then has to bend round a sharp curve which results in breaking at a lower loading than normal.

Wire halliards on drum winches are forever in trouble. If the wire is about 3 mm ($\frac{1}{8}$ in.) in diameter it is worth automatically recommending renewal. The wire is cheap enough, and at this diameter, what seems like little visible damage actually reduces the strength by a third. Such thin wire is much more vulnerable than larger diameters because the individual strands are so tiny. It almost needs to be passed under a magnifying glass to be sure that there are no fractured strands.

Reel winches have a bad habit of letting the end of the wire go. The locking arrangements for holding the bitter end of the halliard need a pessimistic scrutiny. Part of the trouble is that some winch makers do not provide much to secure the wire. A single metal-thread screw tappped into a flimsy barrel is asking for trouble, and should receive it, in the form of a few slashing phrases in the surveyor's report. Nothing libelous, of course, just a keen line in innuendo.

Sails

A large, clean, open space out of the wind and rain is needed for examining sails. If the weather is fine there are often piers that are clean on the top surface, and occasionally convenient lawns. A big clear deck is sometimes a good place to survey a sail. The deck need not belong to the same owner as the sail! A mould loft can be a good place, but it usually needs sweeping beforehand. I have examined sails by spreading them out in a large office and extending them through the doorway into the adjacent hall. Church halls are good too, and in my experience they tend to be well floored and kept extremely clean. Added to this, there appears to be a choice of church halls in almost every town where boats are kept.

But, of course, far and away the best place to examine a sail is in a sail loft. The job can then be done with the assistance of a sailmaker, who in any case almost always knows far more about sails than the most experienced surveyor.

When judging sails it is necessary to temper the opinion to

the future purpose of the boat. What is wholly unsatisfactory for a Class II ocean racer at the top of the points list will serve for many seasons on a boat to be sailed by a careful, hard-up retired man.

The maker's name and the date the sail was made are usually logged in the report, both being important. It is usual to find the information near the tack, though some sailmakers do not always put their names here. The surveyor soon gets to know who are the best sailmakers, but it has to be remembered that good manufacturers sometimes turn out bad sails. Sometimes sailmakers with no reputation zoom to the top of the league in quite a short space of time. This is usually when they take on new management and new craftsmen.

Unless a sail is stowed in a bag it gets dirty, and dirt is a sign of neglect. If there are battens in a sail when it is stored away, this too indicates that the owner has not looked after his equipment.

Sails should be dragged out of their bags as far as possible even if they cannot be fully spread out. The corners usually give the best indication of a sail's condition. Ovalised clew cringles suggest overstretching. Chafe is usually greatest at the corners, particularly at headsail clews. If the sail has been tightened too much at the luff there will be indications of this at the head.

Chafing on headsails occurs where the leech fouls the shrouds. On mainsails, chafe tends to be heavy where the crosstrees rub. It may also be bad on the leech if this fouls the backstay. The stitching usually gives first, so this should be very carefully tested. It ought to be able to stand up to the harshest abrasion by a thumbnail.

The lashings for slides and hanks and spinnaker head swivels are particularly vulnerable. They should be of man-made fibre and show no signs of chafe, elongation or weathering. Because of their importance, and the ease and cheapness with which they can be renewed, there should be no hesitation in condemning any lashing or seizing which is slightly defective.

Even when the sail and sail bag have no date stamped on

them, it is usually possible to tell a certain amount about the age and history of a sail. For instance, different-coloured stitching shows that repairs have already been carried out. With age, Terylene cloth hardens and this is a sure sign that the sail is getting to the end of its useful life. If the luff wire shows signs of rust it can be fairly easily renewed, but where the rest of the sail shows widespread signs of wear and tear it is probably more economical in the long run to have an entirely new sail.

If there is a big tear in a sail it is usually best to let the sailmaker decide what action should be taken, unless, of course, the rest of the sail is clearly wearing out. Spinnakers quite often have multiple small tears near the bottom. These are seldom important, and a spinnaker can be perfectly satisfactory even though it has quite a large number of small darns and patches.

Just occasionally a sail is found with weak corners. There may be a lack of doubling, or at the head of the sail a cringle is occasionally put in with inadequate cloth each side of it. I have surveyed a whole suit of sails in which there was not a single reliable headsail even though they were all only a year old. In each case the head cringle had been hammered in at a point where the sail was so narrow that there was no adequate width of cloth on either side. The sail was designed so that the load of the halliard was taken partly on the cringle and not on the luff wire alone. As a result these sails tore right out at the head in severe weather.

In practice the great majority of sails need a sailmaker's attention, at least for local restitching or chafe repairs. Just occasionally a sail is found to be beyond repair, or so new that it can be used without any maintenance.

Testing Sails Afloat

Much the best way to survey a sail is to set it on the boat it belongs to, and examine the set with the boat underway in moderate conditions. If the sailmaker who originally built the sail cannot be present, then one who is familiar with the type of sail should be invited along. It will be usual for him to be given the job of repairing and modifying the sails he inspects, so the probability is that he will not charge for inspection.

Testing afloat in this way is unusual, partly because it is so time-consuming, partly because so many sales take place when boats are ashore for the winter, partly because few owners care enough. It could almost be said that sail testing under way is more nearly in the broker's province than the surveyor's, since a trial sail prior to purchase is organised by brokers when a demonstration of this type is required.

Incidentally, there are some regions where little love is lost between brokers and surveyors. The arguments used tend to be puerile but perhaps not surprising; the two professions are in opposing camps. A typical broker's contention is that surveyors kill sales by adhering to absurdly high standards, or by imposing their own personal preferences, or by having biased opinions. Some surveyors reply that brokers have been known to sell rubbishy boats to inexperienced innocents, compounding the crime by hiding defects and suggesting that a survey is not necessary.

Reverting to sail testing afloat: this practice is most favoured when a competitive racing boat is changing hands. The sails form a substantial part of her value and race-winning potential. However, as replacement of sails, or major alterations or repairs, can be costly, such examination is justified for any type of boat where the price is taken to imply usable sails. Shape and the fit on their spars can only be really determined by testing afloat. Some sail lofts have masts set up ashore, but these are no true substitute for tests afloat. Also, the majority of test masts are for headsails and spinnakers only.

In practice it may be easier to hoist and set a sail than to spread it out on a clean dry surface. The sail should be examined progressively as it goes up, especially on a big yacht; otherwise defects may be too high up to be seen clearly. A pair of binoculars are good for examining a sail, especially if used from a launch running alongside. However, this degree of inspection is outside the surveyor's normal work and would be carried out only if specially requested or arranged by the buyer.

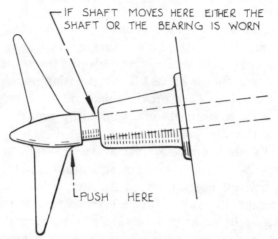

A propeller should always be heaved upwards to see if there is wear at the point where the shaft enters the hull. The wear may be in the shaft or the bearing, so the shaft is withdrawn for examination. This is a good time to check the engine line-up, though final lining up must be done afloat.

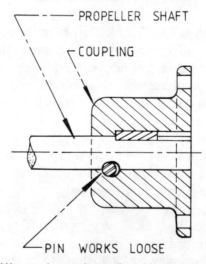

Propeller shafts should be properly secured to couplings with a taper on the end of the shaft and a locked nut inside the coupling. The cheap substitute which depends on a pin driven into a hole bored half into the propeller shaft and half in the coupling is dangerous because the pin works loose.

Systems

Engine and Sterngear Installations

The survey of an engine is a marine engineer's job, and in practice is not carried out in ninety-five cases out of a hundred when a hull survey is done for an intending purchaser. The normal procedure is for a hull surveyor to assess the quality of the original installation, note how much externally visible wear and tear has taken place, and perhaps most important of all, ensure that the mechanical and electrical equipment has an acceptable level of fire and explosion risk.

In almost every case the area round an engine is inaccessible unless the vessel is big enough to have a separate engine room. For the most thorough type of survey the engine thus has to be lifted out, so it will normally be sent for a full overhaul at the same time.

Standard of Installation

The surveyor has to have a knowledge of basic engineering and boatbuilding to assess whether engine bearers are adequate. As a general rule bearers are of the longitudinal type, and should be at least twice the length of the engine with a minimum overhang beyond the engine of at least one half the engine length. This is the very crudest of rules, and should be taken mainly as a primitive guide for anybody who has a shortage of knowledge in this sphere. Diesel engines punish their bearers more than petrol power units, and a check should be made to see if there has been a change of engine from petrol to diesel since the original construction.

A small engine, of say 5 hp or less, can be installed on quite short, basic bearers, particularly if the engine is a petrol one. But once size starts to creep up there should be good athwartships stiffening, in the form of brackets between the ship's side and the engine bearers. Telltale cracks in paint and fibreglass can be detected along the base of the bearers if there is inadequate athwartship strengthening.

Occasionally the bearers themselves are athwartship members, and in this case they should have some sort of fore and aft stiffening such as chocks joining the forward and aft bearers, except under engines of about 5 hp where the bearers may be adequate on their own.

Fibreglass bearers should not take the feet of the engine directly. It is extremely difficult to make such bearers accurate, and it is bad practice to grind the tops away for alignment. A typical good fibreglass bearer will consist of some form of hard core fully bonded in, not only on each side but at each end as well. To this there should be secured steel angle-bars to take the engine feet, bars which extend well fore and aft and have a minimum of three fastenings even on the smallest engine. If the fastenings are inadequate or are beginning to fail it is usually possible to detect movement between the metal angle-bar and the fibreglass.

On engines of more than 30 hp the moulding where the engine bearers meet the hull should be very fully carried out, with no suggestion of a sharp interior angle. The bonding should be continuous along the whole length of the bearer as well as fully round each end.

Whatever type of bearer is used, and regardless of the material used in the hull, the engine bearer tops should be of metal or hard wood. Examining the structure round the engine paws may show that the feet have dug in, or may even indicate very slight movement suggesting that either undersized bolts have been fitted or the bolts are slightly slack or have become bent. Holding-down bolts should have locking nuts and should not be deeply corroded. Coach screws should never be used to hold engines down. It is particularly bad practice to put this type of fastening through an engine foot into a wood bearer encased in fibreglass. Where coach screws have been used, the surveyor may have some trouble recommending a suitable cure. It is suggested that a paliative, but certainly not a full cure, is to replace the single coach screw by three or four. This is done by coach screwing down a metal plate on to the engine bearer top; on the plate is a welded vertical bolt to take the engine foot.

The stern gland greasing arrangements should be examined for accessibility. Give the grease cup a sharp twist fore and aft and athwartships to make sure it is rigidly secured; tap the fastenings through the gland face into the stern chock to make sure that they are tight and have not corroded.

If there is a remote greaser make sure the piping is secured firmly at each end and clipped up at 20 cm intervals. This pipe should not be kinked and it should be searched for cracks at any sharp bends and at the end junctions. The type of grease in the reservoir should be examined, and if this reservoir is awkwardly placed, stern shaft wear must be suspected.

The standard of installation is often indicated by the starting arrangements. The battery ought to be fairly close to the starter so that the linking cable, which must be of a suitable heavy gauge, is short. This cable, like all others, should be secured every 15 cm (6 in.) and ideally there should be an isolating switch on top of the battery, though this switch may be located elsewhere.

The hand starting should have ample room all round, with space enough for a man with a large hand to work easily. The surveyor should fit the starting handle, and in the case of a diesel engine put the decompression levers to the open position. Having made sure the engine is out of gear, it should be turned over by hand. Turning a petrol engine will show any lack of compression.

Wear and Tear

Many marine engines have a patina of rust, but generally speaking this is not serious until it reaches a point where the basic metal is chipping away. Exhaust manifolds are particularly liable to heavy rusting since paint will not stay on. Once the corrosion becomes deep seated, a new manifold is essential. Light chipping with a hammer will show if the manifold has reached the end of its useful life. Light tapping on bolts and nuts will show whether they are deeply corroded and need renewal.

The propeller shaft should be gripped and moved energetically vertically and sideways to detect any wear. If there is $\frac{1}{32}$ in. of wear, renewal is due. Where the propeller shaft is held by a rubber bearing, since the material of the bearing is slightly soft, it is possible to move the shaft minimally even when there is no wear. Naturally this amount of movement is not significant.

No propeller shaft should be unsupported for long lengths, where the engine is well forward of the stern gland. As a very rough guide, there should be a plummer block every 2 m (6 ft). There may be shaft wear at the plummer block, so the greasing arrangements and the type of grease should be looked at. It is also important to check the fastenings of the plummer blocks since here again coach screws are seldom reliable.

All coupling bolts should be tested for tightness by gently tapping with a hammer. It is not usual to put locking nuts on couplings except where the engine is a very high performance one. Gentle tapping of the keys in all the keyways will show if there is any looseness.

In passing it is important to remember that propeller shafts are occasionally installed undersize, particularly when the original engine has been replaced by a larger one. If in doubt the best plan is to consult the engine makers, remembering to tell them the material used for the shaft.

Engine alignment is checked by undoing the coupling bolts. However, if the boat is ashore misalignment is quite likely since

The damage to this propeller occurred in one summer. It was due to an electric current leakage which would have been halted if the batteries had all been turned off when they were not in use. The propeller must be badly out of balance as a result of this erosion, and the shaft bearings should therefore be checked for wear.

The blade sheered off this propeller in normal service. If the intact blade is examined carefully, lines in the metal can be seen exactly opposite the break, suggesting that the other blade is also weak.

the boat will settle and change shape marginally once she is put afloat. For this reason alignment can only truly be checked once the boat is afloat. Misalignment cannot be excused on the grounds that there is a flexible coupling since this type of join is only reliable if the initial line-up is accurate. If the coupling is broken when the vessel is ashore and there is misalignment of more than 1·5 mm ($\frac{1}{16}$ in.) for every 6 m (20 ft) of boat's length, the indications are that the hull is too flexible, or the alignment will be adrift when the boat is put back afloat.

Everything should be tested for rigidity; for instance the batteries should be so well secured that even if the craft is turned over 90° nothing moves. The easiest way to discover the efficiency of securing arrangements is to put a foot gently on the battery and apply steady, firm, relentless pressure. Fuel tanks should also be examined for slackness. Perhaps the most famous case of failure here was the occasion when *Bloodhound* had to drop out of a Fastnet race because her whole fuel tank broke loose and discharged its contents into the bilge. This is an instance where the cost of a pre-race survey would have saved about eight times the surveyor's fee, since the expenses incurred in putting a yacht of this size into a major race amount to at least that sum.

If there are any signs of wear on any of the drive belts of pumps, fans, etc., these belts should be condemned. They are relatively cheap, but if they break underway the engine becomes inoperative. It is important to double check alternator drives, because this type of auxiliary is often heavy on belts, since the same size of belt which has in the past been used on ordinary generators is now expected to drive an alternator which requires more horsepower to turn it. A rule laid across the diameter of the driven wheel on any auxiliary should exactly line up with the face of the driving wheel on the engine. If there is misalignment of the two, belt wear tends to be much quicker. The cure is sometimes the insertion of washers at the support bolts of the auxiliary item.

All the electrical equipment should be checked for corrosion, particularly if the item is located under a hatch, or anywhere else where water can drip down. Sometimes surveyors recommend waterproof 'skirts' or covers which are open at the bottom to protect electrical equipment from splashes and drips.

It is usual for surveyors to list equipment which is important but appears to have been lost. It is surprising how often engines with hand starting dogs have no starting handles, simply because they are heavy, so keen racing owners tend to leave them ashore for a season or two and then lose them.

Fireproofing

All engines and electrical equipment should be fitted in such a way that the chance of fire starting is reduced to a minimum. The Ship and Boat Builders' National Federation (SBBNF) recommendations are a good basis; they condemn horrors like plastic fuel piping. Filters should have metal bowls, not the plastic or glass ones which have become popular over the last few years. The fuel filler should be on deck and fully sealed all round so that any spilt fuel cannot run into the bilge. Fuel tank breathing pipes should discharge on deck, and not into the cockpit or worse still into the cabin.

The surveyor should note the number, type and location of fire extinguishers, and make comments on their external condition, including any renewal dates which may be shown on them. A good type of extinguisher has a dial showing its internal condition, and if this has reached the dangerous stage this is something to note. If a fire breaks out and licks around the base of the only two available extinguishers, it is going to be impossible or extremely painful to put the fire out.

Ventilation

In extreme circumstances, lack of ventilation can kill a crew, simply because the products of combustion from fuels include carbon monoxide which suffocates anybody on board. In addition, if there is no flow of air through the hull then various forms of damage ensue. In a wooden boat the trouble is most likely to be serious, resulting in various forms of rot. But even in a fibreglass or metal boat, lack of ventilation brings in its train different troubles varying from an increased rate of corrosion to spreading mildew, rotting cushions, unpleasant smells, headaches for the crew and so on.

There used to be a famous ocean racer which was forever in the news but seldom in the prize list. This was always a mystery to me until I discovered that she had an unusual ventilating arrangement which looked after the owner's berth and navigating area but did not feed fresh air to the rest of the boat. As a result her crew suffered from thick heads whenever they turned in, but their complaints were not appreciated by the owner. She changed hands, but her racing success did not improve since the new owner always used the same bunk, and always navigated, as the previous owner had. A good surveyor would have spotted the defect and pointed this out, so that the second owner at least would have been warned and his racing results should have been improved.

Ocean racers need particularly good ventilation because they have large crews and are driven hard to windward so that they get wet inside. The internal moisture can only be disposed of by free-flowing fresh air. As an extremely rough guide it is suggested that there should be at least one 4 in. diameter cowl, in a suitable box vent, for every two crew.

Much the same thing applies to craft intended to work off-shore. They need special arrangements which can be fully sealed in extreme conditions so that they are virtually submersible. In fact, for deep-sea work it is no bad thing to have a craft which can be totally sealed off like a submarine.

Inspection of metal cowls is likely to show that they have dents and cracks at the seams. In many instances it is cheaper to replace them than to repair them. Steel cowls tend to corrode at deck level, and occasionally an economic repair can be achieved by simply cutting the stem off above the corrosion, always provided that the cowl is sufficiently high.

The modern type of plastic cowl is rightly popular, but wears and becomes loose so that it can blow overboard quite easily if it is cheaply made. The best plastic cowls have screw in sealing plates so that if the cowl is taken off or blown off the hole can be blanked off by screwing the plate in position.

Mushroom vents made of plastic should be suspected; they cannot support the weight of a child. The vulnerable crossbars supporting the spindle sometimes break on one side only, and the damage can only be seen from beneath. Repairs are awkward and it is normally cheaper to renew the fitting.

To be effective, ventilation needs an inlet and an outlet. This means that every locker, every compartment, every enclosed space should have at least two holes, ideally situated at opposite ends of the space so that the cleansing, drying air blows the full length, absorbing moisture as it goes. This ideal is rarely achieved and when found is often an indication of either careful ownership or good original building. Examples are seen in the ventilation louvres at the top and bottom of toilet doors, slots in the companionway boards or doors, concealed vent holes at the end of settees and through concealed sides of lockers, and so on.

Lack of ventilation is easily detected since it results in mildew growth on almost any surface. It also shows up in the form of corrosion round metal fittings and electrical components, also little puddles in the bottoms of lockers, discoloration of lining and upholstery material, peeling paint and so on.

Electric fans are seldom a comprehensive cure to ventilation problems on small boats because they only work when there is plenty of electrical capacity, and this means for a third of the time when the crew are aboard. During those long periods when the boat is either laid up or not being used, electrical ventilation is seldom operative and is therefore useless. The fan motors should be flameproof or sparkproof and this feature should be noted on their manufacturer's nameplate. If no mention is made of the safety of the fan its name and number should be taken so that the manufacturers can be consulted.

Forced or natural ventilation should be ducted to below an engine space, particularly where a petrol engine is installed, to remove the petrol fumes. The fan switch as well as the fan motor must be sparkproof. The same need for safe ventilation applies to bottled gas installations.

Lack of ventilation is generally fairly easily cured. For this reason it is not something which condemns a boat, unless it has already done serious damage and the boat has other defects which stem from lack of airflow.

Plumbing

To make a thorough examination of all the piping and seacocks, as well as all the other components which make up the waterworks of a boat, it is necessary to take everything apart. This is not normally done for a survey, and if an owner calls for it to be done the surveyor will make arrangements for a ship's plumber to dismantle everything prior to the inspection.

It is fairly easy to assess the general standard of the plumbing installation by looking for such features as the neatness and uniformity of the piping, the type and location of seacocks, the quality of the basins and lavatories, the way these are fitted and so on.

The seacocks should be tested to ensure they are free and yet not too slack from excessive use. There should be a seacock at every pipe connection to the hull, even those above the waterline. A properly fitted seacock has some form of doubler or stiffener regardless of what material is used for the hull shell. There are a few exceptions to this, for instance a strong steel shell does not necessarily need a doubler, particularly where there is a good flange on the seacock.

All piping should be examined to make sure not only that it is in good condition but also that there are no leaks and that the material is suitable for the job. Soft plastic piping is not suitable for hot water, and if clear plastic is used for fresh water it should be the 'food quality' type. This has a faint mauve tinge which distinguishes it from the ordinary commercial quality. Plastic piping should be fitted without kinking and where it has to be taken round sharp bends, metal elbows or angles are needed.

Pipe clips which show signs of rust should be condemned

since they may not last another year. Once corrosion bites deep into them they lose their strength, and for most purposes it is better to replace galvanised clips with stainless steel ones.

Cockpit drains should be crossed except in the rare instances where the cockpit sole is very high above the water-line. The seacocks on these drains are almost always hard to reach and as a result they are neglected and often found to be seized. A seacock which is completely inaccessible is no use at all, and is as dangerous as one which is seized open. The surveyor sometimes has a choice of recommendations in a situation like this. Some seacocks can be made accessible by extending the handle, others need the handle not only brought up but also angled over with a universal joint in the extension. Occasionally, all that is needed is an access hole or panel cut at the foot of a quarter berth.

At one time there was a fashion for fitting lead piping in small craft. Among the techniques used, the lead was belled out at the end and the flange at the end of the pipe nailed direct to the hull. It is a miracle that this technique survived for a week. It looks risky and it certainly is. The fastenings through a lead flange seldom grip tightly, the lead corrodes, and it is soft and extremely vulnerable so that if anybody drops a hammer against it a dent and even a hole can result. Even on very well-built boats from top-quality yards lead piping with lead flanges and no seacocks are occasionally found, but whoever the builder the answer is the same: total condemnation.

Where possible basins and sinks should be checked to see if flooding back is likely when the boat heels or rolls. These fittings should also be given a jolt to make sure they are tightly secured.

WCs should be checked for cracking, particularly round the base flange, which gets damaged when the clamping bolts are overtightened. The holding-down bolts should be checked because they are awkward to fit. Some yards get round the problem by only putting in two out of the four fastenings! If steel coach screws or bolts are used the chances are that they will be well corroded. They should be renewed, because nothing is more disconcerting than to be sitting on a toilet which suddenly breaks from its moorings. The pumps wear fairly quickly and one result of this is leaking round the stem. The best models have glands which can be tightened and also repacked, just like a stern gland. The clevis pins and other linkages should be checked for wear, the seat and cover examined for cracks, and so on. If a WC has three-quarters of the possible faults, then it is sometimes cheaper to fit a new one than to repair the existing one.

There is one make of WC which is flushed by dropping the lid and sucking the contents out with a diaphragm pump. There have been reports of small children working the pump while sitting on the lavatory. The result could be dangerous. This suggests that the pump handle should be far enough from the WC so that children cannot reach it while sitting on the pan.

Tanks

All tanks, whether for fuel, water, sanitary fluids, lubricating oil or just gin, have to be examined for rigidity and corrosion.

Any tank should be able to stand the surveyor's foot pressed relentlessly against it from any direction. Regardless of the type or size of craft, the tank should not be able to move even a small amount. It is no excuse that a tank is very heavy, and that the vessel seldom puts to sea. In practice, craft which operate in well-sheltered waters sometimes go aground so that they heel over at alarming angles. Under these conditions no one wants the tanks to start charging about.

Heavy tanks should have some really rigid chocks or pillars to prevent them sliding forward in the event of collision or running aground suddenly. Tanks below a cabin sole should be chocked and supported so that when anybody walks on top of them they do not joggle sideways, or dent downwards on the top. Whatever securing method is used, it must be able to stand substantial reversing loads. There will be times when the boat rolls continuously, perhaps for days on end, and the contents of a half-filled tank build up a considerable swinging momentum. To give an example, if the tanks are secured to a carline or beam by lugs welded or brazed to the tank's side or top, the welding must be fully continuous all round. Any securing lugs on a tank should be examined very carefully for the beginnings of cracks, particularly at each end of the lugs. Where straps are used round the tank, they should be held by more than one or two screws. Even a two-gallon tank cannot safely be suspended from a pair of screws at each end of two straps.

Metal straps around a light tank of brass or copper, or round a fibreglass tank, must be well padded. The padding between the strap and the tank may be wood, but a more usual material is a felt, and occasionally plastic is used. Whatever padding material is inserted, it must be of sufficient length, width and thickness so that no part of the metal strapping can touch the tank. If a metal strap is against a tank, look for local denting and the beginnings of weld failure.

The tank support should not depend on the pipes, though the filling pipe of a small tank may give a useful additional support. In general, the tank must be designed so that it could move marginally, relative to the vessel, without imposing a strain on any of the pipes leading from the tank.

The location of a tank can be important. For instance, no drinking water tank should ajoin a fuel tank or oily sump, and there should be at least two barriers between any freshwater tank and any sewage tank. Water tanks should not be near exhaust pipes or other sources of heat.

Fuel tanks, particularly those holding petrol, should never be placed so that they feed by gravity to the engine. There are a few exceptions to this, since some small engines depend on a gravity feed. In such a case the fuel tank should not exceed two gallons in capacity, and must have a shutoff cock right under the tank. Sometimes this cock is inaccessible, in which case there should be a second cock, located away from the engine, which can be shut quickly in the event of a fire or risk of fire in the engine space.

The SBBNF book on the construction of small craft only applies to boats up to 20 ft. However, their requirements relating to fuel tanks apply to all sizes of craft.

The material from which a tank is made can be important. For instance, copper or galvanised iron or steel should never be used for diesel fuel. Fuel tanks made from fibreglass should be of a self-quenching resin to British Standard BSS 476, or an equivalent. An obvious trouble from a surveyor's point of view is that merely looking at a tank or scratching away the paint surface will not tell him what GRP material has been used. A certificate from the manufacturer, proving conclusively what the material of the tanks is, may be required.

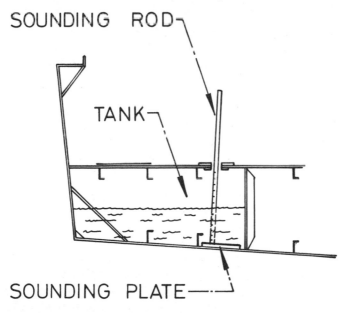

If no sounding plate is fitted in a steel tank it is likely that there will be a lot of corrosion where the sounding rod strikes the bottom of the tank. It is important to examine this area as well as any bottom corners of tanks because this is where corrosion is most likely.

In the same way, it can be extremely difficult to discover whether baffles have been fitted in a tank. In theory it is only necessary to tap the sides of the tank, starting from aft and working forward, and listen to the different sound responses. However, what may appear to be quite clearly a baffle, judging by the dull thump instead of the more vibrant ring, may in fact be nothing more than an internal stiffening bar and not a full baffle right across the tank. Some of the more immoral tank makers put in baffles which are nothing more than wide bands of any scrap metal they happen to have lying around. On a welded tank these show on the outside of a tank, indicating the presence of some internal structure, but only by removing the tank doors and looking inside can the full extent of the tank maker's iniquity be discovered. A baffle, to be any good, must occupy about four-fifths of the height and width of the tank to prevent the fluid surging.

In a major survey it is usual to remove tank access doors, but when examining craft under 15 m (50 ft) or so it is not the universal practice. A lot depends on the instructions from the client to the surveyor, and also the proposed use and past life of the boat.

Tank piping

Most tanks are filled through a screw-down cap at deck level. If the deck opening is not connected to the tank by a continuous pipe any spillage or overfilling of the tank will run into the bilge. This does not much matter when water is being taken on board, but for petrol it is dangerous, and smelly if nothing worse in the case of diesel.

When looking at the deck filler the screw thread should be

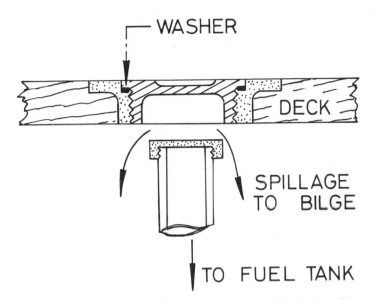

WASHER

DECK

SPILLAGE
TO BILGE

TO FUEL TANK

A common cause of petrol explosions in the bilge is spilt fuel. When filling the tanks it is easy to let some dribble down the side of the filler pipe if there is a gap below the deck. Overfilling the tank is even more serious with this type of installation. The cure is to have a filler pipe which extends right to the deck, so that the pipe cap and deck plate are all one.

examined to see how watertight it is. A poor seal here will allow any seawater or rain running along the decks to dribble into the tank. Washers become compressed hard, and therefore almost useless. It is usual to label deck fillers, and the labels may need checking. I once found a diesel filler clearly marked 'Gasoline', a word which means petrol in most languages. The engine in the boat was a diesel!

In theory, a *small* tank does not need an air pipe, merely a small air hole at the top of the filler. This practice is even countenanced if not actually recommended by the SBBNF. However, it is not entirely satisfactory since the very small pinhole can get bunged up, causing an airlock. Alternatively, the hole may be too big and water driblets find their way through. A far better system is to have a proper air pipe twice the diameter of the fuel takeoff pipe. It should be led to a safe position high up above the main weather deck and turned over in a swan neck with a gauze on the end. In practice this is not always possible, particularly on small craft. Surveyors have to use their experience to judge how well the builder has got round the problem of providing an air inlet to the tank in such a way that water does not go where only air should.

Air pipes on freshwater tanks present fewer problems. They need not be taken up above the weather deck, but they should still be turned through 180° to prevent dirt and dust getting in. They should be led well above the tank level, otherwise they will let water out when the boat heels or rolls heavily.

All piping from tanks should be checked for leaks and security. There should be no sags or looseness in any pipe, so fairly closely spaced strong clips are essential. Pipes must not be asked to bridge gaps without support, and if one does it is worth looking at each end of the pipe where it lands. If anybody *can* put a foot on an exposed pipe, be sure they *will* at some time in the boat's life. It may be necessary to unscrew the clips at each end of an exposed length of pipe to see the back of the pipe for kinks, cracks or nicks.

It is not usual for surveyors to dismantle filters, unless the survey is a very extensive one or the owner asked for it. However, where the tanks are of GRP and there is evidence (anywhere on the boat) of poor resin application, look at the insides of the filters. A badly made GRP tank may give off glass fluff which clogs pipes and filters.

Any vessel used on severe service, such as a pilot boat, should have facilities for isolating individual tanks. It is not unusual to have two or even four tanks all led to one common supply pipe, but there should be a shutoff cock for each tank. Naturally the surveyor tests these cocks, and it is usual to find one cock in three seized tight, even on well-kept vessels.

‖ Equipment

‖ Ground Tackle

Anchors

With the chain, anchors form a 'long-stop' to prevent a disaster when the ship's motive power has failed. Anchors check all sorts of embarrassing situations quite apart from their main purpose of tethering the ship when she is not in use.

Anchor failures and warp breakages form a substantial portion of small craft claims. Insurance companies load the policies of craft moored in certain areas because the anchorage has a bad record, though in some cases there is strong evidence that the local owners are at fault for not using adequate equipment.

Part of the current trouble is that standard craft, both power and sail, are sold with only one anchor. Often enough this is a derisible toy. No boat except an inshore racing craft or a vessel used on very sheltered inland waters, or a dinghy, should have less than two anchors. It is a widespread and unforgivable practice among inshore fishermen and contractors to use boats with only one anchor.

Because sea beds vary, it is common sense to have different types of anchor. For instance, a kelp-covered holding ground is dangerous and only well-proportioned fisherman anchors seem to have the ability to penetrate the weed. A survey report should list the number, type and size of anchors, and possibly comment on their efficiency *vis-à-vis* local or intended conditions.

For specialised work such as ocean cruising three anchors are needed, and for craft over 12 m (40 ft) four anchors are not unusual on well equipped long-range cruisers. However, Lloyds only specify two anchors, and seem content to accept an inefficient pattern like the old 'Admiralty stockless'.

Lloyds lay down the weights of anchor they require for each size of ship. Anchor makers also publish tables of recommended weights. Some of these are wildly optimistic in terms of holding, especially those from America. This is proved by the number of craft which are wrecked when very severe weather strikes the American seaboard. The anchor makers excuse the holocaust by saying that a hurricane is something special. Of course it is, but ground tackle is intended to withstand the worst weather; that is its purpose.

A surveyor's job is to protect life and property. He knows that in any ten-year period there are at least two severe gales in most areas, and properly anchored craft survive these.

Because any body loses weight on immersion, and because anchors have to dig themselves in by penetrating the sea bed, certain conditions have to be fulfilled if an anchor is to work. The points should be sharp, and they should taper slowly. This applies to all makes and shapes. Ideally all anchors should be over 14 kg (35 lb) as below this limit the combination of immersed weight and fluke penetration is known to be unreliable in certain circumstances.

Anchors which show signs of damage or repair cannot be accepted except perhaps as reserves. The arms of fishermen anchors bend or break at the shank, especially if not fully swept in to a reinforced join. Danforths have thin deep shanks which have little resistance to a sideways force. Normally this is unimportant, but if the anchor is deeply embedded and an effort is made to haul it out at right angles to the line it went in, the shank is liable to bend.

Plough anchors have a tendency to crack across the broad

ends of the blades. They also have lead inserts in the cleavage, which means that they cannot be regalvanised without removing and later refitting this ballast.

Regalvanising should be recommended as soon as rust shows, otherwise the anchor will start to lose weight through scaling, the points will become blunt, and the ring will wear fast, quite apart from the poor appearance and mess caused by the rust.

Chain

To survey the chain it should be hauled out of its locker and laid on the ground, on a tarpaulin or duckboards. If it is ranged in zig-zags each 2 m (1 fathom) long the total length is quickly assessed. This length should equal at least four times the depth of water normally used for anchoring plus an allowance for the distance from the waterline down to the clench plate. Further allowance should be made for a heavy swell, since there are regions where this can add 50 per cent to the depth of water used for anchoring. The depth must be taken as the top of high water springs.

In ninety cases out of a hundred the surveyor will find that there is insufficient chain. This is partly due to the practice of selling mass-produced boats with a pitiful length of chain. Another reason is that there is a misleading rumour suggesting that only a scope equal to three times the depth of water is needed for security. Experience afloat and Admiralty tests show that four times the depth is a minimum in bad conditions, and six times in very severe conditions.

Chain link diameter is measured to make sure it comes up to standard. Galvanising adds about 1 mm ($\frac{1}{16}$ in.) so that a chain which seems to be 8 mm ($\frac{3}{8}$ in.) is actually 7 mm ($\frac{5}{16}$ in.) Measurements are usually taken near the anchor end as this is where most wear occurs. However, chain gets reversed to even out the wear, so it is advisable to measure near both ends. The end shackles are notorious weak links, so they should be inspected, as well as the clench plate. On small craft there is a fashion for drilling a hole in a 12 mm ($\frac{1}{2}$ in.) bulkhead, threading a single strand of light line through and securing the chain end with this. If a bulkhead *has* to be used, the surveyor can suggest suitable doubling, with the chain passing twice through the bulkhead. Final securing is achieved by lashing the chain end back to the length which runs up to the chainpipe.

As soon as rust appears on chain it should be sent for galvanising. Rusty chain wears faster than galvanised, quite apart from the mess that rust makes in the bilge.

Anchor Gear

On deck, anchors need chocks and good-sized unworn lashings of man-made fibre. A runaway anchor and chain can produce a spectacular disaster, especially if the chain ends up extending athwartships across the deck, bar-taut so that it cannot be lifted onto the anchor winch gypsy for hauling back aboard. On larger craft the chocks will incorporate some sort of metal hasp or locking device.

Cat-davits and their tackles are located right forward, exposed to spray and the weather. They almost always fail to pass survey, if only because the majority have no means of securing the davit so that it does not swivel by accident when hauling up the anchor.

Warps and Fenders

Warp inspection has been covered under running rigging. Typical lengths and thicknesses are listed in *Designers Notebook* published by Adlard Coles Ltd. It is often difficult to range warps out but they should be inspected in way of any lashings. A warp hung up for a long period is sometimes damaged by the lashing. If it is allowed to swing as the ship rolls, chafe occurs on the outer coils where they rub against the ship's side.

The number, type and size of fenders depends on the home port of the boat, as well as her use. If she is almost always on moorings four quite small fenders may be adequate. But for a permanent berth alongside a rough wall to here must be at least one tubby fender every 2 m (6 ft) and at least half this number on the outboard side. Commercial craft need a profusion of fenders because most craft of this sort spend time alongside quay walls.

Fender ropes should be about two-thirds of the warp diameter. Look at these ropes for chafe and lost end whippings.

Furniture

For the most part internal furnishings are the least of a surveyor's worry, partly because repairs arc normally easy and relatively cheap. More important, defects in the furniture very seldom affect the safety of the crew or the ship, although it is not too difficult to think of exceptions to this.

However, the surveyor's job is to protect his client's investment. For this reason he checks things like the length of the berths and the headroom over seats. If these are inadequate then the boat may need several hundred pounds worth of work before she becomes useful, and if necessary disposable on the second hand market. In one Folkboat I surveyed the longest berth was under 6 ft 2 in. Two were under 5 ft 11 in., and one was under 5 ft 10 in. As the average height of the human race goes up every year, this boat either needs altering or she is bound to be difficult to sell.

If visibility from the helm is extremely bad the surveyor

should note this, since this defect is just the kind of thing which leads to accidents, particularly when coming up to moorings or when racing in large fleets.

It is traditional to condemn cabin soles which are thoroughly screwed down; if the hull becomes even slightly damaged the crew cannot quickly staunch the inflow of water because they cannot get at the source of the trouble. Occasionally floorboards are so dangerous that anyone walking over them disappears into the nether regions. On one yacht I surveyed the floorboards were all fine except for one, and even this lay quiescent until some unsuspecting foot stepped on a particular point. Then the floorboard pivoted up with vicious effectiveness and smashed into one's face, much to everybody's merriment, just like the standard joke about the man who trod on the end of a rake!

A floorboard bearer which is screwed to a bulkhead occasionally has rot on the face against the bulkhead because moisture runs down the bulkhead and collects against the bearer. Bearers are often made of cheap softwoods which are particularly susceptible to rot (see sketch). This defect is found on all types of craft, not just those built of wood, because in many instances soles and bearers are made of wood even if the hull is of a different material.

Another trouble common to all types of hull regardless of material is the sagging floorboard which bears against a tank or electric wiring, or possibly vulnerable piping.

The standard of construction of a boat can occasionally be assessed by looking at the hinges. Brass hinges with steel pins are no good afloat because the steel rusts and binds the hinge. The best builders use large, expensive hinges because these items have a rugged life afloat. Loose hinges are a very common defect even on well-built craft, partly because builders rarely bolt them on.

Steel screws in drawers and lockers should also be noted in the report, since they indicate a low standard of building. Also they will show rust weeps sooner or later, and eventually the furniture may fall apart when the steel corrodes too far.

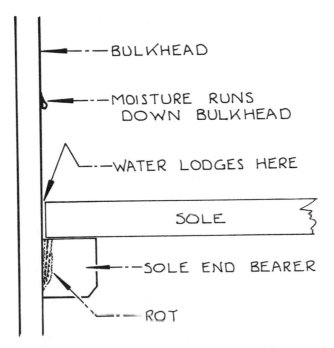

—BULKHEAD

—MOISTURE RUNS
DOWN BULKHEAD

—WATER LODGES HERE

SOLE

—SOLE END BEARER

ROT

A wood sole bearer made fast to a bulkhead is likely to rot, because moisture runs down bulkheads. The small crack at the end of the sole gets dirt in it and tends to hold moisture for long periods. This type of rot is found in fibreglass and steel boats as well as wood ones, when the bearer is wood. If the bulkhead is of a material which is likely to sweat, there is a particularly big chance of rot in the bearer.

A competent builder fits some self-securing device on all drawers and catches on all doors to prevent them coming open by accident. The best builders also round the edges of corners and generally make sure that the crew living on the boat at sea do not become unnecessarily bruised. One occasionally comes across a yacht, normally a big one, which has been fitted out by a shipyard, as opposed to a yacht yard. A notable difference is that the shipyard makes furniture with sharp edges and corners, just like furniture used ashore.

Virtually no boatbuilder puts adequate fiddles round shelves and locker tops. For craft going to sea a 75 mm (3 in.) fiddle is by no means too high. Even boats used on inland waterways should have fiddles throughout the furniture, because another vessel passing at speed will set up a fair amount of motion. Crockery which slides off the cabin table every time another boat goes past can be an expensive nuisance.

Doors and drawers which do not fit may indicate that the hull has been strained. Under a deck-stepped mast on a racing boat it is not unusual to find that doors have been altered, possibly planed away at top and bottom so that they shut even when the craft is driven hard to windward.

The modern tendency to use plastic facings such as Formica has a lot of advantages. However, a very hot pan placed on a Formica-covered board causes the plastic to swell up from the wood. Formica should be glued to wood after a pattern of holes has been drilled in the wood to allow air to escape. Formica which is peeling up looks bad, and because the plastic has a sharp edge it can be dangerous.

Blockboard is used for some furniture. Its edges should be scrutinised because when this material is used it occasionally blots up water and is prone to rot, delamination and discoloration. Wherever blockboard extends down to near the bilge it should be probed with a spike.

Yacht Tenders

Small boats used as tenders to yachts get very rough treatment, and as the majority of yachting accidents occur between the shore and the parent yacht, it is important to examine ships' boats with particular stringency.

It is almost always essential to turn the boat upside down to get a full view of the bottom and then the right way up to see all the inside. In a clinker dinghy cracked planks are fairly easy to detect, but cracked frames are not always so obvious. The most likely place for fractures in the frames is at the sharpest point of the turn of bilge. Just occasionally fractures will be hidden by screwed-in floorboards, or a stringer. It is probably true to say that almost any lapstrake dinghy more than eight seasons old will have at least one cracked plank and three cracked frames. In themselves they may not be serious, but the weakness tends to spread outwards, particularly where the cracks in the frames are in line.

Chafed keels, worn bilge rubbers and eroded metal bottom strips are in themselves not important, though they should be noted. If they are not repaired more serious damage tends to follow. Occasionally a metal bottom rubbing strip gets so chafed that it tears right off, leaving a jagged end. It may also leave a screw protruding which will get bent back and make an oval hole through the bottom. In the same way, chafed gunwales are common and in themselves not serious. It is the damage that will follow if they are not repaired that has to be remembered.

Thwarts should be tested for rigidity. If they are too flexy the topsides are not held properly and various troubles ensue, such as cracking at the edge of the transom. Thwarts badly secured will eventually work loose, sometimes leaving loose fastenings protruding through the topsides.

Far and away the most important part of any yacht's tender is the buoyancy equipment. In many GRP models there is only enough buoyancy to support the hull without the crew. This is totally unacceptable and should be condemned in the survey in capital letters. Plenty of wood yacht tenders have no buoyancy at all, on the mistaken principle that wooden boats float. They do, but only with the gunwales just above water, so they cannot be bailed empty except in a flat calm. Here, too, the surveyor should insist on full buoyancy being fitted, at least under all thwarts. Yachts' tenders should also have some hand-grips so that in the event of capsizing or filling with water the crew can hold onto the flooded boat. More yachtsmen are drowned because of flooded dinghies than for all other reasons put together.

From an insurance point of view parted dinghy painters are a major source of claims. If there is any chafe in the painter it should be condemned; likewise, any part of the painter gear, including the eyebolt through the stem, the doubling at this eyebolt, the joining shackle and so on should all be in perfect condition.

The yacht's name and club or home port should be painted on the yacht's tender, otherwise insurance companies can refuse to pay when the boat is lost.

Inflatables

The hull of an inflatable is made of a cloth which is impregnated and coated with an impermeable material. In time the rubber-like skin begins to come away from the fabric, so that the weave is visible. This is a sign of age and wear, and a clear proof that the boat is becoming unreliable.

The bottom of inflatable craft is vulnerable, seldom being adequately protected against chafe. If the boat is dragged even a short distance over rough ground the bottom shows rapid signs of wear. Even those boats which have pads and other forms of protection on the underside do not have a 100 per cent covering, so the weak spots soon show trouble. This bottom grinding is a main reason why inflatables have to be discarded.

Wear in the fabric is found at the edges of wood floorboards and adjacent to portable outboard fuel tanks. Wherever the shell of the inflatable is in regular contact with a hard component, trouble is to be expected.

A random pattern of little cracks shows that the chemical coating on the cloth is perishing. The appearance of this defect is like the crazing seen on rubber hose, and is just as fatal. If the glue lines are peeling it should not be too difficult to carry out a repair, but the mere fact that the adhesive is letting go is a bad sign. It suggests either poor original construction, or failing glue, or advanced age.

Inflatables are repaired by gluing on patches. The number and location of these gives a very good idea of the past use the boat has had. If the patches are peeling it is almost certainly time to throw the boat away, unless there is evidence that the patches were put on inexpertly. The main manufacturers of inflatables are jealous of their reputation and tend to take trouble over repairs. Peeling patches may be a sign that the wrong glue has been used, or that gluing was done in damp or cold conditions by someone untrained for the job. The cure is to send the boat back to the makers, who will give an expert diagnosis and not let a faulty boat leave their factory.

If the valves are damaged the boat will have to be junked if she is a cheap model. The better makes can have new valves let in, and the bronze valves which are liable to seize can usually be freed. However this is not a job which can be done roughly, as freeing oil will attack some fabrics. This is another instance where the makers are the best judges.

Inflatables are fitted with thin painters, usually ropes far too short for normal use. Any sign of chafe here calls for renewal because of the thin diameter of the rope.

There is a serial number on the better makes of inflatable which makes it possible to find out the age of the boat. These craft have to be considered almost as 'consumable stores', with a useful life of very approximately six years. Plenty last far longer, but the majority succumb at about this age if given the usual amount of neglect and harsh handling. If a surveyor has a mental list of the price range of these boats he will know which are built to a high quality and can be expected to last longest. The cheaper ones sometimes last a single season. A worthwhile test, which separates the sheep from the goats, is to inflate the boat before commencing the survey of the parent craft. If, at the end of the main survey, the inflatable is losing its plump look and getting flabby, something is wrong, and it should be sent back to the makers for their report.

Electrical Equipment

Echosounders, radios, generators and so on do not normally fall within the small craft surveyor's province. These items require a lot of maintenance, because electricity and seawater do not mix. It is usual for specialists to give annual maintenance to all the electrical equipment on any well-conducted boat. Some items like radar and Decca are regularly hired instead of being bought. The hire charge includes servicing, and in this situation a surveyor is seldom called upon to make any comment.

As far as the electrical equipment is concerned, the surveyor's attitude will generally be similar to the approach he takes to the engine: he will look at the equipment externally and assess its quality as well as the standard of installation. His own training and experience will let him see at a glance if the original work and maintenance have been to a good standard.

The sort of thing to look for is neat wiring secured with clips at 15 cm (6 in.) intervals, clips being of non-ferrous materials secured with non-rusting fastenings. All the connections, the insulation and such components as the junction boxes and switches should all be to a good marine standard.

It is quite usual to find that electrical installation is mixed. Often the original installation will be to a good standard but subsequent additions are poor. Sometimes it is possible to detect the reverse. Certain components are totally unacceptable afloat, including domestic and motor-car switches, light fittings, fuse boxes and so on.

A really good installation will have each item sited away from hatches because drips come through and get into the vitals. A well-thought-out electrical plan will ensure that no wires or components can be affected by bilgewater.

The next thing to look for are signs of wear and tear. None of the insulation should show cracks. This applies not just to wiring but also to items like deck plugs which have rubber washers inside and rubber seals externally. These washers and seals crack after a time and so become only partially effective.

If a vessel is to be used for severe service it is sometimes the practice to have an electrical specialist work on board with the surveyor. He will take out as many components as possible and test them 'on the bench'. In general hull surveyors do relatively little electrical surveying themselves. Electrical faults on a wide scale are so common in small craft that they are not considered comparable to structural troubles. Because electricity and seawater are such poor bed-fellows it is part of the normal annual maintenance to make extensive renewals and repairs to the electrical components.

The hull surveyor may examine the battery, but if the vessel is laid up the battery should be out. Its presence aboard is a fault. It should be checked to see if the fluid level is correct and the plates are free from corrosion or warping. The sealing round the top should not show cracks or hillocks, and the terminals should be clean.

Corrosion is the universal enemy. A sample of fuse boxes, junction boxes and other casings should be opened to see if the insidious grime growth has started. On deck the navigation and other lights should be given a gentle but firm shove, to discover if they are still firmly held. They seldom are, largely because there is never an adequate number, size or spacing of fastenings on small craft electrical equipment. It is the cinderella of the chandlery business, so far as adequacy and seaworthiness goes.

Arbitration

There was once a small but popular yard building successful cruisers. The managing director was well known, the boats were built to good designs and on the whole up to a reasonable standard. There were all the ingredients for a prosperous business, and from small beginnings the yard did better each year. But one summer the yard fell out with an owner over the matter of a propeller. The two sides argued long and bitterly and lawyers were brought in by both parties. More and ever more faults, real and imagined, were found on the boat.

The case went to court and was decided upon, but there was an appeal. This was contested so that the matter went on and on up through the courts. The legal fees soared to astronomical proportions and eventually the yard lost. Or did it? It simply went bust, so that the owner had to pay his own enormous legal fees and never did get his boat. All this battle started, remember, over a propeller worth less than the fee for a top arbitrator for one day.

There are plenty of people in the ship and boatbuilding industries who will claim that the business of building and maintaining small craft is so full of technicalities that it is far better to keep out the entire legal profession. They can detail many case histories to prove their point. The attractions of arbitration are that it is relatively quick, normally uncomplicated, and virtually always costs a very great deal less than going to law.

In other technical industries it is practice for lawyers to be called in first who then sometimes, but by no means always, call in an arbitrator. In the boat industry a short-cut is often adopted. The yard or the owner or whoever is in dispute with another party suggests arbitration. Provided the opposite side agree, no lawyers are involved and so the only costs involved in settling the case are the arbitrator's fees. These are split evenly between the two parties, as are the arbitrator's expenses.

One side of a dispute may wish to be represented by a lawyer in putting the case to the arbitrator, and in this instance the other side must be given the opportunity to employ legal assistance as well. In parenthesis, it is worth remembering that in any yacht club there are likely to be quite a few solicitors and barristers. It is worth considering seeking the assistance of a man in the legal profession who owns a boat, since he is likely to have a head start on anyone else in his profession who knows nothing about the intricacies of small craft.

A surveyor who is approached to act as an arbitrator should warn both sides that his ruling is binding to both parties. He works under the regulations of the Arbitration Act 1950 and what he lays down is equivalent to a judgment in court. The only way of appealing against it is to go to the High Court and show that the arbitrator's award is based on a mistake in law.

An arbitrator will normally see the boat involved in the dispute, unless she has been sunk. It could be that the cause of the sinking is the reason for the whole arbitration. The arbitrator will also call for all letters, accounts, invoices, time sheets and so on from both sides. He may interview shipwrights, foremen, managers, as well as owners and crew.

Before he starts work he should get in writing a request from both parties for his services. Each party should state, in the request for arbitration, that they understand that they are liable for half the arbitrator's fees and expenses, and that they agree to be bound by his ruling.

Sometimes the two sides in a dispute cannot agree on a common arbitrator, in which case each appoints his own arbitrator and these two get together and decide on a third party.

If an owner or a yard can foresee the possibility of a dispute it is good sense to let the other side know the risk exists and call for an agreement that arbitration will be used. The actual arbitrator need not be settled, or it may be agreed that an institution such as the Ship and Boat Builders' National

Federation will be approached to put up an arbitrator. Sometimes it is agreed that one of the vice-presidents or the president of the SBBNF, or a committee member of the Yacht Brokers, Designers and Surveyors Association be asked to act as arbitrator. Surveyors make good arbitrators because they are used to dealing with so many boat problems. They sometimes carry out a brief survey of the craft under dispute, to get background knowledge.

When the whole argument is about costs, the arbitrator needs to know the wage rate charged, the overheads or on-costs, and the profit margin. Materials and services such as telephone charges are costed by going to the suppliers, so that independent evidence is gained.

When assessing a repair job it is necessary to take into consideration the conditions under which the work was done. If the boat lies in the open the weather hampers work. A rush job, to get a boat back into commission, is likely to be less meticulous than a more relaxed repair carried out in the off season. If the owner asked for a hasty repair so that his boat is back afloat in time for a race, the yard is not to be blamed if it has to charge overtime rates, or takes reasonable short-cuts, or if the paintwork does not last long because it was done in poor conditions.

Because they are used to standing in the middle, surveyors make good arbitrators. The arbitration must almost inevitably go against one side of the other. Sometimes both sides make disgruntled comments. But both owner and yard know in their hearts that they have saved legal fees, settled quickly and got the correct technical decision. Even lawyers admit that court cases are sometimes lost on a manifestly inequitable quirk of the law.

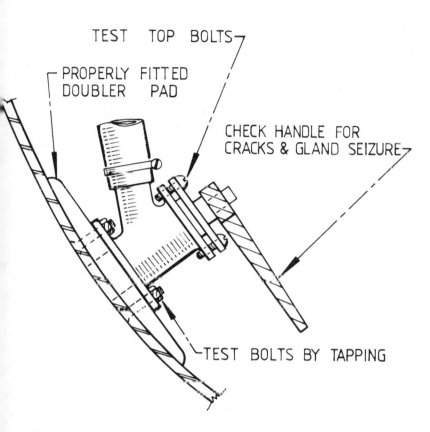

TEST TOP BOLTS

PROPERLY FITTED
DOUBLER PAD

CHECK HANDLE FOR
CRACKS & GLAND SEIZURE

TEST BOLTS BY TAPPING

All seacocks should be stripped off and examined when possible. Sometimes this work is left until after the survey, so the surveyor just taps the securing bolts, taps the gland all over and checks that the handle is in position. If the handle has a crack it suggests that the gland has been very tight and seized at some time. A seized gland needs taking apart for full maintenance and if the handle is missing it must be replaced because it will certainly be needed in a hurry one day.

NOTES ON SURVEYING SMALL CRAFT
IN NORTH AMERICA

by Robert E. Wallstrom, Marine Surveyor

Supplement to *Surveying Small Craft* by Ian Nicolson

This simple work is dedicated to A.E.L., P.L.R., J.D.A., R.S.B., and E.S.B., without whose patience and trust this would not have been written.

R. E. Wallstrom is a partner in the design firm of Brewer, Wallstrom and Associates, Inc., Brooklin, Maine, and is Administrator of Yacht Design Institute, a correspondence school of small craft design, which he and Ted Brewer own and operate. Prior to joining Ted Brewer in Maine, Bob was with the yacht department of Philip L. Rhodes, Inc., the noted New York design firm. Bob has also been associated with the Luders Marine Construction Company of Stamford, Conn., where he was a draftman and loftsman. An active yacht surveyor in the State of Maine, Bob is a member of the National Association of Marine Surveyors, The Society of Naval Architects and Marine Engineers, the Society of Small Craft Designers, and the American Boat and Yacht Council. When not designing yachts or tending to the needs of his 130-year-old farm house, he is acting as the Assistant Fire Chief of the Brooklin Volunteer Fire Company.

INTRODUCTION

One might think that because the laws of physics, hydrodynamics, and biology apply equally to vessels afloat in Great Britain and in North America there would be no difference in small craft surveying on opposite sides of the Atlantic. This belief is reinforced when the surveyor himself is considered. While the Britisher might not be as overweight as his North American counterpart, both walk erect, both have prehensile grasp and have long since shed their tails. They even speak the same language. Or do they?

The North American's cobbler is the Englishman's pie. The former's pie is the latter's tart. Cookies become biscuits and biscuits become scones. When the North American has trouble with his car he might look under the hood, while the Britisher raises the bonnet. As drivers, we might blow our horn at an oncoming truck while the Britisher might use his hooter to warn an approaching van.

Since we are concerned with terms nautical, unless the North American surveyor finds himself in Great Britain with automobile problems or wishes to order tea and cakes, he would not be hard put to make himself understood, for fortunately the nautical language varies but slightly. There are, of course, some differences; our chain pipe is their naval pipe, our rabbet line is their rebate, the bury of our masts is the housing of theirs. But, by and large, aside from variations in spelling, pronunciation, and the occasional term, differences in surveying in countries both east and west lie more in the techniques, tools, resources, professional organizations, local practice, and, of course, cost.

Thus it is our purpose in this supplement not to present a simple translation of terms but to acquaint the reader with the various aspects of the North American survey field and to help the American reader derive maximum benefit from Ian Nicolson's fine work.

In the following discussion, the page numbers cited in the headings refer to the corresponding pages in Ian Nicolson's Surveying Small Craft.

Page 1 – Desirable Qualities

In describing desirable qualities for the owner/buyer or marine surveyor, I feel that a high degree of common sense combined with experience would be another chief asset, as is the good eyesight mentioned by the author. One should know, for instance, that unfair planking may have a hidden cause, that water piping not run level and free from low points may have an ice burst at some unobservable section, that oil dripping from the aft end of an engine gear box might indicate blown or faulty seals, and so on. In short, anything that does not look right to the eye may be the tip of an iceberg of a fault that will mean a great deal to the experienced, thinking surveyor, but little to the novice.

The North American surveyor, the U.S. one in particular, has much in common with a bartender, for he must, as well as fulfill his task in life, upon the request of his client, dispense sage advice on the practicality or suitability of a craft, as well as provide financial wisdom on short- and long-term resale value.

Page 3 – Being Left Alone to Do the Job

Nicolson's comment on the necessity of the surveyor's becoming a bit cantankerous is well taken. I once had a pleasant, professional Captain insist on having me accompany him on a tour about a yard. He introduced me to various workmen, appraised me of local gossip, and filled me with coffee. It was only when I became a bit brusque and stated the necessity for getting on with the survey that I was left alone to begin my task. When the client is about, however, the need for diplomacy in the choice of words necessary to pack him off temporarily is obvious. After all, it is he that pays the tab for the exercise and that makes him worthy of some occasional small talk and the sharing of some trade secrets.

Page 4 – Fees

Fees in the United States and Canada are not established by the National Association of Marine Surveyors (NAMS), the North American counterpart of the Yacht Brokers, Designers and Surveyors Association (YBDSA), but by the local demand and supply for surveyors. Usually the fee system in the United States and Canada is based on the hours or days involved rather than on tonnage, length and beam formulas, or percentage of the overall purchase price.

At the time of this writing, the established surveyor expects about $400 per day plus expenses for his efforts. Travel, writing, or research time, when involved, is also included. The hourly rate is about $60. Again there are departures, and some surveyors can be found who will charge as low as $200 a day and some as high as $600. When air travel is necessary, it is usually by coach or tourist class, again with the possibility of an exception. Adequate flight insurance is also expected and is billed to the client. The surveyor also expects to be well fed and berthed, not lavishly but adequately and comfortably. I have known some content to dine at the local burger dispenser and bunk in a berth aboard the vessel in question.

Some surveyors also charge extra for inspections involving special equipment. An extra charge of approximately $30.00 per hour for ultrasonic testing of metal hulls and using sonic leak locaters is typical.

For those buyers wishing a trial away from the float and comprehensive testing of all machinery and electronics, an extra charge may also be called for.

Pages 4 to 6 – Vessels Awaiting a Surveyor

Since the taking of a deposit on a vessel for sale constitutes intent to complete the sale, pending survey and occasionally other conditions, the vessel is thus withdrawn from the market and cannot be legitimately offered to other buyers. Thus, brokers in the United States are reluctant to take a vessel off the market for any undue length of time while awaiting a surveyor to happen to be in the area where the vessel is located. To do so is to risk missing a better opportunity to sell the vessel, and the old "bird in hand" maxim applies.

Page 6 – Professional Organizations

As in Europe, leading surveyors of the United States and Canada generally belong to a professional organization. The North American organization was originally formed in 1948 as an informal group of Corresponding Surveyors acting under the guidance of the Yacht Safety Bureau for the purpose of exchanging information and knowledge. It became incorporated in 1962 under the laws of the State of New York and is known as the National Association of Marine Surveyors.

Now with over 300 members in 27 states and several Canadian provinces, the NAMS membership is the major listing of surveyors available. Its membership is called upon from time to time to provide information to the United States Coast Guard, American Boat and Yacht Council, National Fire Protection Association, and other agencies whose function it is to write legislation or promulgate regulations for boating safety. The client seeking a surveyor for a given area may direct his inquiry to the National Association of Marine Surveyors, P.O. Box 55, Peck Slip Station, New York, N.Y. 10038, for a copy of their membership list. The non-member surveyor interested in joining the NAMS may write to the same address for a membership application, by-laws, and membership requirements.

NAMS members all have at least five years of experience in the maritime field performing hull, cargo, and machinery inspections, as well as repair, new construction, and damage surveys on all types of vessels. To prevent conflict of interest charges, Association by-laws provide that members may not be engaged as yacht brokers, yard owners, marine vendors, or the like. The Association's credo is, "No surveyor shall take any position contrary to his own knowledge or opinion for any direct or indirect monetary gain or its equivalent." Thus by by-law and credo, the NAMS surveyor must protect the client from the "caveat emptor" attitude occasionally found in some areas of the marine industry.

Pages 6 to 8 – Designers as Surveyors

Frequently yacht designers are called upon to act as yacht surveyors for condition, evaluation, or damage surveys, and while not engaged full time in yacht survey work, they are often more aware of small craft problems than are surveyors whose primary practice may be hull, cargo, machinery, and tow surveys. In choosing a surveyor it is best to make in advance a few judicious inquiries about the surveyor's character, specialty areas, and professional competence.

Richard Henderson, in his book, *Sea Sense*, published by International Marine Publishing Company, makes several worthwhile comments in Chapter Three on the choice of a surveyor and offers many good thoughts on what to look for during the pre-survey inspection of a vessel by the potential buyer.

Page 7 – Professional Indemnity Insurance

At the moment, NAMS members do not hold professional indemnity insurance, although the Association is currently undertaking a search for an underwriter to provide such liability coverage.

Page 7 – Other Organizations that List Surveyors

North American institutions that can supply surveyors are:

Marine Consultants International, Box 2052, Brunswick, Maine 04011

Lloyds Register of Shipping, 17 Battery Place, New York, N.Y. 10004

American Bureau of Shipping, 45 Broad Street, New York, N.Y. 10004

United States Salvage Association, Inc., 99 John Street, New York, N.Y. 10038

Lloyds' surveyors are well known for their thoroughness and meticulous approach, but at times they are a bit dogmatic when concerned with small craft new construction surveys and they no longer do surveys before purchase, only surveys on craft classed to Lloyds. Peter Heaton in his book, *Sailing*, says of a Lloyds survey, "The cost is not high but they open the ship right up, removing the ceiling and taking samples of all suspicious parts of the vessel for inspection. It is the cost of putting this back that makes a survey rather more expensive." On the other hand, he agrees that it is a very thorough survey.

Surveyors from the American Bureau of Shipping and the United States Salvage Association, Inc., are primarily concerned with ships, barges, tugs, oil drilling rigs, and other large commercial vessels.

Marine Consultants International survey all types of craft anywhere in the world.

Page 10 – The Line Between Refitting and Repairs

My own criteria, and those of several other surveyors, on judging the difference between upkeep and repairs, lie more toward what and how it should be on a proper yacht, and more importantly, how great a hazard the fault is to life and safety at sea. For example, faulty engine instruments, cracked portlight lenses, and foul bilges would not be tolerated on a proper yacht. A leaking fuel line, badly cracked swaged terminals, and thread-like keel bolts are a hazard to life. The emphasis is, of course, more on the latter type of deficiency.

Page 12 – Certificates of Seaworthiness

Such certificates are rarely requested of the North American surveyor and then only for vessels making a canal or particular ocean passage. Then, as with their overseas colleagues, they are given with limitations, restrictions of service, and for a given time period.

Page 14 – Preparation for a Survey

Nothing is more frustrating to the surveyor than to arrive at the survey site and find that "Murphy's Law" has been invoked and that the vessel's keys are lost or otherwise unavailable; that the spars have not been taken down for survey and remain bundled and racked twelve feet above the floor, necessitating a monkey act on the part of the surveyor; that the winter cover and frame have not been removed and remain snow covered and ice bound to the vessel until the warm spring; or that the batteries were not marked with the vessel's name and are hidden among the other two-hundred batteries all quietly being trickle-charged.

Such occurrences naturally upset the tone of the affair and make proper survey virtually impossible. In such cases, the loser is the client who should have taken the responsibility to ensure that the surveyor will have proper access to the vessel, that the cover is removed, that the spars are unracked, unbundled, and placed properly for inspection. While this is rarely done, the cost of such simple, advance preparation on the part of the client will be returned in the form of a more complete and detailed survey and may eliminate the need for a return visit to the site by the surveyor.

Page 15 – Floorboards, Lining, and Ceiling Removal

The North American surveyor rarely calls for the removal of ceiling or head liner. Of course this is of less necessity for FRP vessels and perhaps this accounts for the rarity. Inside ballast is almost never removed, although I quite agree with the principle that it should be. It is essential that the owner of the vessel give his written permission before any integral part of the vessel is removed for inspection and that the buyer give a written order to the yard authorizing such work. All such work must eventually be paid for, and a proper yard will wish to know in advance to whom to address the bill.

Page 16 – Fuel Tanks, Full or Empty

There seems to be no standard practice in the United States for having fuel tanks of stored vessels either full or empty. Yard practice varies, and I would say it lies more to having the tanks pressed up.

Page 16 – Removal of Tanks and Engines

Only on the rarest of occasions are tanks and engines moved about for survey, and then only on larger vessels when this sort of movement can be accomplished without massive tearing up of arrangement and structure. On older fishing vessels, particularly carriers which have ice holds, a surveyor may request the removal of ceiling in way of the ice hold so that he may view the timbering and the inside of the planking.

To call for the further removal of structure or machinery, plumbing or electrical gear, would bring forth an aghast wail from the client or owner envisioning the evaporation of large sums of capital only to enrich the yard owner's coffers and produce little of worth to himself.

Page 16 – Partial Surveys

The North American surveyor is in accord with the feeling that a partial survey of a vessel is next to meaningless, although on occasion nearly all have been called upon to perform such a partial survey. Then it is usually limited to assessing the machinery or electrical installations or the hull alone. In these cases the client generally has a firm knowledge of the condition of all other areas and is seeking specialized counsel on a specific problem.

Page 20 – Sources of Error, New Boats

On several occasions I have been called upon to conduct surveys on vessels abuilding, and, based on my experience, I can attest to the importance of having adequate designer or surveyor supervision over the vessel during the building period. For instance, I once found on a large steel vessel that a builder had cut only $\frac{3}{4}''$ (1.15 cm) limber holes in the metal floors and in other areas had omitted them entirely. Yet, the bilge suction intake was a pipe of 1.61″ I.D. (4.09 cm). Thus, in the event of a leak, each frame bay between the leak and the suction inlet would have to fill to the top of the floor before the bilge pump could begin to reach its full flow. In this case the added volume of water could have been some 600 gallons (2,280 liters) or some 5,000 pounds (2,250 kg) before the pump could begin its full flow of 140 gallons (532 L) per minute. In a single compartment, this would have been tolerable, but had this condition been extended to another compartment, the added volume of water and resultant free surface effect when the vessel heeled would have been enough to, as it is said, "ruin your day." To further complicate affairs, the bilges had not been cleaned and I managed to remove some five pounds (2.25 kg) of assorted rubbish from only one small area of the bilge. Such small trash could have easily dammed up around the bilge suction intake, severely limiting the free passage of water to the strainer. I even found a piece of plywood about 4' x 6' (1.2 m x 1.8 m), which had to be sawn into four smaller pieces before they would pass through the access hatch.

Even today, with the state of the FRP boatbuilding art considerably advanced from that of its formative years, we still hear stories of, and occasionally see, vessels built by large well-known companies, both in the United States and in the Far East and Europe, which come unstuck at bulkheads, engine girders, berth and counter flats, maststeps, and centerline taping. In some cases, employment of the designer to check scantlings and construction and of a surveyor to inspect the building process could eliminate many of the problems encountered by the owner after delivery of a vessel.

Some builders are reluctant, however, to allow a surveyor on their premises. Thus, the only way a prospective buyer can gain information about the quality of the builder's product is to make a search of the area's surveyors for knowledge of the vessel's reputation. Common sense should dictate this be done in any case.

Page 23 – Taking Samples
Rarely will the North American surveyor go about drilling holes and taking samples for analysis, for to do so without specific permission would invite angry owners to an open season on surveyors. There will, of course, be an exception and that is when the surveyor must drill several small holes in the bottom of a steel vessel in order to determine the shell plating thickness.

Page 31 – Tools for Wood Surveying, Spikes
The fine set of brad awls of which the author makes note may be purchased from Woodcraft Supply Corporation, 313 Montvale Avenue, Woburn, Mass. 01801, for a very nominal amount. In any case, send them fifty cents for a copy of their catalog, which shows one of the finest collections of woodworking tools available today.

For tapping and digging, I find the Miller's Falls awl, no. 270 C, to be handy. To preclude accidentally impaling oneself, a simple leather belt holster can be fashioned, something similar to the rig the ice men used to wear.

Another handy tool for wood boat surveying, I might add, is a common window-jimmy, such as the Red Devil, no. 4050. It's handy for sheeting off loose bottom paint and scraping away oil-soaked dirt often encountered in the bilges, to say nothing of the tunking and prying occasionally done.

Page 32 – Tools for Steel Surveys, Hammers

Equivalent hammers available in North America are the $1\frac{1}{2}$ pound and 3 pound Surface Protective Hammers available from U.S. Air Tool Company, P.O. Box 160, New Hyde Park, N.Y. 11040. The hammer has a shot-filled head for heft and Nuplaflex tips available in three hardnesses: soft, medium, and hard. Again, for an interesting catalog write USATCO; they carry a wide range of tools not generally seen in the local hardware or marine supply store.

I also use a light four-ounce hammer when light tapping is called for. It is a Blackhawk, HT 1450. It or its equivalent can be found in almost any good automotive or tool supply house.

The use of hammers is certainly not restricted to steel survey alone, for the heavier hammer with Nuplaflex tips can be used to sound the planking of wooden vessels for loose or poorly holding fastenings without causing even the slightest blemish to paint work. The lighter hammer is useful in sounding along the stem, horn timber, and garboard when looking for soft wood along the rabbet.

Page 33 – Gauges

For the measuring of plating, I have found that the Starrett hook rule, H-610-N, is as good an instrument as can be found. I reads in sixteenths of an inch (1.58 mm) and will pass through a 3/8″ (9.5 mm) hole.

For other thickness measurements, I have a Mitutoyo dial caliper, no. 505-629, which I use on reachable thicknesses when a larger, more accurate instrument can be used. Both instruments can be had for modest cost from any machinist's supply house, or from Ben Alprin Company, P.O. Box 1686, 555 Lincoln Street, Lewiston, Maine 04240.

Page 33 – Drills

The Black and Decker cordless $\frac{1}{4}''$ drill, no. 7077, would be a good choice of self-powered drills. There are, of course, similar models of other manufacture.

Last but not least is a small pocket magnet which I habitually carry. It is useful in searching out bits of iron piping in otherwise non-ferrous piping systems and to help distinguish an otherwise undistinguishable bit of metal.

Page 33 – Portable Lights

There are a variety of good lights available, varying from the mechanic's standard to the drop light with a 50 foot lead of at least 16-gauge three-wire, which is available nearly everywhere from Sears to your local automotive supply store.

For those desiring the finest portable light, they would be pleased with the nearly unbreakable and slightly more expensive 40 watt fluorescent wand, no. 05-A-106, available from USATCO.

Curtis Industries, Inc., Curtis Boulevard, East Lake, Ohio 44094, offers a "Spot and Trouble Light" with a 50 watt, 12 volt bulb and a 25 foot cord with alligator clips for attachment to the vessel's battery system. This light might be handy for the owner's tool kit, but perhaps a bit too frail for the rigors of survey work.

Page 36 – Miner's Type Light

For those prefering the miner's style battery light, Kohler Manufacturing Company's "Wheat Light" has a rechargeable battery which is alleged to give twelve hours of non-fading light. It is available as a cap light (5100-G2) or in a belt style (160 G1). The battery is carried on the belt. The "Wheat Light" is available from the National Mine Service Company, P.O. Box 1438, Berkley, West Virginia 25801.

My own preference for lights is a 110-volt Reflecto Clamp Light by Pacific Electricord with a heavy duty bulb and a $8\frac{1}{2}''$ reflector. Its 25 foot cord and my 100 foot extension cord provide me with plenty of light except in the most distant reaches of a yard. The three-cell Eveready "Captain" flashlight takes care of the smaller jobs. The advantage of such simple rigging is that both are cheap, so if either or both get a bit bashed I don't feel too badly.

Page 38 – Marking Trouble

An alternate to the felt tip markers which I have found successful is the Dixon lumber crayon in black or yellow colors available from most hardware stores.

Page 41 – Fairness

Some production builders, in an attempt to keep tooling costs to a minimum, forego the time and expense of fully lofting, full size, a new design. They do this by lofting the sections only, using the architect's offsets as a guide, and do not fair them true by drawing in the waterlines, buttocks, and diagonals. This often results in flat spots in section, humps and hollows fore and aft, and excessively hollow waterlines near the forward waterline ending.

Page 46 – Keel Bands

Keel bands, called shoes or worm shoes, are usually of wood on U.S. vessels. Only on one occasion have I seen a steel shoe and that was on a heavy displacement motor vessel built in England, and it was in rather scabby shape.

Bronze has also been used for shoes and, as can be expected, stands up much better than iron.

Page 59 – Spread of Rot

This little known fact about rot is indeed true and appears to be known by only a relatively few, no doubt due to the paucity of information on the subject available to the layman. While I have never heard of anyone called "Dry Rot Mary," I did have the rare privilege of working with a fellow who, in retrospect, might well have been called "Dry Rot Charley." He was a grizzled old boatbuilder who used to take fiendish delight in sprinkling from a Copenhagen snuff can, which he always carried in his bib overalls, bits of brown rot saved from jobs past into the bilges, nooks, and crannies of vessels in winter storage. In so doing he felt that he was insuring a generous work load for next year's repair work.

Decay spores are indeed microscopic, being about two to four ten-thousandths of an inch in length and are thus easily borne by wind, sea, or any other transport. I am told that these spores are present in the atmosphere at all times, thus it is unlikely that the occurrence of locally infected wood would increase the chances of infection of unaffected wood. The simultaneous occurrence of a moisture content between 20 percent to 30 percent for most woods and a favorable temperature between 40° to 100° F (4° to 38° C) are the prime reasons for the development of rot, especially in a poorly ventilated region. There is a greatly accelerated rate of decay when the temperature reaches the neighborhood of 75° to 85° F (24° to 30° C). Thus vessels in winter storage with wet bilges suffer most in early fall and late spring when the day temperatures often reach those noted. Circulation-inhibiting winter covers, it might be suggested, should not be set in place until the daily daytime high temperature remains below the minimum of 40° F, as a proper ventilation is a deterrent to fungus growth. In practice, many northern yards, by dint of work load, must commence framing and covering as soon as vessels are rendered for storage, even as early as Labor Day. Preferably, covers should be removed in the spring at the moment temperatures moderate to highs of 40° F.

Page 63 – Dry Rot

Dry rot (*Merulius lachyrymans*) is primarily a European fungi and is rarely seen in North America. Unlike its Yankee cousins (*Poria incrassata* and others of the *Poria* species), who can tolerate temperatures well in excess of 100° F (38° C), this fungus is destroyed at 77° F (25° C).

In cutting out rot of any form, it is important not to be content with local excising about the affected area. Radical surgery is in order, with removal of wood as far away as 18 inches to 2 feet (45 to 61 cm) with the grain and 4 inches to 5 inches (10 to 12 cm) alongside the damaged area. The reason for this is that the fungi are equipped with tube-like veins called *Rhizomorphs*, about 1 inch (25 mm) in diameter and one foot (30 cm) in length which can travel along the grain in search of life-sustaining moisture.

In addition, the neighboring surfaces of exposed timber should be doused liberally with a wood preservative, such as warmed coal tar creosote, pentachloraphenol, copper napthanate, or other organic solvent preservative. Coal tar creosote does interfere with subsequent painting, therefore it should be used only where finish is unimportant.

Page 72 – Laboratories

The United States equivalent of the Forest Products Research Laboratory is the Forest Products Laboratory, Forest Service, U.S.D.A., P.O. Box 5130, Madison, Wisonsin 53705. The Canadian equivalent referred to by the author is the Western Forest Products Laboratory, 6620 N. W. Marine Drive, Vancouver, B.C. Many state universities have a school of forestry and would be of help to those seeking information locally. In Maine it is called the School of Forestry Resources, University of Maine, Orono, Maine 04473.

An interesting, informative packet called *Timber and Plywood in Boatbuilding* can be obtained from the Timber Research and Development Association, St. Johns Road, Tylers Green, High Wycombe, Buckinghamshire, England. Contained in the packet are data sheets on species strength properties, new wood construction, repair, timber preservation, wood borer prevention, and much more. Another excellent resource is the U.S. Navy's wood series, *Wood: A Manual for its Use as a Shipbuilding Material.* A three volume series, it is now out of print. Try a large library. Another government handbook is the *Wood Handbook*.

Page 75 – Yellow Pine
The yellow pine referred to here is not the yellow pine we in the United States know as Southern yellow or longleaf yellow pine, both of which are rated durable to very durable.

Page 78 – Caulked Seams
Stopping is what we know as seam compounds, either applied by caulking gun or broad knife. What is known as knifing stoppers would be our trowel cement.

Page 79 – Caulking
Bob Steward's *Boatbuilding Manual* (International Marine Publishing Company) contains a short dissertation on caulking, smoothing, and the use of polysulfide and silicone caulking compounds.

Page 83 – Rebate
Rebate is the British term for rabbet.

Page 83 – Rooves
Rooves are small copper washers used when copper nails are clenched.

Page 100 – Nameplates
In Britain, the builder of the vessel is not necessarily the hull molder. A large firm such as Tylers supplies hulls to a variety of builders who complete and market them under their own trade name. Foreign-built vessels in the United States are by import law required to have a plaque stating the country of origin. All quality builders the world around place plaques aboard which state the builder's name and the hull number, and frequently such other information as the designer and class name.

Now builders worldwide who are building for the U.S. market must, by the terms of the Federal Boating Safety Act of 1972, place a H I N (hull identification number) on the starboard side of the transom or to the starboard aft when there is no transom.

To date there have been over 2,600 manufacturer identification codes assigned by the agency responsible for the enforcement of the Act, the U.S. Coast Guard. For the occasion when the surveyor does not find a builder's name plate he may direct an inquiry to the Commandant, (G-BD 2/43) B2PT, U.S. Coast Guard, Washington, D.C. 20590, or the local U.S. Coast Guard District Boating Safety Officer for the name of the builder.

The labeling requirements are fully detailed in Subchapter S (Boating Safety) of Title 33, Code of Federal Regulations, or in Boating Safety Circular 2-73. Briefly described, the H I N may consist of three random letters that often, but not always, may look like an acronym for the company name or initials. For instance, SYC indicates Scheel Yachts, Inc. and HRH, the Henry R. Hinckley, Co. Characters 4 through 8 may indicate the hull class and number, i.e., 40145 in the case of the Hinckley Company would indicate Bermuda 40, hull 145. The next and last four characters, usually numbers, indicate the date of construction or certification, i.e., 0374 would indicate March, 1974. In some cases the last four characters may be a combination of Arabic numerals and letters. In this instance, character number nine will be the letter H followed by the last two numbers of the model year. Character nine will indicate the month, i.e., A = August, B = September, C = October, etc., through L for July. To complicate things further, the builder may add additional designations after the regulation twelve H I N characters by separating them with a hyphen.

Page 105 – Testing Laboratories

There are several testing laboratories available who are equipped to perform destructive testing of FRP samples. Two which come highly recommended are the Wolfson Institute, Southampton University, Southampton, Hampshire, England and the Reinforced Plastics Testing Laboratory, 212 Bangor Street, Lindenhurst, N.Y. 11757. They regularly perform tensile, compression, bending, resin/glass ratio, and void content tests of FRP samples supplied them by several large U.S. fiberglass yacht builders. They also provide consultant services for the U.S. Coast Guard. For survey purposes, the most common test they perform would be the resin/glass ratio and void content test.

Page 106 – Oil Scum Problems

Oil scum damage can also occur as pitting and occasionally as a softening of the gel coat. This usually occurs following an oil spill of a less refined or unrefined petroleum product such as bunker or plain crude. I have been told this pitting only penetrates two or three mills and can often be carefully buffed out. If the damaged areas are not too large and the adjacent gel not badly faded, a craftsman skilled in gel repair can make an almost unnoticeable repair. I have seen a lightly faded red hull which had an 8″ (20 cm) hole stove in her topsides repaired with the damaged area being virtually unnoticeable.

Page 108 – Gel Repairs

Great care should be taken in the selection of a firm to be entrusted with gel repair, as there are many who have only the slightest knowledge of gel handling and application but would be most willing to give it a try on someone else's yacht.

Page 110 – Flaw Detection Process

An inexpensive flaw detection process used by some FRP builders is a simple one which utilizes a colored dye called Dycum Blue, a toolmaker's dye quite akin to Prussian blue, which is painted or rubbed on a plate and on which lines to be machined are scribed. When used to detect flaws in FRP layups, it is rubbed on thinly with a piece of flannel. Any flaws, i.e., cracks or porosity, will collect the dye and will stand out proudly. The drawback to this system is the clean up with acetone afterward. Usually, this test is only done where there may be stress concentrations such as near chain plates, stem head fittings, etc.

Page 129 – Leaks in Fiberglass Boats

The tracing down of hull-to-deck connection leaks can often be one of the most frustrating of events. Trying to find a leak by virtue of the water test mentioned by the author does little except show up the broad expanses where there are no leaks. Any type of leak is difficult to trace down because the point of egress inside the boat is usually downhill and from inches to many feet from the point of ingress. For the most part, unless such leaks are serious and disruptive, they are simply ignored by the bulk of owners, for corrective action to stem such leaks may be difficult, costly, and not always fully effective.

Fortunately, a new device is making its way into the industry which could be a great asset in the tracing down of leaks. It is called the "Sonic Leak Locator" and is distributed by BOATLife, Inc., 65 Bloomingdale Road, Hicksville, N.Y. 11801. Not a toy by any means, it utilizes a tone generator which emits an inaudible high frequency sound. In use, the tone generator is placed in various locations inside the vessel to be tested. A wand-shaped receiver is then passed about outside the hull-deck connection, fixed portlights, deck fittings, watertight hatches, and the like. At the point of any leak, a whistling sound is heard in an attached headset.

A degree of caution must be used in the interpretation of the signal that indicates a leak around companionway hatches or the tops of opening port lights. The signal, while indicating a sound leak, may not indicate a leak through which water may pass. Again, the common sense spoken of earlier must be applied to determine whether there is a water leak or a normal sonic leak.

The device is not restricted to marine applications since it is also used in the automotive industry to detect leaks in new cars and trucks. The receiver, less the tone generator, can also be used to detect leaks in any air pressure or vacuum system, such as tires, air brake and vacuum lines, air ducts, and the like.

Page 135 – Don't Spare the Hammer

I recently had the unhappy occasion to view another surveyor's error of omission which came about because the hammer was spared. A large steel ocean racer began to develop paint problems shortly after a condition survey and subsequent purchase, and another surveyor was called upon to investigate the situation and present a recommendation to the owner.

After several strong blows with a surface protective hammer in way of the suspect area, sheets of paint and trowelling fell away to expose a rusty, badly corroded area of plating, some nine square feet (.81 m^2), where the plating had been eaten away to a point where it looked like fine, Belgian lace. Prior to the hammer blows, the surface appeared quite innocent except for a small area of raised paint. This would indicate that the cosmetic painting and troweling had been lately added to conceal the damaged area from a prospective buyer. The owner thus saved the considerable expense of accomplishing repairs to the detriment of his own purse. Thus the seller said, in effect, *caveat emptor*, and now the buyer, and perhaps the original surveyor, face repair costs which will run to the several thousands of dollars.

Page 138 – Locating Test Holes

Another important consideration to make in advance of the drilling of holes is to be sure that before the hole has been drilled it can be reached from inside the vessel. For every bolt to be installed from the outside, there must be adequate and reachable hand space for a nut and lock washer on the inside. Failure to plan ahead may well place the hole on the unreachable far side of frames or longitudinals which run between frames. Such occurrences do nothing to round out a surveyor's day. Do not forget that any bolts used to plug test holes must be galvanically compatible with the metal of the hull.

Page 138 – Thickness Gauging Equipment

Automations Industries, Inc., Sperry Division, Shelter Rock Road, Danbury, Conn. 06810, manufactures a line of ultrasonic digital readout thickness gauges and accessories. Their model G-2 operates on 110 volts A.C. and is about 3″ x 13″ x 15″ (7.62 x 33.0 x 38.10 cm), and weighs about 12 pounds (5.45 kg). Its range is from .010″ to 1.99″ (.254 mm to 50.54 mm) and it is accurate to 1/1000″. They also make a smaller unit, the G-20B, which by being more compact and 12-volt-battery powered, is much more suited to the rigors of field usage that surveyors would impose upon it, and its range and accuracy is that of the G-2. For reasons of price alone, there are few surveyors who are equipped to perform ultrasonic thickness testing, but Marine Consultants International of Box 2052, Brunswick, Maine 04011, USA have worldwide facilities, including an office at A. Mylne & Co. Silverhills, Rosneath, Dumbartonshire, UK.

Persons requiring testing that necessitates use of such an instrument and who are not disposed to make such an expensive purchase might contact a local Lloyd's or American Bureau of Shipping representative, or shipbuilding firms such as Bath Iron Works, Electric Boat Company, or the like, which have departments specializing in ultrasonic testing. There are also commercial firms that specialize in only thickness testing, one of which is the New York Testing Laboratories of 81 Urban Avenue, Westbury, L.I., N.Y., which has experience in small craft hull testing.

When testing for thickness using ultrasonic gauges, a degree of common sense and caution must be used when interpreting the readings. The gauges, if not placed on bright metal or paint work which is tightly bonded to the metal, will show a less than dependable reading. The condition on the far side of the plating will also affect readings taken on the near side. Heavily scaled and corroded surfaces will often give readings in excess of the true plating thickness. I recall seeing results of an ultrasonic thickness test performed on a young, lovely, but badly neglected steel auxiliary which showed readings of .155" to .160" (3.93 mm to 4.06 mm) when the plating was only .118" (3 mm) – a difference of plus .037" to .042" (.889 mm to 1.01 mm). The interior of the once proud Dutch beauty was so far gone that shards of rust hung from her deck beams and gussets. Her floor flanges could be effortlessly broken away by hand.

Page 149 – Steering Gear

Another consideration nearly as important as proper lead and alignment of wire to sheave and quadrant is proper tension. There should be no slack or sag in the wire except that which might be ascribed to catenary sag. Proper tension in pounds is difficult to determine but has been unscientifically characterized by one manufacturer of steering gear as "sounding like a dull twang when struck."

Sheaves should also have wire guards to prevent any momentarily slack wire from jumping from the sheave groove and falling loose, possibly to foul itself.

Quadrants should also be investigated to determine the existence and suitability of quadrant stops. These important items serve to protect the steering system against damage at times when the rudder may be put hard over with great force, as when backing down, or when the helm is put over and the force of water against the turned rudder takes charge, wrenching the rudder to full helm. Damage to hull, rudder fairings, and the steering system itself can occur when there are no, or insufficient, stops. On sailboats they should be located to restrict total travel to about 60 to 70 degrees, and on powerboats, total travel to 90 degrees. Many vessels have been equipped with hard rubber rudder stops which have been noted to pit where they are struck by the rough, sharp edges of the quadrant, thus allowing a degree of over-travel by the rudder. Henry Keene of the Edson Corporation suggests having the stops made of an easily replaceable, semi-durable wood.

Page 162 – Chainplates

Here in the United States and in Canada, it is considered good design and building practice to install toggles always on shrouds and stays.

Page 176 – Wood Spars

In addition to testing for tightness of fastenings, the surveyor would do well to withdraw one or more for each cleat and winch base to ensure that, while they may be of the proper gauge, they are also of proper length. I know of a case several years ago where, on a comparatively new boat, a halyard winch pulled off a mast, striking and severely injuring one of the crew as it went sailing by. In that case, the fastenings were of proper gauge but were not of sufficient length.

Page 179 – Standing Rigging and Rigging Screws

The use of Norseman products is by no means limited to England, for their "swageless" fitting system has long been used in this country. Though not as popular as the common swaged terminals, they have been tested and approved by Lloyds, who have found they are stronger than the wire to which they are attached yet they do not crack after a few years. The noted yacht rigger Alan MacDonald says simply, "They are the best," and that anyone going offshore on extended passages should have their rigging so equipped. Their greatest advantage is the ease with which the terminals may be installed, for the process is simple and easily accomplished with only the tools found in a well-found tool box.

Norseman terminals are available through mail-order firms such as Manhattan Marine and Electric Co., Inc., 116 Chambers Street, New York, N.Y. 10007; and West Products, 161 Prescott Street, East Boston, Mass. 02128 (ask for the West Catalog too, it's a pocket-sized dandy); and of course through yacht riggers such as MacDonald Yacht Rigging, Marina America, Stamford, Conn. 06902. The most prominent United States manufacturer of steel rigging is MacWhyte Wire Rope Co., 2982 14th Avenue, Kenosha, Wisc. 53140. Ask them for their catalog Y-5. For cordage, Samson Cordage Works, 470 Atlantic Avenue, Boston, Mass. 02210 or Columbian Rope Company, 316 West Genesee Street, Auburn, N.Y. 13021 are the best known.

Suppliers of wire and rope advertise in the yachting, boating and small craft magazines and trade publications.

Page 179 – Corrosion of Stainless Steel Wire and End Fittings

I agree with the author's comments on the necessity of replacing swaged end fittings which have developed hairline cracks. All too frequently, builders pass them off as minor in nature with vague assurances to the owner that there is nothing to worry about. It happens all the time. While it may be that one or two small cracks are not a worry, like little rabbits they grow and multiply and often go unnoticed until one squally day, while trying to beat off shore.

Useful in the detection of small, undiscolored cracks is a dye penetrant called Spot-Check, manufactured by Magnaflux Corporation, 7300 W. Lawrence, Chicago, Ill. 60656. The test is to spray on the penetrant, which comes in aerosol spray cans, allow a short time for penetration, wipe the surface and what dye remains in the cracks becomes visible to the eye. There are many other applications for dye penetrant in small craft survey work and afield in industrial areas as well, and there is no reason why this test cannot be applied to the detection of flaws in FRP construction.

Page 180 – Gashers
Gashers are what we know as whiskers. Under the circumstances, as anyone who has run afoul of one knows, gashers is a much more appropriate term.

Page 181 – Talurit Fittings
The Talurit fitting is the British equivalent of what we know as a Nicopress fitting.

Page 182 – Their Rigging Screws/Our Turnbuckles
Practice here is for the designer to include the factor of safety (fs) of 2.5 to 4 in the spar and stay calculations. As with the Norseman rigging mentioned by the author, the wire, toggle pin, turnbuckle, and swaged fittings used here are all keyed together, thus our wire sizes can only be assembled with the proper swaging, toggle pin, and turnbuckle.

Page 182 – Turnbuckles With Lock Nuts
Rod Stephens of Sparkman and Stephens has pointed out in a three-part article for *Yachting* Magazine (January, February, and March 1974), that when turnbuckles with lock nuts are tensioned, the lock nuts frequently slack up, and when the lock nuts are turned up so as to be sufficiently tight, they cause additional, uncalculated stress upon the turnbuckle threads.

Page 186 – Sails
By and large, sails are only given a cursory examination by the North American surveyor who in the examination pays close attention to wear on head boards, slides, and pistol snaps, seizings, run-ins, reefing points

and batten pockets, without unbagging and fully flaking out the sails. On well-maintained vessels, sails are usually sent off to the sailmaker every year or two for care and maintenance. The yard office can frequently be a source of information on this and other points of vessel maintenance.

On the occasion when a full survey of sails is requested, many surveyors charge extra, since the work of manhandling a suit of sails from any well-found ocean racer or large motorsailer from bag to floor and back is considerable, time consuming, and requires the assistance of a helper, as well as proper area.

Page 187 – Dating of Sails

U.S. sailmakers nearly always imprint their names or symbols on the sail but rarely the year of manufacture, but on sails used on ocean racers and some class or IOR boats, measurer's notations often may be found which can indicate to some extent the age of the sail.

Page 189 – Surveyors vs. Brokers

How true this is. I don't believe that there is a surveyor in practice who has not had an annual encounter with a broker over one of the surveyor's condemnations. The broker's position tends to be, "Well it works doesn't it?" The surveyor's position must be founded on one of the various accepted standards which he is guided by. Of course, in the event of a law suit, the "it did work, didn't it?" argument is not at all a strong enough defense with which to protect one's good name and assets. But then it is seldom that the broker is the one facing litigation.

Page 191 – Engines

Some *good* yacht yards perform, as a matter of course, compression tests on the engines of vessels layed up for the winter, and I have found that this information can be had for the asking from the yard superintendent or yard manager. Often times this data is provided on a special yard form which will contain other helpful information relevant to the condition of the vessel and its components, i.e., number, manufacturer, and condition of batteries; numbers of pumps and equipment that have been winterized by yard personnel; as well as pertinent comments based on the workmen's observations. In cases of doubt, I never fail to suggest to my client, and occasionally urge him, to retain a good engine mechanic to perform the tests and examinations necessary to assess properly engine condition.

Page 193 – Stern Gland Lubrication

By and large the stern gland grease cup rates as one of the most neglected of lubricated fittings, for I have yet to find one which shows signs of being recently refilled.

Page 194 – Plummer Block

A plummer block is what we would call a pillow block. For slower turning shafts, a babbitted sleeve bearing may be used. In which case, the bearing cap should be removed and babbett metal examined, for higher temperatures and rotations can damage or destroy the bearing metal.

Page 194 – Shaft Sizes

For data on the shaft relationship, the reader may refer to *Skene's Elements of Yacht Design* by Frank Kinney, which in Chapter XV shows nomographs on shafting size and bearing spacing.

Page 196 – Misalignment Indications

Another guide to possible engine misalignment is when the engine will not run up to its maximum or sometimes intermittent RPM or shows a higher than normal block temperature and lower oil pressure temperature. Simply put, the engine showing these indications is working harder than it should and accomplishing less.

Page 197 – Fireproofing/U. S. Standards Agency

The U.S. equivalent of the S.D.B.N.F. is the American Boat and Yacht Council, 15 East 26th Street, New York, N.Y. 10010, which publishes a large, loose-leaf book called *Safety Standards for Small Craft*.

Page 198 – Fire Extinguishers

All too frequently I have found that a vessel's complement of fire extinguishers is far less than desirable. Having been through one experience at sea aboard a new vessel making its delivery trip on which an engine room fire blossomed, I now heavily stress the number, condition, suitability, and accessibility of fire extinguishers.

Many yachts still carry carbon tetrachloride pump extinguishers, which have been outlawed for use aboard ship since 1 January 1962.

This type is not as effective as CO_2 or dry chemical extinguishers, and they can be deadly to one's good health.

Required maintenance commonly overlooked are the large bottles of CO_2, which are by law required to have annual maintenance and hydrostatic testing every five years. All too frequently the fixed systems are overlooked with no thought to operability of the remote pulls or the adequacy of the charge.

Lack of proper ventilation is a common finding on yachts of nearly all manufacture. When combined with owners who negligently leave items stowed away for the winter, such as wet or damp life jackets, mattresses, clothes, dock lines, and rodes, a condition is produced which provides lovely growing grounds for mildew. Normally, mildew is difficult to remove, but one product is becoming known as an effective remover. A fungicide which kills the spores on contact and removes the stains as well, Minute Mildew Remover is a product of U.S. Continental Laboratories, 7206 Alder, Houston, Texas 77036.

Engine rooms are also common sufferers from lack of ventilation. Engines have been known not to run up to the potential RPM because of the lack of air necessary for proper engine aspiration. High temperatures in the engine space create engine operating inefficiency, heat overflow into the arrangement, and, in a few cases, make the deck above too hot to walk on barefoot. High engine room temperatures even have been known to warp teak decking above.

The ventilation problem does not cease when layup season arrives, since form-fitting winter covers, while they are neat and tidy and don't flap in the wind, often lack the suitable vents needed for proper drying circulation of air to hull interiors. Such covers should be equipped with rain-proof ventilators and ducting aimed into the prevailing wind. Ducting should be carried below decks at each end of the vessel to promote optimum air flow about the vessel's interior.

Page 205 – Tank Standards

While the SBBNF rules apply only to the construction of craft to 20 feet (6 m) in length, our ABYC standard for tanks (H-24) is applicable to small craft of any size which are not otherwise bound by Coast Guard regulations.

Standard H-24 provides that baffles should occupy 70 percent of the height and width of a tank. They should also be spaced no farther apart than 24″ to 30″ (60 to 75 cm), although many designers feel they should be 18″ to 20″ (45 to 30 cm) apart.

Page 206 – Tank Piping

Our standard H-24 varies somewhat from the author's comments in its description of what is a suitable vent size and how the vent should be terminated. It states that the tubing should have a minimum I.D. of 7/16″, or if hose is used, 9/16″, and that removable flame screens should be installed at the outlet. The standard calls for a manual shut-off to be located as close to the tank as possible. I always also call for another valve to be located at the engine in a readily accessible location. A flexible hose section should also be installed between rigid piping and the engine to absorb engine vibration. Since it is not our purpose to reproduce Standard H-24, it is suggested that the reader procure the *Safety Standards* volume for H-24 in its entirety.

Page 209 – Ground Tackle

Anchors – there are as many opinions on what is the best anchoring system as there are nails in a keg, and I am going to refrain from trying to pick any good single anchor as the best. Far too many novice yachtsmen are content to settle for the sage wisdom of the non-seagoing showroom sailor and blandly accept the anchor and rode which comes as part of the equipment package, whereas the wise sailor will seek knowledgeable advice from a multitude of sources before deciding on the system he will have aboard.

Where a CQR will not bite on a hard sand bottom, a Danforth or Herreshoff might, and so it would seem that there is ample reason to have one of each aboard and at least two, perhaps three, anchor rodes, with and without chain, so that there is the potential to mix or match in the search for a good holding anchor on strange bottom.

Page 216 – Use of Formica

Formica is now very often installed in broad panels on bulkheads and vertical flats, sometimes can be seen hanging loose like a becalmed square sail. This is due to a bonding failure that occurs when the Formica, which has a different coefficient of expansion than that of the material to which it is bonded, wants to come about more than the backup material wants to go, as indicated by the author's example of a hot pan causing a swelling. My experience, though, is that no amount of re-gluing will suffice, and the cure is to remove the panel entirely. If a bit of luck is at hand and the sheet is not destroyed in the doing, it should be reinstalled in narrow widths of 24″ (60 cm) or so, leaving a small expan-

sion crack between strakes. Further descriptive information can be
obtained by writing the Formica Corporation, Evandale Plant, 10155
Reading Road, Cincinnati, Ohio 45241, for their specification FS
4.05-73, "Wall Surfacing Field Applied."

Page 218 – Inflatables
   If I were buying a used vessel with an inflatable raft aboard which
was in anything but a new certifiable condition, I would automatically
consign the more than likely frail craft to the town dump or perhaps to a
shallow pond where youngsters might use it as a play craft. Too frequently, inflatables are filed and forgotten, left in their cannisters or
cases and not checked or maintained until the day the worst has
occurred and the inherently frail craft is all that is between you and
drowning. We have all recently read of stories where the shelter
entrances of inflated craft were too small for those in the water with
heavy clothing and life jackets on to gain entrance, or the bottom being
rotten and buoyancy chambers being too porous to retain sufficient
pressure. The reader can well imagine the consternation of those wallowing
in heavy seas trying to keep their boney knees from going through the
bottom while huffing over the inflating tube or pump. Where there is any
doubt, chuck it. The astute seafarer (or those who are short of breath
and have boney knees) will have his raft certified annually by a U.S.
Coast Guard approved inspection station or by the appropriate
manufacturer's approved inspection station.

Page 220 – Electrical Standards
   A good standard to be guided by will be found in ABYC's Safety
Standards E-8 and E-9.

Page 221 – Batteries
   When examining batteries, a small volt-ohm meter such as the 1000-
ohm multi-tester from the Radio Shack Corporation and a hydrometer,
which is a cheap simple tool, are handy aids in determining battery condition. Each cell should produce about 2.12 volts; thus a fully charged
12-volt battery should read $12\frac{3}{4}$ volts and should read approximately
1.212 on the hydrometer, with the hydrometer giving the best indication
of each cell's condition and state of charge.

Page 222 – Arbitration
   I quite agree with the author's comments on arbitration and will add

that all too frequently it is not begun at the proper moment. The proper moment, in my opinion, is as soon as it is clear that there are irreconcilable differences of opinion between the parties, rather than allowing these differences to drag on for months, even years, before a settlement is attempted. During that time, records are lost or destroyed, workmen move on to other jobs or die and the memories of all are less than clear. I further subscribe to the theory that the arbitrators should be selected from the ranks of knowledgeable, seagoing folk aware of all facets of our business rather than a beach-bound arbitration association which may have no background for a particular type of disagreement. It would be advantageous for this mutually acceptable board to be chosen at the time of the signing of an original agreement or contract when all heads are clear and level, rather than in the heat of dispute when tempers are all but calm.

The American Arbitration Association with main offices at 140 West 51st Street, New York, N.Y., is a nationwide organization dedicated to the principle of arbitration rather than litigation as a means of settling differences. The Association, with regional offices across the country, maintains a categorized card file with many thousands of names of persons who are professionally competent in their own fields and who are, by virtue of professional pride and interest in their fields, willing to undertake, often at no charge, the task of arbitrating a settlement between disputants.

Arbitration begins when parties file application for arbitration with the Association. They are then supplied with the names of a number of persons capable of assisting them. From this list they choose a mutually acceptable arbitrator. On occasion more than one arbitrator might be assigned, depending on the nature and complexity of the dispute. For instance, a dispute involving construction of a large vessel may involve a naval architect, an attorney whose speciality is contracts, and a builder of similar vessels. Thus expertise in three critical areas of the dispute is assured.

Fees are modest, especially when compared with legal fees; naturally the usual expenses are chargeable.

For a wise and fair conclusion to a dispute it is necessary for the disputants to select the arbitrator(s) with great care as the experience range of the potential arbitrators suggested by the Association may cover a broader spectrum than the problem at hand may require, and thus the disputants should seek those with expertise closest to the problem at hand. This, by the way, is the wish of the Association and to achieve that end they will actively seek persons with the expertise necessary by recruitment and from other geographic locations.

I have an old friend who agreed to have a relatively minor disagreement on a very substantial piece of work settled by a leading U.S. arbitration board. The upshot was that he was deprived of nearly his entire fee and considerable skin besides when the arbitrators found excessively for the other party. This was due, in my opinion, to a decision based on unwarranted conclusions made by gentlemen with little or no acumen in the design branch of the marine field.

CONCLUSION

In conclusion, I must state that information contained in either of these works, when assimilated by the reader, should not be construed as a sufficient education by which a buyer might avoid the necessity for retaining a professional surveyor, or for the amateur to suddenly turn professional. The buyer, owner, amateur, and professional surveyor should treat these works as an additional resource, a part of the whole, available on the subject of pleasure or commercial boating, design, construction, and maintenance, and not as a single, all-informative volume on the survey field.

The reasons for this are manifold. As the author has said quite early in his work, "it takes years for the surveyor to learn how to do a deep survey," and the surveyor must have an intimate knowledge of yacht construction. I would amend that somewhat to say he must have a good knowledge of all areas of the small craft spectrum – that is to say, knowledge of construction in all building mediums and knowledge in small craft design which would provide insight into what is good form, scantlings, necessary factors of safety, and so forth. Time offshore on working and pleasure vessels, sail and power, would also be valuable. Training in all of the areas mentioned – construction, design, and the practical experience of being at sea, when combined, should produce the best educational base on which to rest the surveyor's mantle. Hopefully, experience in all fields would also provide the surveyor with the high degree of common sense I spoke of earlier, for without it a good measure of the surveyor's judgements may be quite valueless.

For the buyer's part, an opinion rendered by an impartial surveyor retained for the survey of a prospective purchase would be completely objective, free of bias, and will not have been subject to the coloring or the glossing over of items as might be the case had the buyer conducted his own survey. Buyers, no matter how well versed, who feel capable of performing their own pre-purchase surveys, might do well to remember the adage, "a lawyer who argues his own case has a fool for a client."

A further reason for retaining a surveyor is that he will supply his client with a written survey containing firm opinions, conclusions, and suggestions, and in the event of serious faults, provide his client with evidence with which the client can decide whether to decline purchase or negotiate with the owner from a more advantageous position. Since most offers given on used vessels are given on a "subject to survey" basis, the seller and/or broker will want to see hard evidence in the event that the buyer declines to purchase because the vessel has failed to pass survey.

As a guide to such buyer/seller negotiations, Peter Heaton in his work, *Sailing*, offers this sage advice, which I must agree with. He suggests that the buyer's "relationship with an owner should be like that of a millionaire with an adventuress, courteous but careful."

INDEX